THE BATTLE FOR PUSAN

THE BATTLE FOR PUSAN

A Korean War Memoir

ADDISON TERRY

LARGE PRINT
Oxford

First published in 2000
by Presidio Press Inc.

Published in Large Print 2002 by ISIS Publishing Ltd.,
7 Centremead, Osney Mead, Oxford OX2 0ES
by arrangement with Presidio Press Inc.

Maps credited to T. R. Fehrenbach,
from *This Kind of War* by T. R. Fehrenbach,
Macmillan edition, 1963.

Cataloguing in Publication Data is available from the Library of Congress

ISBN 0–7531–9736–7 (hb)
ISBN 0–7531–9737–5 (pb)

951.9042

Printed and bound by
T. J. International Ltd., Padstow, Cornwall

This memoir of an old soldier is dedicated to the men and boys of the 27th Regiment and the 8th Field Artillery who did not return. Their dedication to duty, to our unit, and our country shall not be forgotten. Those of us who returned to live a free and fruitful life shall forever be in their debt.

Contents

Foreword

In my lifetime which has consumed ninety-one years I have committed just about all of my time to military matters. My readings as a boy were centered on military history. My studies at West Point were anchored by the great military classics. My senior officers provided ongoing instruction in the tactics and art of war. Yet when I was committed to aerial combat in China there were great surprises and I found that with all my study and indoctrination there were many challenges which had no school solution.

As a cadet at The Academy and as a student officer at Randolph Field I always wondered: All of this is speculation; what's real life combat like? In my book *God is My Co-pilot*, I tried to relate my combat experiences in the skies of China and Burma to theories that I had read about. But I quickly discovered that mortal combat must be lived to understand.

When I started to read Add Terry's *The Battle for Pusan*, I thought that it would be just another old soldier's war story. It isn't. The manuscript was written in the fall of 1950 and the winter of 1951 in a hospital ward at Fort Benning; written while the wounds still hurt and the young memory still fresh. It rushes the reader from hill to hill. The sound, the heat, the mud, and the fear overwhelm you. The surprising and significant command decisions that were in the hands of company grade officers are not unlike the freedom of action associated with fighter pilots.

The performance of the 27th Regiment is remarkable. General Walker's use of his regiment as his "fire department" is legend. And it's not without humor. It clearly recites the day to day, hour by hour modus operandi of our Army in 1950. It has frozen the events in print that molded great men who stood alone on the mainland of Asia against the first Asian Communist army to engage the West. *The Battle for Pusan* is a great read.

Brig. Gen. Robert L. Scott Jr., USAF (Ret.)

Preface

The following account of my experiences and the actions of the 27th Regiment of the 25th Infantry Division and the 8th Field Artillery Battalion in the first days of the Korean War was written in late 1950 and early 1951. I was recovering from gunshot wounds in the Fort Benning, Georgia, Army Hospital. My recall was very keen, and the recorded dates, places, and people are accurate.

The Pusan Perimeter was held for eighty-two days. Until 15 September, the date of the Inchon landing, the issue was in great doubt. The ROK (Republic of Korea) army attempted to establish a line of defense across the entire peninsula, however, it was pierced by the North Korean army in great numbers. By 15 July 1950, the ROK and the American armies were hard pressed to provide an intermittent MLR (main line of resistance) from Yongdok on the east coast, to Andong, to Sangju, to Taejon, and on to Kunsan on the west coast. At this time, the American forces committed were two regiments of the 24th Infantry and two regiments of the 25th Infantry Divisions. The North Koreans were breaking through repeatedly with Russian T34 tanks and self-propelled guns. Our forces had no tanks and only towed artillery at this point in the campaign.

The "perimeter" was not established until 1 August 1950. It ran from Pothang on the east coast to Chingdong-ni on the south coast. This was an area of about eighty-five miles north and south and perhaps sixty miles east and west at its broadest point. In general, we were holding the extreme southeast tip of the Korean peninsula.

The 1st Cavalry Division and the 2d Infantry Division joined the 24th and 25th Divisions. The 5th Marine Regimental Combat Team arrived in early August.

In the meantime, the American press was forecasting a Korean Dunkirk. Many of us on the ground thought the forecast might be right. What we did not know was that the Inchon landing was being staged and that we were holding the entire North Korean army at bay in the south while the X Corps, consisting of the 1st Marine Division and the 7th Infantry Division, was preparing for the Inchon landing on 15 September. Three months to the day after the North Koreans launched their surprise attack, troops of X Corps recaptured Seoul, on 25 September 1950.

This manuscript was completed in about mid-March 1951. In June 1951, I was posted to Fort Bragg, North Carolina. The manuscript was packed with household goods and sent to Fort Bragg. In midsummer of 1951, I was again hospitalized and the manuscript, along with all my other belongings, went with my wife and small son to our family home in Macon, Georgia. After being dismissed from the hospital, I went on to further duties. The manuscript was not seen or thought about for forty-seven years.

In July 1998, while engaged in the disposal of old files and the storage of files and office furniture in a barn on our farm in Washington County, Texas, the manuscript was found. It is presented here, just as it was written by a twenty-three-year-old lieutenant, fresh from the battlefield. It is an accurate account of what happened and how we fought and prevailed in Korea. The burning impression on me after reading the yellowed pages, was the remarkable and emotional devotion and loyalty we developed for one another and our outfit. The battlefield accomplishments and esprit de corps of the 27th and of the 8th Field Artillery were a life-shaping force on me. I shall always be proud to say that "I am a Wolfhound."

Acknowledgments

I wish to thank Edward F. Haye, a pure civilian and old friend, who painstakingly plowed through the yellowed and poorly typed forty-seven-year-old manuscript. His editorial suggestions, spelling, and grammatical corrections were sorely needed. His observation that the book would have a non-military reader appeal was a major factor in my decision to seek a publisher.

I want to recognize Col. Alexander P. Shine, Commandant of Culver Military Academy, for his careful review of the manuscript for accuracy of matters dealing with military organization and terms. His suggestions and recommendations contributed greatly to the authenticity of this memoir.

A great deal of thanks goes to Mr. Noel Parsons, Editor-in-Chief of Texas A&M University Press, for directing me to Col. Robert Kane of Presidio Press, my publisher.

Mr. E. J. McCarthy, Executive Editor of Presidio Press, has been a great mentor. The many hoops and hurdles between the manuscript and the published book were a surprise to me. His patience and availability gave me great comfort.

And finally to my wife Becky, who endured a full year of total immersion in editing, researching, authenticating, and gathering of exhibits with patience and good humor.

Glossary

Here follows a glossary of terms, words, nomenclature, and expressions found in the book. The soldiers spoke a special language of military jargon, Japanese (all had been on occupation in Japan), and English.

Able, Baker, Charlie, etc.: The army's military communications alphabet in this time frame. We would refer to A Company or Battery as "Able," B, "Baker," etc.

Azimuth: The bearing to a target. The army used a 3600 mil measurement in compass bearings.

BNT: Beginning nautical twilight. Patrols were normally sent out at least one hour after BNT. The troops would be confined to a dark area to allow their eyes to adjust to darkness before departing on patrol.

Rations, B: These were the rations prepared by the company or battalion mess. They were issued in No. 10 cans of things like green beans, potatoes, flour, sugar, powdered milk, and other staples. A complete hot meal could be prepared from the rations. They were cooked over propane stoves carried by the mess truck under the command of the mess sergeant. A good mess sergeant would "trade" for eggs, fresh vegetables, fruit, or anything else locally available. We would feast on Bs in reserve positions or rest areas.

Rations, C: This was a combat ration. Each man was to receive a box of C rations per day. It contained toilet paper, cigarettes, powdered coffee, tinned biscuits (hardtack), canned fruit, and different entrées such as spaghetti and meat balls, chicken stew, beans and franks, beef stew. These items were all in cans about the size of a Vienna sausage can. There was a small bar of chocolate and a small bar of soap. The problem with this ration was that it came in a box, about the size of a shoebox. Now, how in the world is a soldier going to carry this? What occurred was, the boxes were broken open immediately, the cigarettes, toilet paper, soap, chocolate, coffee, biscuits, and fruit cocktail were consumed or put in pockets. The balance was left in the box in the hole. If we stayed in a position overnight, the rest of the food may have been consumed. If we moved out, the food was abandoned. I learned early in the campaign to open the boxes at the CP and take out the entrées (except for beans and franks, the favorite). Also, I collected all the cigarettes from all the nonsmokers, including me. I entrusted the cigarettes to my driver who had the most opportunities to go to the rear. He "purchased" all kinds of things with these, from fresh peppers and melons, to replacement crystals for our radios. When we were in a static position, I opened all the canned meals and poured them in a big copper pot we had liberated. I then dumped all the sugar, salt, and pepper in after them and all the hot peppers I could find. This would be brought to a boil at about 0200 and word would go out on the soundpower for one man from each hole to come back with two meat cans for a culinary treat. It was hot, it was food, and it sure as hell woke them up.

CP: Command post.

Column of ducks: A route-march practice with two columns of men single file on either side of the road.

EE8: The telephone we used. It was in a carrying satchel about twelve-by-eight-by-three inches. It had a crank you turned to activate the bell at the other end of your line. It was basically a World War I piece of equipment, but it worked.

ENT: Ending nautical twilight. Patrols would normally return to friendly lines before ENT. BNT and ENT times were sent down by regiment each day.

FPL: Final protective line. As the company commander laid out his perimeter he would assign a sector of fire for each crew-served weapon and each rifleman. These fire sectors provided for crossing fire from all weapons to present a wall of fire at knee level completely across the company front. The FPL was fired only as the enemy was within 100 to 200 yards of the MLR. The FPL was usually fired by colored flare, as the noise and confusion of battle would not allow radio, telephone, or voice command. Each night the FPL flare color was changed, i.e., red, green, blue, etc. When the troops saw the flare, they knew that they were to direct their weapons onto their assigned FPL sector and fire without stopping until the attack was turned, the ammo ran out, or the position was overrun (See Appendix).

Fire for effect: The command given after adjusting fire on a target, usually at least three rounds of all guns or tubes. Adjustment was normally done with the two center guns of the battery.

GT: Gun target line.

How able: Haul ass.

Hood: What Plummer and I called each other. Don't know why. It started in Jinmachi.

Hiokko: Phonetic spelling of Japanese word for rapid departure, as in "Let's hiokko the hell out of here."

Halazone pills: Pills issued to place in your canteen when you were forced to drink water of an uncertain source. It was to kill harmful bacteria. It made bad water taste worse.

HE: High explosive. The basic mortar and artillery ammunition.

MLR: Main line of resistance. This was the position on the land that each unit was assigned to defend, from platoon to company, to battalion, to regiment, to division. (In my experience we never had a division, and most of the time we were an isolated battalion.)

Meat can: The can a soldier's canteen fits into. It has a folding handle and holds about a pint. The canteen is in a webbing sack that fits on the cartridge belt.

NFL: No fire line (friendly troops from this point to guns).

OP: Observation Post.

OPLR: Outpost of least resistance. This was the most forward position of the perimeter or line. The mission of the troops manning the OPLR is to deceive the enemy as to the true location of the main defensive positions and to cause the enemy to prematurely go into his battle formation and attack the wrong terrain. Also, this provided an artillery and mortar target after the OPLR withdrew and the enemy "bunched" at its location. The target area would have been preregistered and a TOT could be fired.

OT: Observer target line.

Sukoshi: Japanese for small, little.

Soundpower: A newer telephone issued to the infantry. No box, power in handset. Good for short range. You could whisper, hiss, or whistle to get other party to pick up line. Good at night when you did not want a phone ringing to give away your position.

TOT: Time on target. A prearranged registration involving all firepower available to the command. In our case, this would be the 105s, the 4.2s, and the 81s. Because all the pieces firing were at different ranges, their firing times had to be mathematically calculated so that the rounds would arrive at the target at the same time. Hence "time on target."

Takasan — pronounced "Toxon": Japanese for a lot, whole bunch.

WP: White phosphorus. Ammo used for adjusting fire (made huge white plumes) and frequently mixed with HE when fired "for effect." Also it was very effective against armor, setting it on fire.

WEAPONS

60s: The mortars at company level. They were in the Weapons Platoon and were employed as the company commander required. The 60mm had about a 2,500-yard range. These were the only indirect-fire weapons at company level.

81s: The mortars in the weapons company at battalion level, 81mm. These mortars were sometimes assigned to support separate companies as a "section" of two tubes and sometimes employed as a battery of six tubes supporting the entire battalion front. Range of 5,000 yards.

4.2s: The heavy mortar of the infantry. They were in the regimental heavy weapons company. There were six tubes. The 4.2 (i.e., 4.2 inches in diameter) is a very effective weapon with about a 6,000-yard range, and very high trajectory.

105s: The basic Army howitzer assigned to support every infantry regiment. There were three firing batteries to an artillery battalion and each battery supported an infantry regiment. There were three infantry battalions to a regiment. There were six guns to a battery. These guns provided indirect fire (over hills) and had a range of 12,000 yards.

Light .30s: These were the machine guns at company level. They were in the Weapons Platoon and assigned to the rifle platoons as the situation dictated. They were normally employed in pairs at either end of a perimeter. For example, if a platoon was dug in around a hill covering a front of 600 yards, the light .30s would be set up at each flank to provide a cross fire across the front, particularly for the FPL. A light .30 squad always carried two barrels so that the barrels could be exchanged as they got hot from firing. I have seen them so hot that they glowed in the dark and the riffling was ruined. (The situation was so frantic that the squad could not stop firing to change barrels.)

Heavy .30s: This was the water-cooled 30-caliber machine gun in the Weapons Company. They could fire for extended periods with the water being circulated through the "jacket" surrounding the barrel. The heavy .30s were farmed out to the rifle companies as the situation dictated. Their range was up to 1,000 yards.

BAR: Browning automatic rifle. This was a rapid-firing rifle supported on a bipod. Each infantry squad had a BAR team of two men, the rifleman and the ammo bearer. This weapon was used as a base of fire on offense and as the most long-range weapon on defense, 1,000 yards.

Burp gun: The Russian Tommy gun that was used by most NKPA outfits on offense. It had a round, spring-loaded magazine (like a clock) below the barrel. I think of it as a 1930 Chicago gangster-type weapon. It was not very accurate, but with several hundred hostiles firing at one time as they spread over your hill, they poured out a lot of rounds. This is the weapon that got me.

Elephant gun: A Russian towed fieldpiece. Its tube was rifled and long, providing high velocity and flat trajectory. It had large steel shields on either side, forward of the wheels. With the shields as ears and the tube as trunk, it resembled an elephant. It probably had an effective range of about 6,000 yards.

ARMY ORGANIZATION, 1950

A Squad: Infantry, 12 men: 10 riflemen and a 2-man BAR team.

B Platoon: Made up of four squads: 48 men plus a platoon sergeant and a platoon leader, a second or first lieutenant.

C Company: Made up of three rifle platoons and one weapons platoon. The weapons platoon was armed with three 60mm mortars and three light .30 caliber machine guns.

D: The company headquarters consisted of a company commander, a captain, an executive officer, a first lieutenant, a first sergeant, a company clerk, a mess sergeant and three cooks, a supply sergeant and a corporal supply clerk. There is a motor sergeant and six driver/mechanics. All together 17 men.

Total men in a company table of organization: 217.

To the best of my knowledge, we were never up to strength in Korea. I think A Company started out with 186 men. As the war progressed, the cooks, drivers, and clerks became riflemen. I don't remember ever having four lieutenants at one time to command the platoons. There was never an executive officer. For most of the period, I was with Company A and I was de facto platoon leader of the 2d Platoon.

Battalion: The battalion consisted of three rifle companies, one weapons company, and a headquarters company. The rifle company is described above. The weapons company was commanded by a captain. It was armed with 81mm mortars, .30 caliber heavy machine guns (water-cooled) and two 57mm recoilless rifles. It was organized into squads that manned the crew-served weapons. The headquarters company was commanded by a captain with a first lieutenant executive officer. Within the headquarters company was the signal section, the I&R (intelligence and recognisance) Platoon, a motor section, and mess sergeant and cooks. The battalion was commanded by a lieutenant colonel, the executive officer was a major, the S-1, personnel, S-2, intelligence, S-3, operations, and S-4, logistics, all were majors. (In fact, the 1st Battalion only had one major, the S-3, all others were captains.) We operated as a lone battalion most of the time. Seldom was there any unit on our left or right. At times we were employed with the 2d Battalion. There was no 3d Battalion!

Regiment: The regiment consisted of three battalions. The regiment is the oldest numbered unit in the army. Many date back to the Revolutionary War and the 27th, the Wolfhounds, is one of the oldest. It gained its name during its participation in the Allied intervention in the Russian Civil War in 1919. At the time we were committed, there were only two regiments in the 25th Division, the 24th and the 27th (please don't confuse the 24th Regiment with the 24th Division). I was in the 27th. The regiment is the maneuver element of the division. The normal employment would be two regiments on line and one in reserve. Our regimental commander was Lieutenant Colonel John H. "Mike" Michaelis (who was later a three-star general). The army organization manual prescribes for a full colonel to command a regiment. Also, within the regiment, there was a heavy mortar company, commanded by a captain, consisting of six 4.2-inch mortars. These were sometimes employed in twos with each battalion and sometimes as a battery. They were very accurate and I fired them many times.

Division: Commanded by a major general. The division consisted of three regiments. We only had two regiments until sometime in August 1950, when the 35th joined us from Okinawa. It was called the "Triple Nickel." I knew it was on the peninsula, but I never had any contact with the outfit. In fact, I never had any contact or knowledge of any part of the division. Within the division was the division artillery. It was commanded by a brigadier general. There were three 105mm howitzer battalions of six guns each and a 155mm howitzer battery. Normally a 105 battery was assigned to each regiment and the 155 howitzer battalion of six guns supported the entire front.

Attachments: Within the Army were tank and engineer outfits. At times a platoon or a company of tanks were attached to us in supporting positions or on attacks. The engineers were employed for river crossings and other special situations. Also, signal, quartermaster, ordinance, transportation, aviation, MP, and JAG units were in the division.

Corps: A corps is put together by army. It can be as few as two divisions or as many as the army commander likes. Usually three to four divisions.

Army: The army consists of the several corps. In this case we were in the Eighth Army. No corps were established during the Pusan Perimeter stage of the conflict.

CHAPTER ONE

Briefing

On 25 June 1950, I was a second lieutenant, field artillery, posted to B Battery of the 49th Field Artillery Battalion, 7th Division, Eighth Army. The station was Jinmachi, northern Honshu. This was at the time of the U.S. occupation of Japan and its "reconstruction." The post was quite remote, situated in the mountains about twenty miles northwest of Yamagata. It had been an Imperial Japanese Cavalry post. I had arrived in January, fresh from the campus of the University of Florida, where I had earned a master's in economics. The source of my commission was the ROTC at Purdue. I had experienced not a single day of active duty or training since the ROTC days at Purdue in 1948. The 49th Field Artillery was my first posting. I had been shipped directly to Japan upon being sworn in as a regular army officer, an appointment offered on the basis of a graduate degree. To assume that I was green, and at the bottom of the competency ladder, would be accurate.

Nevertheless, I attacked the military career with vigor and managed to overcome my lack of competence with enthusiasm and a great deal of instruction from the seasoned officers in the outfit. Of particular help was Lt. Bill Plummer. He was a senior first lieutenant and had served in the ETO (European theater of operations) in World War II.

The first section of this chapter was written in 1999, after the manuscript was lost for forty-seven years. It is not my purpose to relate the details of the first six months of duty. However, it is important to identify Plummer, Nurse "X," and "Jeb Stuart" as they play an important part in the saga that follows. Plummer was from St. Louis. He had played catcher on a St. Louis Cardinals farm baseball team and had aspirations of being a major league regular. These plans were changed on 7 December 1941. For some reason, we called each other "Hood" (like gangster hoods. Don't remember how this got started). He was a great teacher.

Nurse "X" was a large woman who made up one-half of the medical team at the post. I am embarrassed that I cannot recall her name. The other half of the medical team was Nurse "Y" who was a tall, lean woman. Both nurses were in their middle thirties and had been in the army since the early forties. The nurses were officers and were present at the officers' mess for most meals. Their quarters were next door to mine. The BOQs (bachelor officers' quarters) were one-story structures with a hall down the middle and about six rooms on either side. There was one latrine and one shower in the middle of the building.

Now, why is this important to the story that follows?

It developed that my mess sergeant had stolen an Akita puppy that was from a litter belonging to Gen. Billy Gilmore, commander of 7th Division artillery. When the heat was on to recover the dog, the sergeant generously "gave" the puppy to me. Being the only (and dumbest) second lieutenant on the post, it is clear why I was the logical choice.

I was totally swept off my feet by this little dog. He was the cutest thing in Japan and he absolutely took to me. I named him "Jeb Stuart" after my favorite Confederate general. Jeb was a quick learner, and soon was my constant shadow. He accompanied me as I made my rounds on the post, and, of course, got the attention of the general.

I was called to the CG's office without any idea of the purpose of the summons. I was ushered into the general's office by his aide. I stood at attention before his desk, saluted, and stated, "Lieutenant Terry reporting as ordered, sir." In short order, General Gilmore accused me of dog theft and suggested this might be a court-martial offense. This blew me out of the tub. I had no idea Jeb had come from the general's bitch. I explained the circumstances of my "gift" of the dog. The general stated flatly that he didn't believe me. Boy, was I sweating. General Gilmore allowed that he would have given me the dog if he had known how much I wanted him. Further, that I had possessed him (the dog) long enough to ruin him, and that he wouldn't be good for anything now, anyway. (I think I saw a trace of a little smile here.) I was dismissed and told that I could keep the dog.

Through the late winter and spring, Jeb and I bonded and he became a real army dog. He knew all the bugle calls and participated in all the battalion parades. Everyone knew him and he flourished with all the attention. Nurse "X" was especially drawn to Jeb and coaxed him into her quarters at every opportunity. I discovered that she was purchasing his affection with chocolate candy and this really upset me. I absolutely did not allow junk food in my dog. We had a few words about this situation and Nurse "X" would always promise that she would not feed him candy again, but she did. When I had to go to the field for a few days for training, she would always volunteer to take care of Jeb. I think he probably liked her second to me.

Now, back to Sunday, 25 June 1950. The North Korean People's Army crossed the 38th Parallel and invaded South Korea with great force. Dean Acheson, secretary of state, had stated that Korea was beyond the strategic interest of the United States, as was Formosa. President Harry S. Truman had made no statement about protecting South Korea. General Douglas MacArthur had no plans for the defense of South Korea that we were aware of. No one in the 49th thought that we would be involved.

The 24th Division, which occupied Kyushu, was committed first. The 25th, occupying southern

Honshu, was committed second. (I would be assigned to the 25th.) The folks assigned to the 1st Cav and the 7th Division were drawn from to "fill up the ranks" of the 24th and 25th. (Remember, there are three regiments to a division. In the Eighth Army in 1950, there were only two regiments in each division.) I was ordered out on 2 July. My most pressing question was what to do with Jeb. Nurse "X" solved that problem. She was beating on my door as I was trying to get my combat pack together and report to the RTO (rail transport office). She begged me to let her keep Jeb. She said he would never even smell chocolate and that he would be as smart and sweet as ever when I got back in a few months. So, that's what happened to Jeb.

Plummer was on the roster with me and we were bound for APO 25, Osaka, Japan.

On 2 July we had an order from the Eighth Army in Jinmachi for seven lieutenants, two captains, one major, and 500 enlisted men to be sent to APO 25, Osaka. We boarded a special train of four cars that took us, with blinds down, to Sendai. There our train was connected with cars from Sapporo and several other 7th Division posts. We were speeded south through the night, perhaps 5,000 officers and men all told. We arrived at Osaka the following day at 1700 hours. We were taken to the 25th Division headquarters and told to prepare for air transportation to Korea. We were deposited in the lobby of a hotel that was the 25th Division's BOQ and we proceeded to wait nervously. After much waiting and urinating, we were told that the airport was all socked in — that we would draw quarters and have one more night's sleep between sheets. This was heartening news, because the wooden benches of the Japanese trains had not been too comfortable or clean the night before, and most of us felt as though our part of the so-called police action (which is what President Truman called the Korean War) could be postponed another day.

The following morning we were told that we were to go by train to Fukuoka. We boarded around noon, along with the same enlisted men who had been on the train with us from the north. We pulled out of Osaka for another twenty-hours' ride to the southernmost island of the Japanese group. The men were greatly fatigued at this point, and the ordeal of the trip was beginning to show on everyone. The blessing was that the fatigue relieved the tension, and most of us slept that night in spite of the many tunnels that funneled the smoke into the cars through the open windows.

The train toilets consisted of oblong holes in the floor of the car. It took considerable skill to squat, hold your pants, balance yourself, and hit the hole from both ends at the same time. Many of the "old soldiers" who had taken part in the occupation for several years were quite skilled at it but for those of us who had been on this "island paradise" for only a few months it added considerably to the discomfort of the trip due to our lack of coordination and skill. Finally, it was decided that a latrine orderly would be assigned in every car to see that each individual scraped, kicked, or pushed his own droppings through the hole. This abated the menace considerably.

Outside of a few hundred Japanese casualties, due to flying C ration cans from the speeding trains, the trip was uneventful. We arrived at Fukuoka at 0600 the following morning and found only the Japanese station agents there to meet us. The little colonel who had taken command of the train in Osaka was considerably upset at the lack of a transportation and reception committee. He promised those of us close to his elbows that there would be some hell-raising when we got to the 24th Division headquarters. After a telephone call, GI trucks began to pour into the courtyard at the station, and a part of what was to become "the famous 27th Wolfhound Regiment" piled into the trucks.

Not knowing what outfit we were, or were to become, we were carried to the evacuated 24th Division headquarters, an old Japanese industrial plant. We were quartered in the barracks that had so hastily been abandoned by that now-famous division. We took baths, ate C rations, and waited. By noon, trucks were lining up to take us to the port to embark for Pusan. The young lieutenant with a siren on his jeep led our fifty- or sixty-truck convoy on a fifty-miles-per-hour trek to the docks at Sasebo. Upon arrival, he received a thorough chewing out by a colonel whom I did not know. But if the troops felt the way I did, the speed and recklessness of the truck ride had relieved some of the tension and made us feel as though we were at least going somewhere. We dismounted on the docks near a very large and formidable-looking transport, stood around for about twenty or thirty minutes, and then learned that this was the wrong boat. We climbed back into the trucks, went about two miles down the dock area to where two small Japanese inter-island ferries were making a head of steam, obviously preparing for a voyage. These little ships had three decks, the lower A deck being only two or three feet above the water and measuring from stem to stern only 100 or perhaps 110 feet. On the first ship we packed 465 men and nine officers, including one doctor. We had C rations for three days and a magazine of ammunition for each individual weapon. These were carbines, .45s, and M1s.

A very tough-speaking lieutenant colonel, whom I had never seen before and was never to see again, took command of the ship. The captain was Japanese and his crew was Japanese, Korean, Chinese, and Philippine. The crew was made up of no more than eight or nine men. We waited until dark and made our way out of the harbor across the Sea of Japan. Watches were organized and the strictest blackout orders enforced. The troops were assigned to decks and simply collapsed there. There was no panic, very little tension, just simple fatigue.

My watch was from 0300 to 0500, and was uneventful. I was relieved at 0500 by Lieutenant Howard, went back to B deck where my gear had been deposited, and passed out into a most restful sleep. The next morning Lieutenant Plummer got a wrestling hold on my foot and shouted, "Get up, Hood, we have reached the wild, picturesque, and romantic continent of Asia."

In spite of my weariness, I eagerly jumped to my feet, stuck my head out the porthole: there was Pusan! We were entering the bay and could see the Korean fishing boats passing into the bay carrying on business as usual.

Around the bay were steep and rugged hills, completely naked of trees, and boasting only a kind of scrub grass, red soil, and brown rocks. At the end of the bay was a chaos of gray that materialized into mud-and-stick houses and mud-and-tile business establishments. It looked as though Pusan had simply slipped from the sides of the hills into a pile of confusion at the end of the bay. It completely lacked color. As I think back on Pusan, I can remember only gray.

After about an hour of waiting we took on a pilot and were docked at one of the lesser piers. While waiting to disembark we heard carbine fire. I looked over to where a South Korean sentry was pulling guard over supplies. He was firing at some children who had gotten too close, in his estimation, to the dock area. The children dispersed.

9

Briefly, and with a minimum of confusion, we performed the miracle of getting the same number of troops off that we had put on and assembled them on a railroad siding near the dock. Here we were assigned to our units. Four of us from Jinmachi were to go to the 8th Field Artillery. We were directed to a building that sat on the railroad tracks about a quarter of a mile up the road. As we trudged up the railroad tracks, we noted that there were three other transports docking and two more were visible on the horizon. It made me feel strong.

We reached the building, which had boarded windows, and on the shady side I met Lt. Col. August T. Terry, Jr. (no relation) from New Orleans. He was to be my CO and commander of the 8th Field Artillery. A lieutenant asked for my 201 file and told me to make myself comfortable while I was being assigned. I slumped down with Plummer (from Illinois) against the building. We talked about the other hoods from our post who were being assigned elsewhere. Hood Haegar from North Carolina joined us shortly. After settling down for a few minutes I heard what sounded like crying. Plummer heard it, too. We looked around, but saw no one weeping. The noise persisted, however, so I got up and walked around to the side of the building. As I passed by one of the boarded windows, I was certain that the crying was coming from within.

I looked through a crack in the boards and saw a dozen or so small boys about ten to twelve years of age kneeling in a double row with their hands behind them. A Korean policeman was walking behind the first row, striking the children between the shoulder blades many times with a board two or three feet long and several inches thick. There were a few other Koreans in the room nudging each other with their elbows, pointing to the children in agony, and laughing. I rushed around to the front of the building and grabbed someone (I don't remember who) and asked him if he knew what was going on inside and suggested doing something about it. It was at this point that I learned of a directive that forbade American troops from interfering in any way with Korean civil affairs.

I rushed back to the windows calling Plummer and Haegar. As they arrived we heard what sounded like furniture breaking and the splattering or breaking of a water-filled bag. A door opened and from the room came an adult Korean with his head bleeding and his nose pushed over on the side of his face. A South Korean policeman followed him and kicked him into a corner. The Korean policemen in the room laughed with glee. This was our introduction to our allies.

Someone pulled at my shoulder, handed me a copy of my orders assigning me to A Battery. A corporal directed me to the point where the battery was assembled for loading onto flatcars. I walked to the head of the motor pool and there I found Captain Hull and Lieutenants Record, Anderson, and Carter. I was assigned a jeep and trailer, a driver, Private First Class Toras, and a radioman, Payne. I was to be an FO (forward observer). Army T, O, and E (table of organization and equipment) calls for a lieutenant, a reconnaissance sergeant, a commo corporal, and a Pfc. driver. However, we were fighting at two-thirds strength and I was very happy to have two able-bodied men with or without training.

The battery was loaded on flatcars, each driver blocking his own vehicle, and the South Koreans tying them to the cars with rice-straw rope. (It seems that Americans do not have the knack of tying heavy vehicles with rice straws.) We moved out of Pusan at 1700 and rattled northward. Our orders were to advance up the east coast of the peninsula, seek out, and engage the enemy. Upon close inspection of our train, many of us professed great doubt as to its ability to transport us. The engine was an old Japanese model that had huge patches riveted on the sides of its boiler. From the sound and appearance of its wheels, it was evident that the Koreans had yet to discover the circular variety. The flatcars on which we were perched were in harmony with the surroundings. Some were from China, some from Japan, others of unknown origin. They rattled, vibrated, shook, and traveled as far sideways as they did forward. We attempted to get comfortable and then devoured our C ration meal, which was beginning to taste familiar by now.

Just before dark we came to a halt in a small Korean city. The local schoolmarms and schoolchildren were on the station platform in force, half of them with U.S. flags, the rest with Korean ones. They marched up and down the side of the train waving the flags in cadence, singing Korean songs, which most of us felt might be the local equivalent to "You Came a Long Way from St. Louis," or perhaps "I'd Love to Get You on a Slow Boat to China." After a few minutes our train rattled out and darkness dropped around us. The capacity of our little engine for speed was unbelievable. I am sure it attained sixty or seventy miles an hour on many of the downward stretches. As it became dark, the troops began to get trigger happy. All up and down the train there were occasional bursts of fire. We (officers and NCOs) made an effort to bring the firing to a halt, but due to the noise of the train and the hazard of going from one car to the other while the train was in motion, our efforts had little effect upon those "juvenile delinquents" who were to be the heroes of our beachhead.

CHAPTER
TWO

Heartbreak Highway

We arrived at Uisong the following morning after a train ride that I am sure I shall never forget. The vehicles were unloaded from the flatcars and we were off to the war. I joined the infantry, the 1st Battalion of the 27th Regiment, at once, and I was never again to spend much time with the 8th Field Artillery. Captain Beard was our liaison officer, and we were to become big buddies in the course of the campaign. Captain Logan E. Weston was the company commander of Able Company, the company I was to later learn like the palm of my hand. Lieutenant John Buckley, from Augusta, Georgia, was the executive officer of the company, and Lieutenants Font, from Puerto Rico, Scroggens, and Braum were the platoon leaders.

The 1st Battalion went into a perimeter around Uisong that first night and the 2d Battalion was sent to Yongdok on the east coast.

The following night, after sending motorized patrols far to the north, we moved into position at Andong, twenty miles farther north. We went into position on the road leading northwest to Yochon and Chongju. From there we worked patrols for several days, fighting skirmishes at every opportunity. We made contact with the ROK (Republic of Korea) 8th Division and fought closely with them. It really seemed as though we were fighting a rather decent war. The casualties were light and the enemy had shown us no artillery or armor.

While at this position, I received my third man, Homes. He had been in my battery in the 7th Division in Japan, and I was delighted to have him. He was a wiry little kid from New Jersey. He was a natural to fit in with my big radio operator, Payne, who was from West Virginia, and the driver, Toras, who was from Hawaii. I felt as though I had the most colorful command in the theater. We all got along well from the beginning, and although the fighting was not too rough at the very start of the campaign, I felt that I had an outfit that would be sticking right in the hottest part of a firefight when the going tightened up.

On the morning of the fourth day at Andong, Lt. Col. Gilbert Check, CO of the 1st Battalion, and Lt. Col. Mike Michaelis, CO of the regiment, climbed the hill to my OP to look over the battalion front and to inspect our positions. Colonel Check was a slight little man with a quiet confidence about him. I guessed his age to be somewhere around thirty-five to forty. Colonel Michaelis was tall and slender. His hair was a silver gray, his skin as clear and smooth as I have ever seen on a man. He was extremely alert and spoke distinctly. He was thirty-eight. The two stood above my hold and discussed the campaign, and I eavesdropped for all I was worth. From what I had gathered from their conversation, the outfit was to leave shortly. This proved to be the case. We got the order to move out at 2000 that evening.

The battalion assembled on the road back at Service Company and was put on trucks. The column rendezvoused with a motorized column with the 2d Battalion aboard at Andong, and after we had crossed the Naktong River, we were joined by the 8th Field Artillery Battalion. This made a column at least five miles long. To me it seemed as though we had an enormous task force. The column moved south, lights blazing, to Uisong, then turned west to pass through Kunwi and several other towns that had no name and no meaning for us. In all the towns the civilians were lining the road, even after midnight, in tight little groups, watching us roar past. They made no sound and no one waved. They just stood solemnly at the side of the road and watched with poker faces as we rode by. There was no light, other than that which was made by our headlights, and these cast exaggerated shadows on the mud walls of the villages. Occasionally the cry of a baby from within a house or the frightened bark of a dog could be heard, but nothing more. The column roared on into the black night. Its destination, anyone's guess.

By 0200 it had started to rain, and this not only added to the misery of the trip, but also to the hazard. We were in a particularly mountainous region, and the rain had made the red clay roads deathtraps of oozing mud and water. Two trucks were lost over the edge of a precipice and most of their cargo of men were lost. On several occasions I felt certain that we were going over the side also. Our quarter-ton trailer was overloaded to the breaking point, and more than once it had slipped to the side, pulling the jeep around at right angles to it.

It was about 0300 when we had a surprise. We entered a large city. After taking two or three wrong roads, we wound up in a big marketplace. In the pouring rain I spotted a wet MP on guard in front of a rather sturdy building that had evidently been taken over by our forces. I called to him from our parked vehicle and asked what town we were in. "Taegu," came back his muffled voice. I looked around at the others in my party in surprise. What the hell were we doing back in Taegu? We had really covered some territory in the last few hours' motor march. The column began to move again. We cranked up and followed. In a few minutes we were out of the city and on another seemingly endless, muddy road. The rain continued to beat down and the fatigue and discomfort of the troops mounted. I sat in the puddle of water that was my seat, miserable, tired, and puzzled over why we had left our sector and had gone all the way back to Taegu and then northwest. Our destination and our present location was a complete mystery to me. The only logical guess for our movement must be related to the action that had taken place on the west in the 24th's sector. Because we had learned of none of the unfortunate battles at the Han River, Suwon, Osan, and so on, we had no idea of the critical state of our position.

The column came to a stop at around 0430 and we simply sat in the rain and soaked until 0600, at which time the column cranked up and we moved on again in a generally northwesterly direction. We passed through many towns and villages that meant nothing to us, and changed our general direction from west to north and then from north to west several times. We completely turned around twice, and by 1400 I don't believe there was a soul in the outfit who had any idea where we were. The significant thing, as I saw it, was that there was more and more military traffic as we moved forward, and all the vehicles were from the 24th Division. Another condition that pointed toward our nearness to some action was the thousands of refugees who streamed east and south. It was obvious that things were not going too well. A few of the troops of the 24th had been questioned by our men at rest breaks, and the tales they told turned our blood cold. They told of tanks, artillery, and mortars that supported thousands of yelling North Koreans who charged on toward them, indifferent to their own casualties. They told of entire battalions being wiped out, and artillery positions and regimental CPs being overrun. They told of the aid stations being run through by tanks, and of the enemy shooting the GI wounded as they lay on litters.

All of this came as a shock to me. The Reds had not shown us any strength in the east and we had held them for five days. We had seen no tanks or artillery. I was surprised to hear these tales of the apparent abundance in the enemy forces. Frankly, seeing and talking to these troops from the 24th frightened us. After I had been in the thick of things a little while I learned to laugh at the stories of men from other outfits, but at this time I hung onto every word and noticed that the others in our column did likewise.

By 1630 hours we had reached a town that seemed to be a hub for roads going in all directions. We stopped here for some time. The rain had stopped so I took this opportunity to put on some dry socks. It was while we were here that I first heard the word *Taejon*. It was on everyone's lips and I gathered that it was an important town. I asked a 24th Division truck driver, who had a flat tire, about it, and he told me that it was where the 24th was holding. He mentioned something about the Kum River and a hell of a fight developing around its banks and Taejon. I was soon to learn a lot more about the Kum and Taejon.

At this place Captain Weston's jeep refused to start and he asked to ride with me. When he climbed in the front seat with me he started talking. He turned out to be a herald of information. He said that he had just come from a command group meeting and that the battalion was going into position on an important road running north out of Okchon, which was a few miles east of Taejon and south of the Kum River. This really didn't mean too much to us because we were not familiar with the location of these places, but we at least had the satisfaction of knowing where we were going.

We spent the remainder of the afternoon grinding over the mud-and-water roads, splashing through dirty mud-and-stick towns and villages, and waiting in our vehicles at the side of the road. No one ever seemed to know why we stopped or how long we would be there. It is the most amazing maneuver the army practices. This waiting. We did more waiting than anything else that afternoon. The rain would stop then commence again. The roads gathered more and more water and the fatigue of the troops gathered more weight. It was dark and we continued to wait and drive. There were more mountains and treacherous turns, there were fords, made uncommonly deep by the rains. Vehicles broke down, went into a ditch, fell over cliffs, and flooded out. The men complained, cussed, caught colds, and vowed that they would "shoot that sly, damn recruiting sergeant" if they ever got home.

It was nearly midnight when the column pulled into a field near a small village. The troops piled out of the trucks and the trucks returned from whence they came. Able Company was assigned an area to the east of the field, and after putting out security guards, they sacked out on the wet ground. No one seemed to mind the dampness after twenty-four hours in the rain, and it was only minutes before the exhausted regiment was asleep.

At 0600 I opened my eyes to find all kinds of activity taking place. It was obvious that the outfit was to make a move. The troops were busily adjusting packs, checking weapons, drawing grenades, and so on. I got up with much creaking and stretching to find that my crew was already up and functioning. They had let me continue to sleep, although the others had been awake for some time. I had walked over to the jeep to get my toilet articles and put my blanket in the trailer when the company runner came up to me and said that Captain Weston wanted me to report to him at once. This I did.

"We are going to the regimental CP for a briefing, Terry. Are you ready to take off?"

I replied that I was and we marched off through the field, across the road, past a few houses, and into a schoolyard. We entered the school to find Colonel Michaelis, Colonel Check, and the other company commanders along with Captain Beard, the liaison officer. The briefing was exactly that, brief. What it amounted to was that the NKPA (North Korean People's Army) were pressing hard on the front of the 24th at Taejon and all along the Kum. There was a real danger of them breaking through our crust, and after that running on to Pusan, for there was nothing else to stop them. Our regiment was to go in on the right of the 24th and prevent them from being flanked by the use of a secondary road. The 1st Battalion was to be about ten miles to the east on commanding ground in the mountains. That was it. Sweet and simple. I was given a map of the area in which we were to operate. Colonel Check announced that the command group for the 1st Battalion would rendezvous on the road in fifteen minutes to go forward at 0700.

Captain Weston and I walked back to the company area. He suggested that we go forward in his jeep, which was repaired by then, and that my party follow with the company when they came up. I agreed to this plan and dashed off to give my crew the word and to get a can of C rations out of the jeep for breakfast.

The command group assembled on the road in jeeps. Captain Weston and I were the last to show and as soon as we had pulled up in the rear of the little column of four jeeps we moved out. The road ran west for about four miles and then formed a junction with the north-south road we were to defend at Okchon. Here we turned right and proceeded north until we reached a point some four or five miles north of the town. Here the valley, in which the road ran, was only about a mile wide, and a ridge ran down to the road from the major hills on the west side. On the east, the hills were high and extremely steep. It was here that it was determined that we would engage the NKPA.

The command group dismounted and went to the crest of one of the lesser hills on the east of the road. After a terrain survey Colonel Check assigned to Able the ridge running perpendicular to the road on the west and the extremely high peak from which the ridge spilled. This peak was the outstanding landmark in the entire area and it was only about half a mile off the road. Baker Company was given an area that included the road at the place where the ridge ran down to it, and a front of about five hundred yards running up the hills to the east of the road. Charlie was given the crest of the hills on the east of the valley. The CP and aid stations were to be located at a schoolhouse that sat behind a little knoll about half a mile behind our most forward positions, but protected on the flank by Charlie.

At this, the group broke up and each company commander, with his FO, went to reconnoiter the area assigned to his company. Captain Weston and I made our way down the hill we were on and up the ridge that was to be the area in which most of the company was to be stationed. After checking the ridge we investigated a little hill to its rear that we named Sugar Loaf Hill. The company CP was to be located behind the hill, and the motor pool (only four jeeps and trailers, counting mine) was to be in a group of small scrub trees that were also in the area. Captain Weston decided that the only place for me would be that prominent peak and he assigned it to me along with a squad of men to protect it. It was obvious to both of us that by controlling that

23

peak we could control the entire left flank of the battalion. It was also obvious that observation from the peak would in all likelihood extend for several miles up the road. Thus, I was destined to draw this prominent landmark for my position.

The captain glanced at his watch and noted that it was about time for the company to arrive. They, of course, were making the march on foot, and we had taken just about enough time in our reconnoitering to give them time to catch up with us. The captain asked me if I would go out on the road and guide the company in when they arrived. He was going to look over the area a little more closely.

I made my way down to the road after a couple of falls in the rice paddies (I was trying to walk the little dikes that divide the paddies). I sat down in the ditch and waited. There was no sign of the troops, but the I&R Platoon passed by on a motorized reconnaissance up the road. I glanced at my watch. It was 1100. I looked around for some shade, but I couldn't find any. I took a few sips of water out of my canteen and fiddled with my carbine. I looked up at the peak that I was to man and dreaded the climb. It was at least a 75-degree climb most of the way and in places it looked as though it was straight up. There were really two peaks instead of one, but the lesser peak was nothing more than a projection of the primary one. On the very top of the pinnacle there was what appeared to be a rather flat surface, perhaps fifteen yards in diameter. There was no vegetation on the hill other than grass, and there didn't seem to be much of that. It was mostly rocks, or at least so it appeared. I sat there and eyed the hill and fretted about getting up it and being supplied once there. Frankly, I didn't want to go up the damn thing.

I happened to glance up the road to the north and noticed dust. My first thought was to run. I thought the NKPA were ahead of their schedule as we had figured it, and I was not in the frame of mind to make a one-man stand. Then I remembered the patrol that had gone up the road in jeeps just a few minutes before and I wondered why I had not heard firing. Then it dawned on me that something had been said about the ROK 3d Division withdrawing through our positions, and I reasoned that this might be them. Still, I didn't want to gamble and I had no way of being sure. Maybe the patrol had seen the enemy first and had taken to the hills. Maybe the ROK outfit had taken another route. I was about to jump into the paddies to hide when I saw what appeared to be an American jeep leading the column. Of course, the patrol had gone out to meet them. That was the reason the I&R Platoon had been sent out, to prevent us from firing on the ROKs. Just the same, I reasoned that I had better make ready to jump in the paddies, in the event my assumptions were incorrect. I moved up to the edge of the paddies and made sure that I stayed in a prone position.

As it turned out, I had guessed correctly and the column was the retiring ROK division that had been expected. As they came closer, and I was certain of their identification, I sat up and watched them go by. They were completely on foot except for the GI jeep that was leading them. There seemed to be no brass with them at all and the highest grade officer I spotted was a captain. They had many oxen that were loaded with wire, ammo, C rations, and 60mm mortars. There were a few oxcarts also. The outfit came down the road in a column of ducks and they were stepping pretty lively for a bunch who had been in constant battle for two weeks. They were mostly equipped with M1 rifles with a few carbines and grease guns. They all wore rubber shoes and their uniforms were a green cotton that was obviously a copy of our fatigues. On their heads were every conceivable type of headgear, but the most popular seemed to be the GI plastic helmet liner without the steel helmet. It was really a motley, yet tough and hardy, group that passed by me that morning.

Our infantry met the ROKs at the road junction and there was a mess as the two bodies of men tried to pass each other. It was accomplished, however, and in our favor. Several of the ROKs broke ranks and joined our outfit in hopes of getting better chow. We let them stay with us. This was a crazy war.

When Able Company reached me I gave each platoon its relative position and they took off for it.

I got in my jeep when my party drove up, after telling the other company jeeps where they were to go. I reasoned that the easiest way to get up to my peak was to drive the jeep to the point where the ridge nearly reached the road. I would take what equipment I needed from the jeep there, and with the help of Holmes and Toras, we would get the wire laid from the road to the peak. I told Payne to lay wire from our starting point on the road back to the battalion and Captain Beard. Then he was to leave the jeep in the company motor park and bring up some chow to our OP on the peak. When he reached the top, which I did not expect would be before 1700 or 1800, I would send someone else down to stay at the company CP. The following morning we would rotate again. This way no one member of the party, other than myself, would have to remain on the OP all of the time and with each rotation we would have a fresh supply of water and rations.

Payne said that he understood what he was to do. He commenced splicing the end of the wire I was going to lay up the hill with another roll that he would carry back to the liaison officer in the battalion. Toras, Holmes, and I loaded ourselves up with the radio, wire, map board, and our weapons with ammunition, and we started our climb.

The 2d Platoon had already reached the ridge over which we walked to get to the side of our peak. Holmes had accurately named it "that bare-assed son of a bitch."

"God damn, Lieutenant, you know what I told these guys when we turned up this road and I spotted that bare-assed son of a bitch?" asked Holmes. "I said that I would bet these guys a bottle of sake each that we would be out on that bare-assed son of a bitch. That's exactly what I said, sir."

"Boy, oh, boy! I wish you would keep that beeg mouth shut," said Toras dryly with his Hawaiian accent. "If you would stop guessing how we were going to fight this goddamn war, maybe we wouldn't be put on so damn many bare-assed sons of bitches. This son of a bitch, she is the worst yet."

I kept on puffing up the hill trying hard not to appear tired. The sun was burning down and each step hurt. We came to the place where the 2d Platoon had set up their CP in a big erosion ditch. I stopped and tied our wire to a little bush and asked them to connect us into the company net when their wire got up to them. They agreed and we went on. Soon we reached the end of the ridge and the bare-assed son of a bitch towered above us. It was, as I said, damn near straight up.

Here we took a break before starting to claw our way up. The rocks were loose and would pull out of the hill as we grabbed hold of them, then they would roll dangerously down on the unfortunate character who happened to be bringing up the rear at that moment. There were a few bushes to hold on to, but they couldn't be trusted. As soon as you would develop a little confidence in hanging on to the bushes, one would pull out and a ton of rocks and dirt would start sliding down upon you. We were wringing wet with perspiration, and as we became covered with the falling dirt, it stuck to us most uncomfortably, turning to mud the sweat that ran down us. The grade seemed steeper as we progressed, and the packs with the heavy parts of the radio on them threw us off balance. In fact, I thought many times that I would surely be pulled over backward.

I began to fret about the squad that was to come up with me, and I wondered if I should have gone back to the company CP to check with the captain before mounting this hill. We climbed on. We stopped often for breaks and we cussed a great deal. It was 1600 before we ever reached the top. To our surprise we found that the flat-appearing area on the top was a grave. In its center was the mound where some past Korean had been buried sitting up cross-legged and looking over the valley he had lived in. This turned out to be the customary manner of burial. The plot was nice and grassy as though it had been cultivated.

To the north of this major peak was a saddle and then another smaller peak that was a kind of knoll. There was only about a ten to fifteen foot difference in their elevation. I knew full well the fallacy of occupying a too-prominent landmark such as this, so I decided upon digging in on the lesser of these two peaks. I picked a spot a few yards below the crest, so that we would not be silhouetted, and announced that we would dig in there. It was on the north side of the hill, and because the hill dropped away so steeply on both sides I had a good view in every direction but south.

I noted to my surprise that to the west and north was a huge town with several roads and a railway coming out of it. After inspecting my map, I was sure that it was Taejon. Damn, I didn't realize that we were this close. The town was probably fifteen miles away with mostly mountains in between, although there was a north-south valley running parallel to the one we guarded about five miles to the west. This valley ran into Taejon. I could see trucks moving up and down the road that ran through the valley into Taejon, and Holmes swore that he could hear artillery coming from that direction. Out front we could see the road twist and turn up our valley for at least ten miles before it was lost in a tumble of hills. To the east we could see over the top of the hills that were the eastern boundary of the valley. There was nothing there but a jumble of hills, the area in which the 2d Battalion was digging in.

I decided that I would dig a two-man hole at the spot selected on the front of the hill and have Holmes dig another one behind my knoll in the saddle for himself and the radio. He could run a remote to the hole up front. While we were thinking out this operation, the squad came straining over the crest of the hill. The squad leader's name was Freddy and he made a hit with me from the first. I had seen him in the company before, but this was to be my first contact with him. He was only an eighteen-year-old kid.

Along with his squad, Freddy had brought the 4.2-inch mortar observer and his radio operator. This made the hill a rather well-manned position. Freddy put his men in a perimeter around the top of the peak and everyone started digging holes. The mortar observer, a sergeant from Orange, Texas, asked if he could move in with me and let his radio operator dig in the saddle with both of my men. This sounded like a decent suggestion to me, so we followed through with it.

The sergeant and I got started immediately and by dark we had a pretty decent hole, about five by three feet and around four feet deep. This was large enough for us to squat in and have our heads a foot below the surface. The dirt we took from the hole and placed around it also gave us added protection. I put my mosquito bar (netting) over this fresh dirt, which was piled noticeably on the green grass and we got some grass from the saddle to plant on the mosquito bar. Then we put a shelter half over the hole, anchoring it to the knoll that rose steeply in the rear, and propped it up in front with our bayonets and a pack-board. On this we planted more grass. This completed, the hole showed no raw dirt to give us away and we had a slit about a foot high from which to peek at the enemy, unseen.

Holmes and Toras had their hole dug and had run the remote from the radio to us by the time our hole was complete. It was then that I realized how late it was getting and how thirsty and hungry we were. Payne had not appeared and the wire was not through on the other end. I cranked on the EE8 (field telephone) repeatedly every few minutes expecting that the wire might be in. After dark, at about 2140, I got an answer. It was the 2d Platoon on the ridge below. They had tied in with me and could connect me with the company, but the line to battalion was still out. I asked them to put me through to the company CP and shortly I was talking to Captain Weston. "What can you see up there?" the captain asked. I gave him the picture.

We spent a quiet night. We worked on a two-hour watch system and most of us got at least four hours of much-needed sack time.

It was first light when we heard a light .30 start to chatter below us on the ridge. A few M1s were fired and then all was still. Everyone on the hill was awake at the sound of the first round and we waited nervously for what was to follow. It was still dark, however, and there was only a hint of light to the east. The dew seemed extremely heavy, and I felt chills run up and down my frame in the dampness. We waited but nothing followed. It had probably been some trigger-happy kids, the mortar sergeant suggested. I agreed with him, but continued to keep my eyes and ears open for any indication that the sergeant was wrong.

It was 0540 on the dot, for I had just looked at my watch, when the crap hit the fan below. The sun had come up in a big orange ball and with its light we could see for miles, but not below us. There was a thick fog or mist clinging to the valley and we could observe only about two or three hundred feet down the hill before the thick white mist began. It was extremely dense, and the only other landmark we recognized was the top of the hills across the valley that peaked out of the mist.

Below in the white fog there was a helluva firefight in progress. Machine guns, M1s, carbines, mortars, burp guns, elephant guns, and several other kinds of weapons that I had not yet learned to identify by sound were engaged in a death-lock struggle. From our perch, we could not see a thing, but the noise of the battle came up to us clearly. This was undoubtedly the heaviest firefight the battalion had ever been engaged in, and its intensity conveyed to us clearly the frantic nature of the struggle. The firefight continued and the mist began to lift. It rose out of the low areas and crept up the hill until it completely engulfed our position. We could not see more than a couple of feet with the mist all around us, and the thought that the NKPA might be climbing up the hill with the mist was in the front of everyone's mind.

The sergeant spoke, "Those little slant-eyed bastards will be sticking their stinking heads through that fog any minute, Lieutenant, you wait and see. We have had it." He took a grenade out of his pocket and placed it on the side of the hole for immediate use. I did the same thing, following his lead.

We waited. The fire below seemed to be slowing down somewhat and there seemed to be fewer small arms and more mortars. We listened. The sound of small arms stopped altogether after a few more minutes. "What does it mean, Lieutenant?" asked the sergeant.

"Beats the hell out of me, Sarge," I said truthfully. I really had no idea, but the most likely explanation was that the enemy had run our people out of their positions, and that the battalion had withdrawn and the NKPA had moved in to consolidate and regroup. If this was the case, we were really hurting. There was nothing to do but wait and see.

"At least we'll get our share before the sons of bitches get us," mused the sergeant. "Those little slant-eyed bastards are going to pay heavy for this Texan's boots," he commented, more to boost his own courage than mine. "I just wish that we had more grenades," he said thoughtfully.

"Don't get your ass in an uproar, Sarge," I suggested. "This fog will rise and we will find the battalion down there dug in just where we left them, you wait and see." This cheered me up considerably and I believe that it had the desired effect on the sergeant. I wondered how the others were getting along in our little perimeter. There was no sound from any of them. Then I thought of the phone again. Maybe I could get an answer now that the firefight was over. But what if the enemy was down there now? The phone ringing would only cause them to notice our wire running to the top of the hill. Maybe they would think that we had bugged out with the rest of the battalion if the phone seemed dead. On the other hand, if the battalion was still in its position down below, I wanted to know about it and learn what had been going on. I wrestled with the thought for several minutes and decided to risk a call to find out what the score was.

I cranked the EE8 vigorously and in a few seconds I heard the familiar voice of Sergeant Miller say "2d Platoon."

"Oh, hell, Lieutenant, the goddamn gooks hit us with everything including the kitchen sink this morning. We had a hell of a firefight, as you heard. Our casualties were pretty heavy, but we held, and the gooks must have lost thousands. You just wait until this fog gets out of your way and you will see the little slant-eyed Yankees piled out there in front like cordwood. How are things with you?"

"Quiet as a mouse, but jumpy as hell."

"Well, I guess your turn will come later. They always try to flank after a frontal assault fails, you know. We are depending on you to let us know what is taking place over there on the left flank and to hold that high ground."

"Don't worry about us, Sarge. When it gets too hot for everyone else it's just right for us. Say, what about sending a man down for water and chow. You won't shoot him, will you?"

"Hell, no. Send him on down. We will be looking for him. I have a man who has to go back to the CP and they can go back together."

"Okay, I'll send him down. How about the line to the CP? Can you put me through to Captain Weston?"

"Nope, that wire was cut by the mortars, but I have a man running it back for the break. It should be spliced and in operation in a few minutes. I'll call you when it's through."

I said "Okay" and hung up. I called to Toras who answered through the mist and in a moment came crawling around the bare-assed son of a bitch to our hole. I told him to make his way down the hill, following our wire, until he reached the CP of the 2d Platoon. He was to proceed from there to the company CP. There he would find Payne and send him up with water and rations. He was to remain in the area and look after the jeep and equipment, but first he was to run our wire back and get it tied in with the battalion. Toras said that he understood and slipped off into the mist.

I felt better now that I knew for certain that Toras was on his way back to the CP and that he would have the wire in shortly. Payne should be up in about two hours at the most and we would have rations and water.

"Lieutenant, the mist is clearing. You can damn near see the ridge the 2d Platoon is on." This was the sergeant. I glanced down and could see the vague outline of the ridge running out into the valley to our right. The mist was lifting. We sat there on the edge of the hole and strained our eyes in an effort to pierce the mist that still clung to the sides of the hill. Then — it was gone — the mist was gone and you could see for miles. There below was the valley with its ridge, its road, the positions dug in, the men moving around, and out to the front — there was the "cordwood," just as Sergeant Miller had said.

The sergeant and I looked for a long time. There were bare places along the road and ridge where enemy mortars had lobbed in tokasan rounds. There in the paddies and on the road to the front were more burned and bare places where our mortars had returned the fire. Along the road were lumps that could be nothing else but bodies. On our end of the road litter jeeps were plying back and forth from the edge of the perimeter to the aid station in the schoolhouse in the rear with their cargoes of agony.

The other men on the hill, Freddy's squad, came over to the east side of the peak and gaped into the valley below. I yelled a warning about staying off the skyline and not moving around so as to attract attention, but it really did little good. A GI is curious first, cautious second.

I got out of the hole and went around to the place where the radio was set up and where Holmes and the radio operator for the mortar sergeant were set up. Holmes had bad news for me. As usual, the damn obsolete radio would not work. I trimmed the aerial and did all the other fiddling that I knew of to try to get the thing to function, but to no avail. The mortar operator had a SCR 300 (a reliable infantry radio) but, for some reason, it would not work either. This was really a pickle. Here we were on this hill for the sole purpose of keeping the battalion informed of the situation to the front and the left flank, and we could not even communicate with them. If there were enemy tanks coming down the road, I could not even get the artillery to fire on them for lack of communication. I cussed bitterly and told Holmes to keep the radio open just in case we could receive someone else's call. It might give us a clue as to what was going on, even though we could not transmit. I went back to the hole, wondering where the hell Payne was and why the hell the wire was not in.

I asked the sergeant if the phone had rung, hoping it had and that we were in touch with the battalion, but this was not the case. I cranked the thing to see what was going on in the 2d Platoon and to find out if Payne had passed by there yet. I got the 2d Platoon, but no news of Payne. I hung up, took out the field glasses, and began to search the area out front for some sign of enemy activity. There was nothing. From appearances, there was nothing but dead enemy soldiers for miles. I looked to the left to Taejon. I gulped. There was an air strike in progress and it looked as though a dozen or so planes were giving the place the once-over. Smoke was beginning to spiral up into the sky, and if I listened carefully, I could hear the "booms" of artillery or bombs — I was not sure which. On the road running south of Taejon there was an awful chaotic muddle. There seemed to be vehicles going in both directions and troops appeared to be clogging the road. At this distance I could not tell which way they were going, but from the general appearance of confusion it was safe to guess that they were withdrawing. Then I noticed that mortar and artillery rounds were bursting all over the road and rice paddies over which the 24th was trying to withdraw. I watched this scene with horror.

The sergeant had his glasses on the road to Taejon also, and his only comment was, "There goes the 24th, bugging for all they are worth."

I picked up the phone and cranked it vigorously. Someone in the 2d Platoon answered and I asked him to put me through to the company CP. I was connected with Captain Weston. "It looks like a general withdrawal on the 24th's front. The Taejon highway is loaded with troops and vehicles and the gooks are plastering them with mortars and artillery. Pass the word on to the colonel."

"Well, that's news," came back his voice, calm, as if he were only mildly interested. "I'll pass the word on to battalion. Keep us posted of any new happenings on the left as well as to the front. You are the eyes of the battalion, you know."

"Yep, I know. What the hell is the story on Payne? He hasn't come up yet with water."

"I don't know, but I'll check for you."

"Please do. We are really hurting up here."

With this the conversation was closed and I turned back to watching the fiasco to the west. More rounds seemed to be falling among our troops now, and the confusion seemed to be growing. Then the sergeant called my attention to something we had not expected. There were tanks coming up from the rear and east of the Taejon road, cutting into the withdrawing troops with murderous fire. It looked as though all the troops that were able had abandoned the road and their vehicles for the paddies and the high ground beyond. Our planes were doing what they could to assist the ground troops, but there were just too many targets. From the outskirts of Taejon black blotches that moved indicated the enemy were following up their advantage. Our aircraft attacked the advancing Reds repeatedly in an effort to give the 24th time to put more distance between itself and the advancing enemy. It was really a pathetic sight. There seemed to be no resistance being offered to the NKPA. All was a mad rush to outdistance them.

It was at this point, when we were most concerned about the welfare of the 24th, that our whole battalion was hit by a TOT (time on target) that really sent us rocking. We received at least fifteen rounds on the hill simultaneously, and the entire area below got the same treatment. Then followed a steady bombardment that chilled everybody's ass. The sergeant and I hit the bottom of our hole. The rounds seemed to burst right on top of us, and the concussion from the bursts would shake the ground and jar our insides, yet no one got hurt in the fifteen minutes that followed. This little episode proved to me most conclusively that the best place to be when there was incoming mail was in your hole.

Down on the ridge and in the other sectors things had not gone so well. When the barrage had lifted, calls for "medic" could be clearly heard from the area below. We could see litter-bearers making their way to the rear with the wounded and there were many walking wounded who were staggering back toward the aid station.

I glanced up the road into the NKPA territory and lost my breath. There were tanks on the road at about five thousand yards, coming our way. I grabbed the phone and cranked the handle frantically. Someone answered in the 2d Platoon, and I asked him to put me through to the company CP. I got the CP and asked the operator for the captain. There was a pause, and then, "Captain Weston speaking."

"This is Terry. Can you put me through to battalion yet?"

"Nope, the wire is still out, but I can reach them on the 300."

"Well, you better start reaching. There are tanks coming down the road. The coordinates are 64.3-52.1, but their position is changing every minute. Relay on to the battalion and see if they can fire a mission for me, using you as the relay."

"Okay, hang on."

I listened as he called the battalion over his radio. I heard him talk to the colonel and give him my account. Shortly, "Okay, Terry, give your mission."

I gave him the azimuth and coordinates of the tanks' position and asked for the center platoon with WP (white phosphorous) in the adjustment. I listened as my commands were forwarded on to battalion, where they had to be relayed by Captain Beard back to the artillery. This was really an awkward and time-consuming method of communication, but I was lucky to have it. After about five minutes, I finally got the "on the way" over the telephone. I heard the rounds whistle through the air on their way over, and then heard a couple of muffled explosions way out in front. I waited, but there was no white smoke. I couldn't imagine what had happened to the rounds. I was about to decide that they were lost when two white columns of smoke rose from behind a hill way out to the front, over and to the right of the advancing tanks. I made a large adjustment and waited while the fire commands were being relayed back to the battery. During this wait the NKPA mortars began to let us have it, and it was here that disaster struck. One of the mortar rounds cut our wire. We were without communication.

The mortars were coordinated with the tank attack and I spotted the NKPA infantry coming out of hiding in the hills to the front at about two thousand yards. This was it, and it looked as if the enemy was prepared to meet a division instead of an under-strength battalion. I saw the rounds that I had ordered fall harmlessly in the rice paddies beyond the tanks. There was no more artillery fire on our part after this. The Reds continued to advance. Our 81 and 60mm mortars were in action, but they didn't seem to slow up the advance, even though they did cause casualties. The hill appeared to have only one mortar concentrated on it, and although we drew a round about every minute, it didn't cause much more than nervousness. It did keep us in our holes, however.

The tanks, in the meantime, were coming down the road at full speed. They were only about a thousand yards down the road from our most forward position now. The 81s and recoilless .75s were firing on them and getting hits, but it just didn't stop them. There were eight tanks in a column with about fifty yards between each tank. The Red infantry had hit the dirt and they were waiting for the mortars and tanks to open a hole for them, just like in the training manual. I felt so helpless and vulnerable sitting up on that hill, observing the NKPA attack and yet unable to fire the six howitzers that were sitting somewhere back up the road for my use. This was a hell of a spot.

"Jesus Christ, Lieutenant, we have had it," commented the sergeant. "Just look at those tanks! They are doing at least thirty. How the hell we going to stop them?"

"Just wait. When they get a little closer we can open up with those new 3.5-inch bazookas the battalion got the other day. There are bazooka teams all over that road," I assured him and myself.

The tanks opened up now. Their big 85mm guns crashed into the positions on the ridge and on the hills on the other side of the road. The first tank virtually ate up the road, and in seconds it was at the point on the road where the first defenses were dug in. I could not tell what casualties the tank had inflicted, but they must have been great. I saw the back blast from a bazooka twice, but they did not get a hit and the tank evidently got them, for the tank had now passed the first road defenses and was pouring fire into the exposed rear of the ridge the 2d Platoon of Able occupied. The second tank burst into our perimeter without opposition and contributed to the fire of the first. The other six tanks came barreling down the road and the first two moved on, switching their fire now to the east side of the valley where Charlie Company was located. The mortar fire continued throughout this action and the NKPA infantry made their play. This is where the "Wolfhounds" first put their sticking qualities on display. In spite of the mortar fire and of the tanks that had broken through the perimeter and were shooting up the outfit from the rear, the men stayed at their guns. The machine-gun and BAR fire that was served to those NKPA infantrymen was a testimonial to American firepower and guts. The enemy didn't withdraw, however, they were simply killed.

In the middle of this firefight, which developed and marched on before us as though it were a football game and we were in the press box, something occured that shall always be fresh in my memory. The first four tanks had advanced well into the battalion perimeter and they were simply sitting on the road and shooting at us with their 85s, immune to the fire that we returned. Thus far, they had been devoting most of their attention to the rear of the ridge, Sugar Loaf Hill, and the hills on the other side of the valley where Baker and Charlie were dug in. Our hill was only receiving the mortar fire from "faithful Charlie" as the sergeant had named the one piece that plagued us. (I had poked my head out of the hole and was casually observing developments when the turret on the second tank began to swing around in our direction. I watched, fascinated, as the gun came around and elevated until it was pointing straight between my eyes. I remember thinking that my imagination was playing tricks on me and that the tanks were not going to waste ammunition on a little old position like ours. At this point I noted an orange flame leap out of the muzzle of the gun and reflex made me duck, although I believed that we could not be seen after we had taken such pains with our camouflage. At this point there was a terrific explosion that knocked my helmet right off my head and blew off the shelter half, the mosquito bar, the grass, and so on,

45

which we had believed concealed our position. The round from the tank had burst smack on top of the fresh dirt that was piled in front of the hole. It had blown everything that was above the surface to kingdom come. I looked around at the sergeant and I am sure that I was as white as this paper. "Those goddamn little slant-eyed bastards are getting awful damn anxious to get us Texans out of this war in a hurry," the sergeant commented. I nodded in agreement.

Here I did a foolish thing. I poked my head up to have another look. Just as I got my eyes over the edge of the hole I saw that orange flame from the muzzle of the tank again. This time I nearly knocked the bottom out of that hole in an effort to find security. Damn if those NKPAs didn't think we were important targets. With the camouflage gone every enemy soldier in the country would be shooting at us before long.

"Goddamn, Lieutenant, we stick out like a mole on a tit on this bare-assed son of a bitch, with all that fresh dirt shining in front of us," the sergeant complained. "If only we had some communication so that we could hit back at the little bastards."

I didn't say anything; I was too busy just breathing. Those last two rounds had really given me the shakes. The enemy tank fired three more rounds into our position, but the only damage it accomplished was to cause us to be covered with rocks and dirt. Damn if this wasn't a tight spot. And all the time "faithful Charlie" kept arriving every minute, a cheerful little reminder that we had better keep our heads down. Below, everything was in turmoil. I spotted several bazooka teams going out to engage the tanks and then watched them as they were cut to pieces by the coordinated machine-gun fire of the tanks. The lead and second tanks had gone on down the road to the rise behind which the schoolhouse containing the CP and aid station were located. I watched over the rim of the hole as the tanks commenced pumping the shells into the school.

Then, a miracle happened. Out of the blue came four angels in the form of Australian P-51 fighters. They swooped down over the hill, so close that I could see the pilots, and made a strafing run on the first two tanks with their .50s blazing. The .50s did not knock the tanks out, of course, but they did cause some damage. Then the planes made a wide circle and came in over us again for their second run, this time with rockets. They knocked the track off the second tank with a near miss and a direct hit was scored on the first tank, which was set on fire.

While this attack was going on, the third and fourth tanks pulled a tricky maneuver. They backed off of the road into a field on the east side of the road and thus blended in with the terrain. The other four tanks foolishly tried to turn around or back up to the north. They were silhouetted perfectly in the dusty road and were easy pickings for the Aussies, who rocketed them most skillfully. They were all set on fire. When the rockets were gone, the planes came back and strafed the second tank, whose track was off and lay prostrate in the road. Then they flew away to their base for more ammo and gas.

After they had gone, the two tanks that had pulled into the field cranked up and pulled into the road and bugged for the Red lines. They had had enough. A recoilless rifle got a hit on the rear of the last one as it ran for its lines and crippled it. Both tanks made it safely out, however. Six were left, five burning and one hopelessly crippled.

It suddenly dawned on me that the mortars had stopped. The sergeant had come up out of the hole and we sat there looking at the battlefield below us and at the bare spots all around us where the incoming mail had been deposited. "It was a goddamn filthy fight," he was moved to say. I tried to agree, but the cotton in my mouth would not let me. Damn, I was thirsty. I looked at my watch. It was 1330. The engagement had been going on all morning.

"You got any water, Lieutenant?"

"Hell, no. Damn it, we had better get some before long, though, or we won't have the strength to get off this bare-assed hill if we have to."

"Yeah, you're right, Lieutenant."

I cranked the EE8 to no avail. The wire was still out. I decided the time for command action had come. I crawled out of the hole and went around to the back of the mountain where Holmes and the mortar radio operator were sharing a hole. I told Holmes to take advantage of this lull and check the wire. He was to find the break and splice it. Then he was to go back to the company CP and see what the hell happened to Payne and Toras. He was to come back up the hill as soon as he could with Payne and bring with him water and rations. I gave him my canteen and told him to stop by my hole for the sergeant's. This was done and Holmes was off. I felt that I could depend on him.

There were no more Reds, mortars, or tanks that afternoon. By 1600 the wire was back in and Holmes and Toras were back up the hill with water and rations, along with a story that Payne and the jeep were nowhere to be found. We passed the water and rations around and everyone felt better. Outside of a strafing from two ROK jackasses in Mustang fighters, there was no further action until the night hours.

At dark, the battalion moved out, leaving the 2d Platoon of Able as its rear guard. At 2200 we joined the 2d Platoon and bugged out with them to positions four or five miles down the road. The NKPA hit again at dawn and we fought them well, never giving an inch of ground under pressure. That night the battalion withdrew again under cover of darkness, for the hostiles were continually flanking us and we had to withdraw to prevent encirclement. There was no other outfit on either flank now. The 27th regiment was the whole show.

We caught on to the wire problem and each day the communications were better and my shooting was better. We fired 105mm artillery rounds by the thousands at the human sea of Reds that always came forward, and each day I became more skilled. Payne, who showed up the day after the session on the hill, became an excellent wireman, and Holmes became my constant companion on the OP. We killed the NKPA together by the hundreds and Toras kept us supplied with hot coffee and rations, which he always managed to get to us under any conditions, regardless of the enemy fire. Able Company, and in particular the 2d Platoon, became a part of us, and with each day we grew closer. We stood and fought, withdrew, and then fought again — always killing the maximum number of NKPA and suffering the minimum of casualties. The minimum was always high, however, for we were so few in number. Payne was killed. Holmes, Captain Weston, Lieutenant Braum, and Freddy were wounded, as were many others.

There was always the road — "Heartbreak Highway." We fought on the hills around it, swam and waded the rivers that it crossed, burned the towns it went through, ate on it, ran on it, shit on it, and died on it.

Captain Beard loaned me a little Mexican kid, Virgil, to replace the loss of Holmes and Payne. He was good and I liked him. Toras fought gallantly, and he always managed to keep the jeep running and to get the rations and water to me. Virgil kept the lines in. I fired the guns.

CHAPTER
THREE

Two Weeks of War

The shady side of the hill was littered with exhausted men — sweating, dirty — I heard voices just above me. Though half asleep, I identified them as Toras, my driver, and Virgil, my wireman. Toras was looking at the sky and commenting upon its likeness to the sky over Hawaii, his home. Virgil didn't think it looked any more like the Hawaiian sky than that which formed a roof over New Mexico where he came from. To him that was the only thing in this nasty peninsula that looked like home. He said that even the sky in Japan looked the same as that of the States.

Toras commented that he was damned glad that there was something over here that appeared the same as home. Then the two began to reminisce about their homes. Virgil told of his mother, three brothers, and several sisters, and of his father who was a carpenter in New Mexico. Toras talked about his father who had retired on Social Security, which he had earned while working as a stevedore in Honolulu, and of his mother and an indefinite number of brothers and sisters abiding on one of the lesser islands of the Hawaiian group. Toras was reminded of his father's forgetting his Social Security number and what a hectic time he had locating his card and identifying himself. That was why he'd had his Social Security number tattooed on his shoulder at the age of fourteen, so that if he forgot or lost his card he could prove to the government men that he was entitled to his pension.

At this point I dropped off to sleep, while Virgil and Toras droned on, each of them more intent upon his own comments than upon the other's. As I slept and awoke, and slept again, I began thinking about my own home, which I had left only seven months before to begin an army career. I thought of my wife, my boy (who was only one and a half weeks old when I departed for Japan), my mother and sister, my aunts, and my grandmother. I could picture my family home, sitting placidly in the Georgia sunshine. I could hear the quietness that always prevailed while sitting in the swing on the front porch. I thought about the exciting and interesting flight to Asia, the thrill of seeing Honolulu, Guam, Johnston, Kwajalein, and the islands of Japan. I thought about how easy the life of soldiering in Japan seemed to me, the novelty of it all; about the happiness I had dreamed of when my wife and boy would arrive in Japan to live on the post; about the ten-day leaves we would take in the winter to go skiing. I wondered how big my boy was at this time.

★ ★ ★

At this point I could hear mortar rounds bursting in the distance; and as they disturbed my dreams, I began to reflect upon the war that we had been thrown into so suddenly, which seemed to have all the characteristics of a great fiasco. I remembered how excited and shocked we were over the news of the American intervention in the Korean War. How only a few months before that we had been told at Officers' Call that there probably would be a conflict in Korea, but that our State Department had decided we would not intervene. I was curious to know the circumstances leading to such obvious indecision in the State Department. I was indignant over the seeming nonchalance with which we were committed to this action.

It seemed as though our entire Far East Command was being steered from one course of action to another on the individual whims of a small number of politicos in Washington. Then I, who had never attended an army school of any kind, thus never having been indoctrinated into the army's canned policy in relation to politics, thought about the place of the army in politics. It seemed absurd that the army should have such a "hands-off" attitude toward politics. We had men to advise our government, men who had spent thirty years in the armed services and who had gone to our best military schools. I thought that their viewpoints as to what might or might not be necessary and advisable from a military standpoint should be a little more closely scrutinized by our State Department planners — specifically General MacArthur's viewpoint as to the defense of Formosa. For us in Japan during March and April of 1950, it seemed that the secretary of state's pronouncement that Formosa was not militarily nor politically important to our national interest was an open invitation for the Communists to parade into French Indochina and Korea. For if the United States chose not to defend Formosa, which was strategically located on our western perimeter running from north to south along the Aleutians, the Japanese islands, Okinawa, Guam, and the Philippines, we certainly would not step over this perimeter to defend Korea and Indochina.

This Formosa policy certainly did not make any show of strength to the Asian people on our part and brought about a considerable loss of face, which in the Far East is far more important than life itself. The reversal in our State Department's thinking concerning Korea seemed extremely late, and certainly most unnecessarily costly.

At this point, I rolled over on my compass, which had slipped down under my ribs, adjusted it, closed my eyes, and tried to sleep. I thought about that compass. It was an old M2 artillery compass that had been used in the Pacific campaigns during the war, sent to ordnance during the postwar period to be reconditioned, and, in the process, someone had painted the wrong end of the needle white. I thought how fortunate it was that I had discovered this before I had fired any missions.

This set me to thinking of our army's equipment in general, of which our secretary of defense Louis Johnson was so proud. The jeep that my FO party now was assigned had come out of the ordnance depot in February 1942. This was the vehicle on which our lives depended day in and day out. The radio that our party was carrying had come out of a depot in 1943. It was an SCR 610, declared obsolete and replaced in 1946 by an SCR 619, a more compact and efficient model. We had not seen any of these, however. Incidentally, in sixty-two days of combat this particular radio worked for only one mission.

Then I thought of the howitzers to which I sent my fire missions (always over wire due to the failure of radio). Upon these guns we depended more than anything else to stop or slow down the avalanche of enemy soldiers. It was more economical for us to withdraw behind a curtain of artillery shells than a curtain of men. It was up to these howitzers to lay down this curtain, and it was up to me to tell them where to drop the curtain. The heartbreaking part was that in spite of the competency of the gun crews and the fire-direction personnel, the howitzers were all so old that it was never unusual to have from fifty to two hundred yards' dispersion. Not only that, but the guns were truck-towed, and the situation called for self-propelled guns. This was the army that (it had been boasted) "would strike back decisively within an hour after being attacked." I couldn't think of Louis Johnson without thinking of our personnel problems.

Only six months ago many fine reserve officers had been relieved from active duty, not "cutting an ounce of muscle, only the fat." Yet at this very same time, of the four divisions in Japan, not one was up to two-thirds strength. When we were ordered to Korea, it was necessary to rob the 1st Cavalry and the 7th Division to a minimum of cadre in order to fill the 25th. In reality, the forces we had in Korea at this time — the 24th and 25th Divisions — were at two-thirds strength (two battalions to a regiment instead of three). The 1st Cavalry and the 7th Division, which were still in Japan, were in reality without personnel.

It was necessary to fill them up with replacements from the Zone of the Interior before they could be committed to our assistance. This was the "powerful, well-equipped, well-trained, and well-manned Eighth Army" of which our president, secretary of state, and secretary of defense were so proud and confident. This was the army that had been selected by the hand that writes, to hold a beachhead and represent the United Nations in its first adventure in international policing.

Something was shaking me, saying, "Rise and shine, Lieutenant Terry," or rather, "Wake up and urinate, the world's on fire!" It was Lieutenant Howard, who had been with me in the 7th Division in Jinmachi, Honshu, Japan. He and his party had come up to relieve me and my party so that we might get some sleep and food. Toras, Virgil, and I grabbed our equipment and stumbled down the hill, too tired and too grateful for our relief to have much to say. It was roughly four miles down this pathless hill to a small grove where our jeep and trailer were concealed. We piled in, said a silent prayer that the jeep would start, and our prayers were effective. We moved down the road, which was the main highway from Taejon to Taegu, stopping occasionally to ask directions as to the location of Service Battery, 8th Field Artillery of the 27th Regiment. We were told there was hot food, clean underwear and socks, and a roof there for us to sleep under. This was our first opportunity to see what was going on at the rear of our forward lines. It was encouraging to learn that there was actually someone in back of us at this point in the campaign. We passed several artillery batteries of 105s and 155s. We began to see tanks occasionally, usually in groups of two. There were a few half-tracks with quad .50s and twin 40s. It seemed a considerable show of strength compared to what we had seen on our way to the front two weeks ago — nothing.

We found the Service Battery about twelve miles to the rear in a Korean schoolhouse. We drove into the schoolyard, got out of our jeep, and stumbled toward the door. GIs were working on trucks cleaning carbines, loading ammo for the batteries up forward; they began calling to us, asking us if we had seen NKPA, how many there were, how things were going up forward, and so on. A warrant officer stepped from the schoolhouse, grabbed my hand, and said: "Hello, Terry, glad to see you. Come in and let me give you clothes and coffee. Bring your men with you." I couldn't recall ever having seen him before, but in the one hectic day at Pusan it was quite possible that I could not have remembered all of the officers and men I had met when I first joined the 8th Field Artillery. This was the first time we had been with the artillery since landing on the peninsula and, frankly, there were very few of the officers and men of the outfit whom I knew or remembered. I considered myself, and the members of my party, to be infantrymen.

The warrant officer, whose name turned out to be Thompson, called a little South Korean man who knew some English, pointed to the three of us, and told him to get us some clothes and bathe us. The warrant officer took us around to the mess hall, which was set up with a kitchen fly, where we got hot coffee, hot biscuits, and fruit cocktail. Supper wasn't to be served for another hour. We felt as if we couldn't go another step without some food, especially because we could smell it.

The diminutive South Korean came around, stood off at a distance, and waited for us to finish chow. Then he motioned us to follow him over to a well near an apple orchard. The ground around the well was two or three inches deep with soft, slimy mud caused by the water being spilled by previous bathers. Boards were strewn around the well where we could step from one board to another. We took off our clothes, hung them on the apple trees, and stepped daintily from one board to the other to keep our feet out of the mud, although we had walked out of our socks weeks before. Our feet were certainly far more dirty than the mud.

The Korean mounted a wooden chair conveniently placed by the well and began pulling out a long rope containing a bucket of muddy water at its end. He would dump one bucketful on me, one on Toras, and one on Virgil. We each had a quarter of a bar of GI soap, and we began to lather up. We washed our hair three or four times, and then bathed for thirty minutes. We stepped from the boards back to the grass under the apple trees and stood around waiting to dry. We amused ourselves by swatting mosquitoes, which had come out as the sun sank. The South Korean scurried off and reappeared with brand-new fatigues, socks, and drawers. Silken robes could not have felt better.

I borrowed a razor and shaved with what was left of the soap. It felt good. Thompson called me into the schoolhouse and pointed to a litter among several on the floor and suggested that it be my bunk for the night. The thought of sleeping at night, to say nothing of the comfort of a litter, was a most unexpected and gratifying surprise. I met several other lieutenants and sergeants who, to my total surprise, treated me as though I were some hero who had gone through an unbelievable hell. Now I was beginning to see that things were really rough;

at the front, we had thought it was like that everywhere. It was here that we first learned of the fame the 27th had attained. While fighting, we had no idea of the superior job we were doing. We were simply carrying out our responsibilities as ordered. We had a huge meal and — we slept.

CHAPTER
FOUR

Sachon Pass

The sharp rock jabbed into the small of my back. It hurt. Either I had to roll over or move it, but it took too much energy. I opened my eyes and stared up at the hot blue sky. Circling above were at least a hundred vultures. I could hear the clumsy "throp" of their flopping wings and see their big claws tucked underneath their ugly stomachs. I smiled as I watched them. Their presence meant not only that everyone in our platoon was asleep, but also that the NKPA were taking their afternoon siesta, too.

One of the more aggressive birds began to swoop near to the ground now, and I watched it with childish wonder. It made several close passes directed (I assumed) at me and then came straight at my chest. I stared wild-eyed as the bird flapped its wings to stop its forward motion and then settled down, not on my chest, but on the sergeant, who lay dead next to me. The bird began picking at the man's field jacket, which had been placed over his face. I became furious. I swung wildly at the creature with the butt of my carbine and it made a hasty withdrawal, laden with every curse I could bestow in the capacity of my breath, voice, and vulgar vocabulary, which at this time was extensive.

Most everyone on the hill sat up, grabbed his weapon, and looked through wide bloodshot eyes for the enemy. Sergeant (later second lieutenant) Matthews crawled over and grabbed my arm. He looked at me for one hard minute, then smiled. I smiled, too, and rolled back over to get some more rest. I guessed the "police action" was beginning to take its toll on my nerves, too — no, that was impossible — I was untouchable.

I lay there. I wished the graves registration people would come after our dead. They had a lot of business on this hill. Then I thought of the dead enemy soldiers on the hill. This was our job (in the course of the campaign we developed an SOP of collecting all enemy KIAs in our position and depositing them in a ditch for mass burial by engineers). We should bury them — when? The men were tired — perhaps in an hour, perhaps two.

I was dog tired. I guessed I should be though — war was a fast game. It seemed months ago since we first pulled into the placid little schoolhouse below the hill in Chingdong-ni. It was really only night before last, just thirty-six hours ago.

We had come down from the north and had reached the schoolhouse after a twenty-seven-hour truck ride at about 2000. We had learned that we were going on the offensive for the first time in the campaign.

I remembered well the excitement I felt when I was ushered into the little schoolroom where Gen. John H. Church, Colonel Michaelis, and Colonel Check were to brief us. I thought of the cockiness I felt and the eagerness that swept the command group as we sat in the dimly lit room, listening to the attack plans. I remembered the shot in the arm the tank lieutenant gave us. This was the first time we were to have tanks. They were old Shermans, but they looked good to us. The tank lieutenant assured us that he could handle anything that came his way, and we chose to believe him simply because it gave us courage.

Taking the tanker's lead, I gave the rosiest picture I could cook up when asked for the artillery support available. I felt it would help to make the greatest show of confidence possible and it did. Not only did the eyes of the others light up a bit, but mine did also. It seemed as though our mission was destined for success.

The meeting was closed and everyone filed out of the schoolhouse in quiet anticipation. This was going to be a morning to which I would look forward. We were going to attack. Our objective was a pass twenty-two miles away just east of Sachon. After we had taken this pass, we could hold the cork for the southern tip of the peninsula and prevent the enemy from getting any of his heavy equipment through to Masan and Pusan from the west.

We were to jump off at 0530. For a change, I went to sleep that night anxious for the morning.

Toras shook me to consciousness. I opened my eyes on a dark, damp dawn. Toras whispered that he still had a couple of cans of fruit and that I was welcome to share them with him. This brought me up in a hurry. I tied my boots, then picked up my blanket and tossed it into the jeep. I joined some of the other men in tossing muddy water from the well on my face, and then took my canteen cup over to one of the several tubs of coffee that were being cooked all over the schoolyard. Someone promptly filled my cup with the thick, jet-black solution that would put gun powder in any man's veins. I took the coffee back to the jeep where Toras and Phillips had already opened the precious cans of fruit and were nursing their coffee along as if it were the last drink from the bottle.

We sat there eating. The activity of the schoolyard became more intensive, and the noise mounted to a sickening roar. The tanks (five of them) began warming up their motors and the two-and-a-half-ton trucks started droning in from Masan (they were to carry B and C Companies). The men scurried around in the half light filling clips, snapping bolts, drawing grenades, and adjusting packs. The scene reminded me of paintings I had seen of events of the two world wars. *This would never be painted*, I thought. This probably wouldn't even be noted in the papers. This was only an operation by one little battalion with attached tanks and a battery of artillery. This, to the rest of the world, was not noteworthy of mention, but for these weary, lean men and boys in the schoolyard, it was one of the most important moments of their lives, perhaps the last.

A Company was to ride the tanks and D Company jeeps in the front of the column. My jeep was to be the first vehicle behind the last tank. At 0530 we moved out. The attack plan called for motor transport until contact was made. The trucks were to return at the first sign of enemy and B and C were to hoof it from there. Twenty-two miles was a long way to walk and fight, too, and we all prayed that it would be some time before contact was made. Our prayers were answered.

We traveled placidly through the Korean countryside for at least eight miles, enjoying the warmth of the newborn sun and congratulating each other on our good fortune in not encountering any enemy troops. Things were going even better than we had hoped for. The tension eased a little and we began to speculate on the possibility that the NKPA might have been frightened away upon hearing that the "Wolfhounds" were on their front.

Somewhere in the middle of these brighter thoughts, my attention was caught by smoke up ahead from one of the tanks, and then the yells from its excited passengers who made a most undignified departure. It seemed that one of our newly acquired weapons was going up in smoke because of simple operational trouble. To this day, no one knows what caused this oil fire, which put one of our five tanks out of commission, even before it could be committed. Our faith in the invincibility of our Sherman tanks dropped considerably at this point.

The people of A Company, who had been riding the burning tank, squeezed onto the remaining four tanks with their comrades who complained bitterly. The tank crew stayed with the burning machine, assuring everyone that they would rejoin us shortly after exterminating the fire. I never saw them again.

The column moved on past the crippled tank and after a few minutes, advanced into a little village in the center of a large group of rice paddies that were squeezed into a long valley that grew more narrow as it ran west. As the leading elements of our column reached the other side of the village, our L-5 observation plane came winging down the valley and dropped a message (in a small canister with a six-foot red streamer attached). The enemy had been spotted on the road and in a village about a mile up the valley. The picnic was over. It looked as though we were going to have to fight our way to the pass from here on in.

At this point, I decided the best place for the FO was on one of the lead tanks. I wanted to see what was going on, and I wanted to see it first, so that I could get word back to the battery the moment we hit something big. It would take the battery some time to get into position anyway, and I didn't want to lose any time at this end. I jumped out of the jeep and instructed Toras and Phillips to keep me on the air with their walkie-talkies. They were to follow at a respectable distance and to get the jeep in a defilade if things got hot. They were, of course, in touch with the battery with the 610, when it worked.

I scrambled upon the second tank with the men from the 2d Platoon, and we nosed our way out of the village, somewhat more cautiously now. The men of B and C had dismounted and were following us at a reasonable distance like a column of ducks. The two-and-a-halfs had turned around and were speeding east behind us, giving the rice paddies another coat of dust. It was like burning bridges behind us to see those QM boys bugging out to the haven of our lines. We could see the little group of thatched roofs up ahead that were sheltering the enemy, and Lieutenant Buckley decided that we would advance to a thousand yards from the village before leaving the tanks for the paddies. After we had advanced half the distance to the huts, we spotted a few NKPA manning a machine gun, hastily emplaced on the side of the road. Our infantry poured off the tanks and began a flanking movement from both sides. The tanks proceeded on down the road with me aboard. For a change, the enemy was hopelessly outnumbered and they knew it. Before we had gotten within two hundred yards of them, they surrendered without a shot being fired. This was a real break for us. We continued down the road with the men of A Company scurrying through the paddies on each side of the road. As we approached the group of huts, it seemed certain that a rain of fire would start the show, but none came. We reasoned that the hostiles were waiting for us to get into point-blank range, but it certainly seemed as though we were close enough now. There was a teeth-chattering silence that made everyone slow down to a snail's pace. We felt just as though we were walking into the lion's mouth. The Koreans had to be mighty confident to let us get this close without a peep. We were only seventy to a hundred yards away now, and the men of A Company were even closer. The first tank crept around a little crook in the road and looked straight into the courtyard of the largest house. There, kneeling around a cook-fire, were about fifteen enemy soldiers. The lead tank let them have it with three quick rounds of HE (high explosive). The first round must have knocked the pot right off the stove, and the second and third must have blown the fire to kingdom come, along with the NKPA. Arms and other various flying pieces of enemy soldiers were blown all over the courtyard. The men of Able rushed over the wall, and a thunderclap of lead saturated the courtyard. Then, all was quiet. We moved on into the small group of mud-and-stick houses behind the 1st and 2d Platoons. No more enemy could be found. We had evidently hit the advance guard of a larger force and had found them completely asleep. We all prayed that the next group of NKPAs we met would be as careless. These boys had evidently discounted the possibility of aggressive action on our part. They had made a costly and fatal mistake. We hoped that their comrades would be as cocksure.

After the main body of the battalion had reached the town, putting us about 500 yards to the west, we stopped for a break. The men eagerly examined the weapons we had captured and talked seriously about going on to Seoul. We had not suffered a casualty in this action thus far, and the success of the operation was like a hot meal and a good night's sleep. The whole bunch began to act as though we were a group of school kids attending a county fair. I know that I felt this most keenly, and I was not at all unhappy when we got the word to move out a few minutes later. We were eager now. We were highly successful killers and the greed to continue our trade was a force that drove us on with a quicker step and a stronger heart. We were the cats; they were the mice. No one thought of why we were fighting the war, if indeed there was an answer, or of their homes, their dysentery, or where they would sleep that night. All we wanted to do was kill gooks. Kill gooks this minute, kill gooks by the thousand, kill them with hot lead, cold steel, or ripping explosives — but kill gooks. We were accomplished murderers. We were masters of our skilled trade.

I had never seen the battalion so bloodthirsty. I had never been so bloodthirsty. I smiled — it was a dirty, mean smile. I vowed that I would distinguish myself as a killer that day.

We were victims of mob hysteria, but under the circumstances, this was a break. It gave us courage that did not exist and bravery that had long been exhausted.

The column moved down the road now. Ahead were a few small hills that the road wound around in its path up a rice-filled valley. On either flank at a distance of several thousand yards were the ugly bare mountains that surrounded us. These grew closer as we progressed westwardly.

We had covered about a mile now, and we were in rifle range of the small hills to our front. The 1st and 2d Platoons again dismounted, leaving me as the only passenger on the tanks, and began a flanking movement from both sides. We stopped on the road in order to let the men of Able get into position. Once again there was a graying silence. I took out my field glasses and studied the squatty little hills to our front. There were a few small farmhouses and several trees scattered about the grassy knolls. A stray cow was peacefully grazing, but there was no other movement. This was always the case; you could never see the enemy until they were close enough to shove their burp guns down your throat. The men of Able were starting up the hills from both flanks now, and we began feeling our way forward.

At this moment all hell broke loose on the hills. The riveting roar of machine guns opened the show, and then the din developed into a fortissimo as all the small arms of both contestants were put into action. From the tanks we identified machine-gun emplacements from their muzzle blast, and the four tanks began laying down an avalanche of fire on these positions. The men of Able inched forward as the assault fire continued from the tanks. The 4th Platoon set up their sixties, and in seconds mortar rounds were adding to the woes of the stouthearted little heathens. Then there was a purple flare — there were yells — curses — and the men of Able roared over the crest pouring forth U.S. steel — compliments of the Wolfhounds. The tanks took off with a jerk that nearly threw me off my perch and would have made any hot-rod driver sit up and take notice. We dashed around the turn in the road and found ourselves at the foot and backside of the hill from which the NKPA had been pushed. They were coming down the hill headfirst and diving for the ditch on the other side of the road. We got there just in time to let them have it with our .50s. About ten dropped to their knees, throwing up their arms to surrender — they played it smart. The others were cut down like hot butter, except, of course, for the 1 or 2 percent who always get away.

The men of the 1st and 2d Platoons started coming off the hill now. They were exuberant. They had met a force of about eighty men and had completely destroyed and captured them, suffering only two casualties themselves, and they were just slightly wounded. It looked as though we had met a bunch of rookies for a change.

By this time, Baker and Charlie Companies had come up fast from the rear, and they were now around the turn in the road. Immediately to our front the road took a sharp curve to the right, and we could see on the map where it then continued

71

up the valley in a generally straight westward course. The column came to a halt, and a patrol from Baker was sent scurrying up the little hills to our right in order to reconnoiter the road around the bend. It was only a matter of moments before we got a report from them. There was an entire enemy column, perhaps a division, on the road headed east toward us, and it looked as though they were trying to get off the road in order to be in a better position to receive us. They had jeeps and oxcarts (mostly oxcarts) loaded to the gills with equipment. It was decided that we would take as great an advantage of our surprise as possible and hit them while they were still disorganized and wondering what was happening up front. Baker's and Charlie's 60s went into position along with Dog's 81s in the defilade. Wire was run up the hill rapidly for their FOs (radios often fail). The tanks were ordered around the bend with Able partially mounted and the remainder of Able screening the flanks. I called back to Phillips in the jeep and gave him the picture and instructions to alert the battery. It didn't seem prudent for them to go into position just now. This was because we might choose to simply run through these people and the battery would be in a bad fix if it lost its mobility just when the infantry chose to make a dash. Therefore, we just told them to be on their toes.

The first tank had pulled around the hill now, and we could see down the road. Just as we pulled around the turn, the first tank let go with our initial greeting. In front of us for several miles were oxen, oxcarts, infantry, and jeeps. Most of them had managed to get off the road and were struggling in the paddies. The second tank (my mount) and the third and fourth, as they came around into position, opened up with their .75s and .50s with small arms aboard, spraying the flanks. The first mortar rounds could now be heard starting their journey from our rear and shortly could be seen bursting on the road and in the paddies to our front. Their effect was extremely profitable and seemed to have a terrific effect upon the spirit of the Reds. They were on the receiving end of a rolling mortar barrage of perhaps a hundred rounds a minute, plus the flat-trajectory fire of our four tanks and several recoilless rifles that were now getting into action on the hill. We got orders to move on out, and as we did, Baker and Charlie came from around both sides of the little hill on the run.

The NKPA challenged us only with small arms and a few machine guns, which were easy picking for the .5s. It looked as though our first battalion was invincible. Many of the enemy were killed and practically all of their larger equipment was destroyed. As we reached each vehicle or oxcart loaded with supplies, one of the doughfeet would toss a white phosphorous grenade, immediately setting it ablaze. We ran through them like a dose of salts, and in a matter of what seemed like a few minutes, we had reached a point where there was no more equipment in front of us, and the only foes conspicuous were dead ones except for some fast disappearing little black dots on either flank, evaporating into the hills. Of course, there were probably hundreds of wounded as well as sound-but-scared Koreans soaking in the paddies, but we chose to ignore them. Our mission was to reach the Sachon pass and then hold it. We hoped that we had stunned the survivors of this outfit enough to keep them out of our way for a while.

We were called to a halt now to regroup and take account of the situation. We lucky characters on the tanks were quite rested, but those poor devils on foot were ready for the showers. They had made the attack in double-time, but were unavoidably left several hundred yards to our rear. They had to catch up along with the jeeps and weapons carriers. Also, the mortar crews had to march order (displace) and rejoin their respective companies. Another important piece of business to be transacted was the resupplying of ammunition for the small arms, particularly for the men of Able. One of the company jeeps was being brought up from the rear of the column with this important commodity.

This stop afforded me an opportunity to let my blood cool and take notice of what was going on about me. I had simply been a sightseeing passenger the whole trip. I had the equivalent of a press box seat for this engagement and felt like a real piker. I hadn't even fired my carbine, much less fired any artillery, but I reasoned that we were all lucky that we had no cause for artillery.

This morning we were red hot. The men were bubbling over. If they had been promised a clean bed with white sheets, their spirits could not have been higher. Everywhere was loud talk and laughter. There was no fear or panic here. There was no lack of confidence or timidity about these men. They were killers who had dealt the enemy a devastating blow and had suffered only a few casualties themselves. Miraculously, none of the casualties had been fatal. We were an untouchable force.

We would go to Seoul this afternoon, maybe Pyongyang tomorrow. Why had the brass not thought of an offensive before this? What was this fable about NKPA invincibility? To think that this was the same army that pushed us down Heartbreak Highway was unbelievable. Hell, we could run on up to Vladivostok if we took a notion. We were in the full flush of fresh victory. There is nothing so essential to the morale of an army as success in the field. We were an army starved for a victory, battered, and bleeding; until this morning, that is. The effect of this success had the effect of a bolt of lightning. From my perch, I could see this esprit de corps take hold, generate heat, and then erupt. I could feel it. We were an unbeatable team of killers.

The order to move out crackled over the radios, and the men of Able scrambled back on the tanks and the few jeeps that had collected close behind. Baker and Charlie could be seen forming columns of ducks in the rear and the dust began to rise into the hot sky as our hotheaded and hardfisted little task force gathered momentum. Our next stop was to be the pass.

We churned on up the road, which now had a noticeable upgrade. There were still paddies on either side of the road, but they were smaller and more rectangular-shaped; the large hills that ran parallel to the road were growing much taller and closed in upon us as we continued west. I kept my glasses to my eyes, scanning the rugged ridges for signs of the enemy, but all was quiet. There was an occasional group of cattle grazing on the grass that grew on the little pathways that divided the paddies into sections. As we passed through groups of farmhouses, abandoned dogs would bravely bark from underneath the houses, but that was all. There was no other life. The terrain was simply hot, steaming, and still.

Ahead, the road became more narrow and began to twist and turn as it snaked up the narrowing valley. The paddies here were narrow, perhaps only a few feet wide, and they were almost dry. Minor ridges tumbled down from the primary hills and caused the road to make abrupt twists around them. Ugly erosion gullies cut the faces of these smaller ridges, and, from a few, muddy water oozed. In the more moist spots, heavy cane flourished in dense thickets. The grade became quite steep now, and it was apparent that the pass was near at hand.

I searched my map in an attempt to identify our position, but this proved futile. The map had no contour lines and the pass itself was not identified, because we had given it a name only the night before. I put the map back in my pocket and put the glasses to my eyes. As I searched the terrain for enemy, I listened to the talk around me. The men were like children on a hayride. The loud chatter and laughter was clearly audible above the roar of the tanks. No one was concerned. This was a real joy ride. I sat back, stretched out my legs, and leaned on the back of the turret. I smiled as someone asked me if I had gotten my limit for the day, and replied regretfully that I had not.

The tank below us began to twist and jerk as it maneuvered the sharp turns. I noticed that the road was actually carved into the side of the hill on the right. On the left was a drop of several feet into long narrow paddies, broken occasionally by canebrake. Across from the paddies, the left ridge reached up into the sky. Here a stubby nose of red clay plopped down from the right. The road made a circle around its end to the left and then back to the right behind the hill. It made a wide half-circle behind the nose, then left again under a very steep ridge on the right and dense canebrake on the left on the border of the last paddies.

The lead tank was three-quarters of the way around the circle now and entering the tight area between the cliff and the canebrake. I noticed that everyone seemed to quiet down somewhat here, but there was no obvious apprehension among the troops. I made a commo check with Toras and

Phillips in the jeep and they read me "loud and clear." The lead tank now eased into the close corridor that was the road, and we followed suit at an interval of about fifty yards. The third tank followed us at about twenty yards, and the fourth at about seventy. The first tank had disappeared to the left now as we squeezed through the corridor.

Peering into the dark green cane I saw only cane. I looked back at the third tank close at our heels and thought that — wham, wham, wham. Fire lashed out of the canebrake. Our tank shuddered and quaked. There was the ear-shattering sound of ripping metal. I don't remember jumping, but I am certain that I did, for people were already landing on top of me in the ditch on the right side of the road. As our tank ground to a halt, the third tank was forced to do likewise, suffering a direct hit. I took this in as I snapped the safety off my carbine and poured a thirty-round clip into the cane. Everyone else followed suit.

I replaced my empty clip and let go with one of my two grenades. There were three or four more grenades tossed into the brake simultaneously with mine, and then without a command from anyone, we all rushed across the road and into the shattered and splintered cane. There were two elephant guns (51mm antitank guns) and their dead and wounded crews, only a few feet off the road where they had been ingeniously concealed.

Whamp! Whamp! Whamp! Throp throp throp! We began receiving small-arms fire and hand grenades.

The cane cracked about us as fragments rattled through it and everyone dropped to the ground searching in panic for the source of this fire. I looked above us. Across the road on the cliff were enemy soldiers, throwing down grenades and emptying their burp guns. This spot was obviously untenable. We did not have to be told.

We began the military maneuver known as "bugging out." We tried to use the cane as best we could for concealment and began crawling through the mess parallel with the road. Someone had the presence of mind to drop a grenade in the breech of each elephant gun as we withdrew. From the noise we could tell the people on the third tank were having a rough time of it. We crawled on past this noise, dragging our wounded, until we reached the edge of the cane, dropping off into a rice paddy. We were a good twenty yards behind the third tank now and could see across the paddy to the red-nosed hill we had just come around. The fourth tank was sitting on the road, this side of the hill, its turret swinging into firing position. I saw the red flare from its gun, and a split second later heard the round burst on the cliff above us. It was in position to rake the shelf from which the NKPA were pouring the grenades on us, and evidently its fire was quite effective.

After three rounds, it was obvious that this was the time to make a break for a more secure position. I jumped to my feet and dashed out of the cane and across the road under the cliff. The men from the third tank, minus the dead, had already taken off for the collective security of the main body, which was behind the red-nosed hill. I took a deep breath and started the sprint down the covered side of the road. I imagined I could hear slugs thumping into the road behind. Whether this was purely imagination or actuality, I do not know. There was no time to investigate. As I ran, the fourth tank continued to pump 75mm rounds into the cliff and to employ its .50. It seemed that I gained speed as I fatigued. I ran smack down the middle of the road now, past the tank and around the red-nosed hill. Here I found the rest of the battalion: parts of Able lying all over the backside of the hill and Baker and Charlie strung out along the road for half a mile, smoking and eating C rations. That's what I liked about our outfit — never got its ass in an uproar. Some kid, lying luxuriously in the deep grass near the road, rolled his head over and grinned, "What's wrong, Lieutenant? Those little yellow bastards take your tank away from you?"

I just stared at him and dropped to the ground. My heart was beating so hard that it was making an echo in my helmet, and I felt quite sure that my breathing could be heard a mile away. While here, it occurred to me that I came out alone. What had become of the other men on the second tank? I was not responsible for them, but I thought about my job; I was here to direct artillery and I had forgotten. I reached for the walkie-talkie to call the jeep. That's when I discovered that I had no walkie-talkie. It had been lost somewhere in the melee. This was the first piece of equipment I had lost, and I felt bad and disgusted about it.

I struggled to my feet and staggered on down the road in search of Toras and Phillips. I passed about four jeeps and then spotted my crew. There was Toras, making coffee, and Phillips eating fruit cocktail. The jeep was loaded with loot, burp guns, rifles, Russian first-aid pouches, helmets, and so on. They had really had a picnic on the drive up this morning. Toras looked up smiling.

"Hi, Lieutenant! Boy, oh, boy! We really knocked the hell out of them today, huh?"

I said, "Yeah, boy, oh, boy!" I asked Phillips about the radio, and he informed me that he had good contact with Colossal 25 (Captain Beard the liaison officer) and Colossal 21 (the battery exec). I took the mike and called the battery. I instructed them to go into position, and assured them that a fire mission would be forthcoming. I signed off and immediately received a call from Captain Beard asking for a little poop on developments. I filled him in as best I could over the radio and asked if he could start some wire my way. He said that he could and would and signed off.

By now a few mortar rounds were bursting on our side of the hill and small-arms fire could be heard reasonably close. The men of Baker and Charlie were being deployed to either flank, and the fourth tank backed to the edge of the red hill. I crawled into the jeep and drove to the foot of the hill, where the men of Able were being deployed, and where the fourth platoon was setting up their 60s. I thought the jeep, as well as Toras and Phillips, would be safe here. Also, the radio would be close enough for me to call fire commands down from the top of the hill or perhaps use the mortars wire, which was close.

By this time Lieutenant Buckley had Able pretty well organized and was asking Lieutenant Scroggens and Sergeant Burris to get their mortars into action. I slapped Buckley on the back to let him know I was still with the company and hurried on after Scroggens and Burris. They were going up to establish an OP and I wanted to be right with them in order to use their wire. We had worked together often before and they hardly noticed me when I puffed my way up. It was only a short pull to the crest of the little red hill, and as we approached the skyline, we found a couple of squads of the 1st Platoon digging in just below the crest. We dropped to our knees and crawled up to take a peek.

There was absolutely no cover on this patch of real estate, and the only way to see on the other side was to pray and then stick up your punkin head like a curious turkey. This is what we did. Nothing happened, so we took out our glasses to look around. At first it seemed there were no NKs around, but that was always the case until it was too late, so we continued to look over the terrain. The tanks had run the bunch off the cliff and they must have gone somewhere. Also, the mortar rounds that were bursting all over the road behind us had to be coming from somewhere. Lieutenant Scroggens said that he thought he saw troops working on the base of the larger ridge to our right. Burris and I swung our glasses around in that direction. We picked them up also.

There appeared to be four or five platoons working around our right flank at about 1,000 yards. I took the glasses from my eyes and blup, blup, blup — rat-a-tat, rat-a-tat. I dropped to my belly and rolled a few feet off the crest as did Burris. We sat up, then blinked at each other. Where was Lieutenant Scroggens? I jerked my eyes back to the spot we had just occupied. Burris was already on his way back up there. Lieutenant Scroggens was still lying there, face down. I crawled to him and helped Burris pull him down. We rolled him over. There was a bullet hole in the center of his forehead. Able had lost a good weapons platoon leader, and I had lost a good friend. Mrs. Scroggens had lost a husband, and his daughter had lost her daddy.

Where those shots were fired from, I don't know, but I was certain of one thing. There were enemy soldiers close at hand. The mortar rounds that had been peppering the road behind us dropped closer now, and some of the rounds seemed to be falling right in on our positions at the base of the hill where I had left Toras and Phillips. It seemed essential that those mortars be knocked out if we were going to stay around long.

I crawled back to the crest of the hill and began searching for the mortar positions. I saw the NKPA we had spotted previously, still working around our right flank, but no trace of the mortars. I decided I would fire on the infantry for lack of another target. I took an azimuth to them and made a rapid guess at their approximate map position. Burris said that he would stay at our observation point and see that the wire got in. I slid on down the hill to get my fire mission on its way.

As I approached the base of the hill where the 60s were set up, and near where I had left the jeep, someone yelled, "Hey, Lieutenant, they got both of your men!" I rushed to the jeep. Its rear was ripped and twisted, and lying in the ditch. Beside it were Toras and Phillips. Toras was hit in the legs and head, Phillips in the head and arms. Someone had put first-aid packets on them and removed their cartridge belts. Toras was jabbering out of his head. Phillips was unconscious, perhaps dead, I didn't know. Someone said that the aid station was set up about half a mile down the road, but that the aid men were unable to get to them due to the mortar fire. This seemed obvious enough. The road was a boiling mass of dust from the bursting rounds. I saw that there was nothing I could do for Toras and Phillips, except help kill their attackers and get them out of there, so I turned to that task.

One glance at the radio told me that it was out of order. It was thoroughly smashed. I picked up four grenades from the jeep and ducked under the comparative safety of the base of the hill. Buckley had set up his CP just off the road by the red hill. I gave him the news about the radio and my men — he had already heard about Lieutenant Scroggens. He gave me a brief "fill in." Part of the 1st Platoon was still with the first tank, the rest (those with me on the second tank) and a few from the 2d Platoon were missing. The remainder of the 2d, together with the 3d and the 4th, were here on the hill and the fourth tank was just around the corner. Baker and Charlie Companies were down the road about half a mile, and the odds were that they would remain there as long as this murderous mortar fire continued to slice the area between us.

Someone called back for something and Buckley went ambling off. I sat there and reflected upon the situation. Uh-oh. I forgot to mention the troops I had spotted moving around the right flank. I found the company's radio operator nearby. I gave him the poop and sat close to hear him repeat it to the battalion. This made me feel a little better. I sat back. The 60s began to sound off now, that was good, Burris was on the job. There was not much small-arms fire now, and the enemy mortar rounds seemed to be coming in less frequently. A litter jeep came barreling up the road. I got to my feet and started toward it. Too late — the company medic had already flagged it down. He had six men to go on the two litters. I went on to the jeep anyway and told them about Toras and Phillips. The medics gave me their solemn promise that they would pick up my men the next trip. They turned around and drove back through the mortar rounds with their cargo of moaning and groaning men.

I went back to look at Toras and Phillips. They were both unconscious now. Neither one was bleeding excessively, but Phillips had an ugly yellow fluid oozing out of his ears and nose.

I stumbled back to the point of the hill where the road wound around it and where the fourth tank was silently standing vigil. I sat down to wait for developments. Perhaps the wire would be up soon from Captain Beard and I could get a fire mission through. The enemy mortars had almost stopped now and jeeps were starting up the road toward us.

Now small arms began to sound off above us and to the right. Uh-oh. Machine guns started chattering on the right rear. Those people we had previously spotted had worked into position and gone into business. The machine-gun fire was sweeping the road and those who had started up to join us were forced to take to the ditch. The tank's .50 now fired a few short bursts to the front. Evidently the NKPA were working up there, too. I sat there with several others from the company headquarter's group, listening to the din and wondering what I could do. Artillery was out of the question as long as the commo was out. Perhaps I should crawl back to the top of the hill and take up a rifle position.

As I sat there brooding and staring across the narrow little rice paddy on the left of the road, a figure appeared out of the paddy. He had no helmet and his shirt was charred black. His head was bleeding and he held a .45 in his hand. I jumped to my feet and slushed out into the paddy to meet him halfway. He was a tanker. Someone helped pull him up the bank and into the ditch on the sheltered side of the road. He said there were more wounded in a creek that ran parallel with the road on the other side of the paddy. It occurred to me that my best use to the company at this time would be in the role of a medic. I dropped my carbine and field glass (foolishly), reasoning they would only hinder me in carrying wounded and jumped down into the paddy carrying only my .45.

I slushed the fifty yards to the creek that the tanker had come from and slid down the slick bank into the cool water. The water was only a few feet deep, but it was reasonably clear and cool. It ran between the steep ridge on the left and the five- or six-foot man-made bank that held the rice paddy on the right. I had expected to find someone here, but the place was empty. I felt conspicuous and wanted to kick myself for not bringing my carbine.

I started wading up the stream. It seemed as though I were in a world alone now, and as I slushed along, I began to think over my present position and my hasty action. I could have asked that tanker for better directions. Where were the wounded I had come after? Suppose the enemy had killed them or taken them prisoners? What about the NKPA? Would I walk smack into the middle of them? Fat chance I'd have with a .45. Why had I left that carbine? I could feel my nerve turning thin. I stopped, listened, moved on a few feet, then stopped again. I was the army's biggest fool. Why did I come out here? Why hadn't I stayed behind the hill? I moved on cautiously, a foot or two at a time. I stopped — listened — voices. GIs. Where? Out into the stream in front of me burst Sergeant Miller. A gully ran into the stream from the right, and it was from this that Miller had popped. I don't know who scared who the most. In the gully were about ten men, some of whom had been passengers on the second tank with me. Four of these had not been hit. Most of the wounded could drag themselves along under their own power, however. I asked if there was anyone else farther up the gully and they said there was — the tank lieutenant. I wormed on past the others and found the lieutenant about twenty yards farther up, sitting against the side of the gully with both legs shot up and bad burns about his face and hands. There was a young round-faced boy from Able with him. The kid had been shot in the ankle and could crawl, but was staying around to guard the lieutenant. They both seemed mighty glad to see me.

I asked the lieutenant if he could hang on to my neck. He said he could. I laid him on his back and straddled him on my hands and knees. He put his arms around my neck and I started crawling back, dragging him head-first under me. The little round-faced kid followed. I liked that boy.

When we reached the point where the gully emptied into the creek, most of the others had gone on, but Sergeant Miller and another man were waiting for us. Miller came to my assistance and we half carried, half dragged the lieutenant downstream to the place where I had descended from the paddies. The small-arms fire seemed to have increased somewhat, but the mortars had stopped. A couple of the men stuck their heads up but didn't get shot at, so they scooted over the bank and out of sight. This gave the rest of us heart, and the able-bodied began pushing the wounded over the top. This was a painful process for men with broken limbs and torn-out guts, but it had to be done. Once over the bank they could make their own way the last fifty yards. Everyone was up now except for the lieutenant, Sergeant Miller, and me. The lieutenant was hurting bad. Miller and I got under his shoulders and tried to claw our way up the bank with him but, unfortunately, he weighed more than two hundred pounds, and he was just too much for us. We tried this several times, causing terrific pain, but we made no progress. I started thinking about the enemy who might be coming down the stream behind us and panic took a strong grip on me. Miller suggested that he get on top of the bank where there was firm footing and with me pushing and him pulling perhaps we could get the lieutenant out. I agreed to this with my eyes fixed upstream. Miller pulled himself over the bank, then lay on his stomach reaching over for the lieutenant. I got the fireman's carry, or a facsimile thereof, on the big fellow and with much straining and support from the bank, got him within reach of Sergeant Miller. I felt the sergeant's tug, and the lieutenant disappeared over the bank with much pain and moaning.

I clawed my way up the bank and splashed into the muck of the paddy on all fours. After a few deep breaths and a long stare at Miller, which was returned with mutual understanding, we harnessed ourselves again to the pathetic lieutenant. With Miller under one shoulder and me under the other we began that last fifty yards. Rice paddies are hard enough to navigate with your own weight, the muck sucking at your feet as they sink in ankle-deep, but with this extra weight and drag, they were pure torture. I looked toward the road and noticed it was more congested than before and that there were some litter jeeps loading the casualties who had preceded us. Two men noticed us and jumped into the paddy to come to our aid.

In a fraction of a second we heard machine guns to our rear and rounds going overhead, dancing dust where they crashed into the hill, and new casualties. By now we were flat on our faces in the muck. The little bastards were on our left flank now. What were Baker and Charlie doing? Picking daisies while we were being flanked on both sides? The firing continued. Now we heard the .50 from the tank — the firing continued — now we heard more machine guns — U.S. light .30s. Baker was over there, after all. Miller and I decided to chance it.

Please God, let us live a little longer. We picked up the lieutenant and struggled with new strength. A few rounds began to land around us. We dropped in the paddy again, waited, pushed on again, reached the road, pulled the lieutenant over the little bank, and dove for the ditch on the other side — we made it. Miller said the bastards shot the heel off one of his shoes — he had the shoe to prove it.

I crawled down the ditch over cussing, praying, scared men, to where Toras and Phillips had been. They had been evacuated. Thank God. I started back up the ditch just as particularly heavy incoming fire started. They were using all types of small arms on us now. It struck me as being an extremely unnatural affair. Here were thirty to forty men, lying in a ditch, armed, yet returning no fire, while lead thumped into the ground all around them. It seemed that someone should make a token attempt to return fire.

A man near me got careless about his arms, and caught some of that Ural Mountain steel through his right bicep. He let out a wail that I am sure the NKPA heard and then settled down to quiet, nerve-racking sobbing. I took out his first-aid packet and wrapped up his arm. I gave him a drink and put him on his back where we could elevate his arm and still have cover. He bled pretty heavily for a while, but after applying pressure around his arm above the wound and at the pressure point on his shoulder, a clot was formed and I felt as though the bleeding was under control. The man began to calm down, although his carrying on had already unnerved most of the people in the ditch.

The incoming fire slackened somewhat as Baker or Charlie, I don't know which, engaged the flankers with their full firepower. Able's mortarmen got their 60s turned around and began pitching greetings across the paddy to the ridges on our left and the tank opened up with his .50 again. The combined effect chilled their courage somewhat, and it gave the men in the ditch some heart. Some of them actually grew bold enough to get up into firing position and try to pick off some Korean soldiers. They did this without the gusto that they had displayed earlier in the morning, however. The atmosphere was not that created by a group of bloodthirsty killers, but rather one of desperate, God-fearing souls in a fearful struggle to live.

Things seemed to settle down now. There was sporadic firing all around our perimeter, but nothing like an all-out firefight. The Dog Company 81s fired off and on, and the 4.2 platoon fired occasionally. The battery had received orders from someone to go into position when this ruckus first started and the L-5 observation plane and Captain Beard had fired some missions. Matter of fact, it was Captain Beard who earlier silenced the machine guns that had been sweeping the road from the high ground on the right. Lieutenant Buckley slid down off the red-nosed hill and came over to sit in the ditch with me. Litter jeeps started shuttling back and forth along the road again, and the few wounded who were in the ditch were quickly taken to the rear. An enemy mortar round would buzz over occasionally, but coming one at a time they had no effect. The men began trading cans of C rations and I noticed the time, 1400 hours. Time had really slipped by. I began to think about food.

A jeep bounced toward us from down the road, and we could tell from its two aerials that it was the colonel. He was accompanied by Captain Beard. They stopped in front of us. The colonel asked Buck for an appraisal of the situation. Captain Beard already had heard of my predicament. The colonel decided we would push on out after a break, and after air support could be arranged. I was told to take my jeep and go back to regiment and get a replacement radio. I was to take with me an NKPA lieutenant whom we had captured and a load of captured leather satchels containing maps and other data. These had been taken from a vehicle in which some enemy brass had been killed. It was believed that we had some important G-2 information.

I hopped into my shattered jeep and ground off with both rear tires ripped to shreds by the same shrapnel that had hit Toras and Phillips. Miraculously, none of the working parts of the jeep were hurt, although the back end of the body looked like a cheese grater. I drove about a mile down the road to a place where the battalion CP and aid station were located. Captain Hickman stopped me and directed me to a little shack where the G-2 poop was stashed and where the NKPA lieutenant was awaiting transportation. He had been stripped and had lost a considerable amount of his composure. I wondered just how much a lieutenant in the Red army knew. If he was no better informed than a lieutenant in our army, we would get little information out of him.

Captain Hickman began dumping the leather satchels into the back of the jeep with the help of several of the headquarters people. He was still bubbling over with enthusiasm for the mission, and some of his optimism brushed off on me. One of the men gave me some canned fruit and a can of dry rations from his C rations. I thanked him and quickly threw the nourishment down the hatch. I filled my canteen with some water from a well, dropped the halazone tablets into it, threw water on my face, and announced that I was ready. The NKPA lieutenant had already been placed on the hood of the jeep where he was to ride. I climbed into the driver's seat, clicked the safety off of my .45, and took off, feeling very fortunate and grateful that I was going to the rear. It meant that I would most certainly miss the pending attack on the pass. I felt as though the Good Lord was taking a personal interest in me.

I quickly left far behind the clutter of thatched roofs, under which the CP and aid station were concealed, and I roared down the dusty road on my flat tires, giving my prisoner the ride of his life. He gamely clung onto the A-frame in front of the hood and looked straight ahead. In front of me I could see the battery position, with the pieces dug in on both sides of the road. There was a little brass lying beside each piece, indicating that they had done some business and the men were stretched out over the entire area taking it easy. A few men waved as I bounced in, but that was the only welcome I received. I pulled up near the battery executive truck, which was the mobile CP, and greeted Captain Hull and Lieutenant Carter. They asked where I was bound. I told them and they grinned at each other. Seems they had a surprise for me; the enemy had set up a roadblock some distance away and it was suicide to try to run it. The 2d Battalion was trying to break it from the other side, and when this feat was accomplished I could dash through; until that time I might as well sit down and drink some coffee. My first reaction upon learning of this development was to become slightly irritated, but upon further consideration, I decided that it might be a break. Captain Hull told me I could find some coffee at the mess truck, which was parked down the road a piece behind a rise. I left my prisoner under guard at the CP and drove about a quarter of a mile to the place where the mess truck and ammo trucks and trailers were parked. The mess sergeant poured out a canteen cup of the black strength-giver and hauled out some cold biscuits for me. This really hit the spot. Shoot, I might get a full stomach if I continued to run into people with food at the rate I had today.

The sun had been under the clouds for several minutes now, and the sky had let forth some thunderclaps. I covered my cargo as best I could with my shelter half. I topped off my cup with some more steaming coffee and climbed into the back of the mess truck to enjoy it in a dry place. Several others had already taken refuge here and as the rain began to fall in quantity the first sergeant came scrambling into our sanctuary. We exchanged greetings and he immediately asked me how things were going up forward. I gave him the straight poop as I knew it and asked if the boys on the battery's security perimeter were awake. He avoided my eyes and said that he supposed they would be shortly, that a perimeter had not yet been put out.

At this, I blew my top. It was not my responsibility to see that the security of the battery was provided for, but because I was relying on this protection myself, and because I felt some concern for the gun crews and the CP personnel, I went through the roof. "For Christ's sake!" I screamed, "Who the hell do you think is on either flank and your rear? It's two miles from here to the infantry, and they have their hands full. The NKPA have set up a roadblock behind you and they are sitting on the hills watching you from both sides, and we don't even have a perimeter of defense set up!" This outburst seemed to scare everyone, me included. We were sitting ducks.

The first sergeant said something about not realizing the seriousness of the situation and jumped off the truck with a declaration that he would have a perimeter out in jig time. I watched him slop around in the rain collecting men. A couple of kids slushed by carrying a .50, cussing. I knew they must have been giving me hell for causing them to lose their dry spots under the trucks. A few minutes later a man came up to the back of the mess truck and asked me if I could get any carbine ammo from the infantry. Seems it was on short supply in the battery and the first sergeant thought maybe I could turn the trick. I wondered why the first sergeant couldn't ask me himself rather than send this kid, but, hell, I guess it made little difference, although I was privately irritated at the thought of the battery going on an attack without enough small-arms ammo, when there had been plenty available at the schoolhouse. Fortunately, we had been carrying ammo for the infantry in the jeep, and I had about half a case of carbine ammo left in there. I jumped off the truck and started over toward the jeep. The cloudburst was about over now, and there was more of a mist instead of rain. We reached the jeep, and I found the box of ammo under the debris and turned it over to him with some nasty comment about bringing his own ammo with him next time. I was thoroughly disgusted with the lackadaisical attitude these people a short distance off the front had concerning their security. In reality, they were just as prone to be overrun as anyone else in this war. No one was really safe, the front was everywhere.

I climbed wearily into the jeep and drove back to the battery CP. There were no new developments. Everyone was sitting around, smoking and waiting. A three-quarter-ton truck had come in with a few wounded and had stopped, waiting for the roadblock to be cleared. I exchanged glances with the CP group and sat down in the dry spot, under the tailgate. The rain had stopped. I sat in silence, listening to the hum of the radio and the comments of those about me. The cards had really changed since this morning. I thought of the time — my watch said 1500. This day was flying by. The radio began to spout forth our call signs. It was Baker Battery, firing missions in our rear in support of the 2d Battalion, which was trying to crack the roadblock. I recognized Lieutenant Plummer's voice, directing fire for Easy Company. I smiled — this was good — just to hear that familiar voice.

A two-and-a-half rolled up. It was full of wounded. The driver, with a couple of medics, had orders to take the wounded back to regiment, roadblock or no roadblock. I decided I would throw my luck in with theirs. Somebody hustled the prisoner back on the hood of the jeep and I took off, followed closely by the two-and-a-half-ton truck with its load of misery. The few wounded who had come into the battery area in the three-quarter-ton truck had been transferred to the larger truck, swelling its passengers from twenty to twenty-five. We rambled down the bumpy road, watching and listening for a clue that might tip the enemy's hand.

The NKPA lieutenant sitting up front had gotten wet during the rain and the moisture really brought out his odor. Now with the sun shining freshly on his damp body the stench seemed to be several times multiplied; because of his position to my front where the breeze from our forward motion could carry his aroma, the unpleasantness was accentuated.

I noticed a black object down the road which, as the distance grew less, developed into a man. He stood up and waved as we grew near. He was a GI. I stopped and he almost kissed me. He was obviously very glad to see me; he was in the jeep and we were rolling before he stopped exclaiming his good fortune and gratefulness. I asked him what he was doing back here all alone, and he gave me an answer that I never did hear over the roar of the motor and the racket of my flat tires. He was obviously a straggler, and I was tickled to have him under any circumstances. He had an M1 rifle, which was just that much more protection for me and the truckload of wounded.

We rushed on through the paddies and through the several little villages sprawled in their midst. We passed groups of dead NKPA soldiers and overturned and burning equipment, monuments to our morning's progress. Groups of vultures would take to the air as we approached and then settle back to their feast after we had passed.

It seemed as though we had traveled eight to ten miles now and the tension began to mount heavily.

The roadblock could not be far, although I could hear no firing up front. I wondered if the 2d Battalion had broken through. I searched the road, the paddies, the groups of thatched roofs, the ditches. Where was this roadblock? I began to expect each group of dead we passed to suddenly jump to their feet and empty their burp guns on us — the enemy had been known to play dead before. We bounced on. I felt in my shirt pocket, the little condensed edition of the Bible was still there. I thought of Easter Sunday at the post in Japan. How clean we were. I thought about the good breakfast, the neat little chapel, the peacefulness, how the little Bibles had been passed out at the door after the service. Lieutenant Page and I had walked to the club and played pool. We had a lovely dinner, followed by more pool and two sets of tennis. It had been so pleasant that Easter when the little Bible came into my possession. I gave it little thought then; it gave me much comfort now.

We rushed on, the sun shining brilliantly now, drying the road and causing steam to rise from the paddies all around us. The road quickly turned to powdery dust that added to the discomfort of the wounded. We covered another mile — no sign of the enemy. Several hundred yards down the road I recognized the little village where we first tangled with the enemy a few hours before. It was quiet and dirty, baking under the afternoon sun. I had fears that it might be harboring Korean soldiers, and as we approached the group of mud-and-stick houses,

I brought the jeep to a virtual crawl (one never rushes into death). My hitch-hiker signaled the truck in our rear to lag behind so that we might draw the first fire if any were to come.

We crept into the village. There were dead North Korean soldiers lying here and there and a few propped up against the walls that zigzagged around the houses. It was quiet, and although I did not feel as though fear had too firm a grip on me, it was apparent that it had, for my knees were shaking so that they chattered against the steering wheel shaft. We had come about three-quarters of the way through this mess now, and I was about to breathe a sigh of relief when the man next to me noted movement ahead. I hit the brake and reached for my carbine, but it was too late. They had the drop on us. Then I took another look. They were GIs! They lowered their weapons and sat down again — picked up the C rations they had been eating and settled back to enjoy the shade of an overhanging roof and fruit cocktail. I pulled up alongside, and we exchanged greetings. The two-and-a-half roared up behind us.

"What's the deal on the roadblock down the road?" I asked. A freckle-faced, redheaded boy squinted up at me and replied, "As far as I know, it's still suicide to go much farther down this road. The lieutenant and four men got killed trying it a couple of hours ago, and that's good enough for me." He went on eating with the others, six in all. They had a jeep and small arms.

"What's the best way of getting to regiment without running the roadblock?" I asked hopefully, expecting that perhaps one existed. "Well," said the redhead, "you can go the way we came; just take this little two-rutted trail running to the left, and it will take you right to regiment. The road ain't too good in spots, but you can make it." This was better than I had hoped for, a road that circumvented the roadblock and would give us safe passage back to the regiment. The kid pointed to the place where the road snaked out between two houses and ran along a dike in the rice paddies.

We roared off, the two-and-a-half knocking down a wall as it squeezed between the little houses. We quickly left the village behind and hurried on across the broad paddies. To slip off the narrow dike on either side was the sure end for a vehicle, for the paddies were deep in water. This was a particularly precarious passage for the two-and-a-half, its outside dual wheels extending over the sides of the dike. The road continued almost due north, and as we approached the large hills that formed the northern perimeter of this bloody valley the road widened somewhat and the footing became firmer after leaving the paddies. We gained altitude rapidly now, and as we twisted around the hairpin curves, we glanced back into the long valley we had just vacated. There was no movement, and to a less informed observer it might appear as a picture of sublime tranquillity. The motor labored as we chugged ahead, and the Korean seated up front began to get fidgety as the hood grew warmer and there was less breeze from our forward movement.

We passed a group of shacks with tin roofs and an accumulation of machinery suited to mining. There was a shaft and several piles of rock and earth. *A good place for infiltrating NKPA to hole up in*, I thought. We labored on, one crest giving way to another as we continued up and north. I knew the road had to cut back to the right (east) in order to take us to Chingdong-ni, and I was growing anxious concerning this. It seemed as though we were going way out of our way, and I was not sure just how far we could go without running into the enemy. I had the kid with me searching my map for the trail we were on, but to no avail. This piece of real estate was a blank on the map. A good deal had taken place since 1924, the year the map was made.

We reached the crest of the last ridge and the terrain, a rolling plateau, was scattered with clusters of thatched roof villages. There were cotton, pea, and pepper patches here and there, and an occasional farmer out in the fields. This atmosphere worried me. It looked as though most of the population had cleared out, yet there were enough still hanging about to indicate the enemy had already passed through, the people present being sympathizers.

I checked my watch, 1710. We had been on the road a long time. If this was the way to regiment, why weren't there some listening posts out here? Surely there should be troops around someplace.

We churned on, the tires cut to threads. How much farther? The road carried us north through more villages and more cotton patches. The farther we traveled the more apprehensive I grew. What if the redhead did not know what he was talking about? Why didn't I ask a few more questions? Why didn't the road turn east? What if the enemy had come this way since the redhead had come over the road? We would be easy pickings for them. We had to get those wounded men to an aid station quickly; they had come through a grueling ride as it was. I felt my shirt pocket. The Bible was still there.

I noticed the kid next to me was looking a little worried and his head seemed to be on an automatic pivot, looking from side to side for hidden death that might lash out at us at any moment. I had to defecate in the worse kind of way, but I did not dare to stop now. If only I could overcome this damn dysentery, this war would be so much easier. We bounced on; there was a drop ahead, another dip, and we were plunging down a much steeper grade than we had come up — we had reached the other side of the plateau. Below us to the north stretched a broad green valley running north. On the west were high and rugged mountains from which booming mortars and artillery could be heard. Up the valley several miles was a rather large town. Was it in friendly hands? We rolled down the zigzagging road at a reckless rate. What would this valley hold for us? Who would be in this town? We reached the bottom of the hills and raced through the paddies toward the town, the speed relieving or perhaps shortening the tension. Unknown to us, we had been the victims of one of those peculiar twists of fate that occur often in war without rhyme or reason. On this afternoon fate had dealt us a card that could mean death or salvation. The human element in this checkerboard of war had caused us to make a mistake — a mistake that could be fatal. I could not guess or even suspect this error, however, as we sped toward this strange Korean town.

As we approached the outskirts, it seemed as though I had been there before. Down the street was a concrete building with a black roof; written in white letters in English was HAMAN. The redhead was not from our regiment or even our division. This was the 19th Regiment — 24th Division. We had come to the wrong regiment. We were not even in the 25th Division sector, but north and west of Masan.

There was an American-made hospital car in the railroad station. I drove right up to it across tracks and all, the two-and-a-half with the wounded smack behind me.

A medic called out to me, "Stay clear of this damn car, you fool, the engine is backing down the track to hook on to us now." I yelled back, "Don't get your ass in an uproar, I got more customers for your tour."

The wounded were put aboard, Toras and Phillips among them. The train jerked away from the dirty station and the boom of artillery from the mountains. They would be in Pusan in a few hours, Japan in a day, maybe home next week.

CHAPTER
FIVE

Chingdong-ni

We watched the hospital train jerk out of the little station and felt both sorrow and envy for those aboard. We pulled off the railroad tracks with the two-and-a-half, now empty, still following. It seemed imperative that we get some tires, before taking the long circular route through Masan to Chingdong-ni, our original destination. We bounced on down to an area that was being used as the regimental supply point and where the service company of the 19th was set up. I found the lieutenant in command and gave him my story. All he could give me was rations and sympathy. I accepted both. He hustled out some No. 10 cans of peaches, pears, and fruit cocktail. I passed them out to the medics and the driver in the two-and-a-half, and the straggler and I began digging into a can of peaches. They went down mighty smooth.

While stuffing my face I considered the idea of completing the trip on flat tires. I decided to make one more play. I took a last gulp of peaches and stumbled off to find the 19th CP.

A GI directed me into the center of town where the CP was set up in the old police station. I sashayed on down the street feeling a new strength. The place was stuffed with ROK troops. They were everywhere, cleaning weapons, smoking American cigarettes, eating C rations, and telling jokes. Their nonchalance made me mad. I always grew furious when I saw those little ne'er-do-wells sitting around behind the lines while GIs were getting their fannies shot off to save a country most of them had never even heard of before now.

I found the stone police station and entered past several bearded guards. I walked down a short hall and turned left into a large room. The first face I encountered was a familiar one — it belonged to a lieutenant colonel who had come from the 7th Division. We had been on the same train from Sendai to Sasebo in the pipeline to Korea. I had forgotten his name and he mine, but he recognized me immediately and gave me a hearty greeting. (I felt the tires under me already.) It seemed that the colonel was the 24th Division's G-2 and he was at this regiment obtaining intelligence. I was loaded with information. He went over to the situation map and I pointed out our present positions and the route we had traveled during the day. As the story developed the situation took on an extremely rosy glow. A small crowd gathered around the map and they were greatly encouraged by my news. On the map things looked good. Of course I mentioned, "There are a few NKs manning a roadblock back on the road to Chingdong-ni, but it will certainly be cleared soon." They all agreed with me.

While everyone was letting my news soak in and stood around smiling confidently at one another, I cornered the colonel. I told of my prisoner, my G-2 info, and my shot up tires. He sat down and wrote a short directive to the motor officer of the service company. (I was to have the tires.) I took the note he scratched out hurriedly, made a comment about a get-together in Pyongyang, and made a hasty withdrawal. The mission was accomplished: why tarry?

I hurried through the mess of ROKs who were still overflowing in the streets. They irritated me all over again, but I didn't dwell upon this too deeply because of the order for tires I held tightly in my hand. The Good Lord evidently was still taking an interest in me.

I reached the service company area and someone directed me to a lieutenant who had just rolled up in a truck. I introduced myself, gave him my story and written order, and then stepped back to let him cuss a while. After the initial storm he called over a couple of men and ordered them to change my tires. I thanked him just as if he had some say-so in the matter and led the men off to the jeep. They directed me to a maintenance truck parked nearby where the rear of the jeep could be jacked up high enough for them to work on both rear wheels at the same time.

I put the prisoner on board the two-and-a-half, which was standing by, and the medic and drivers took turns pulling guard over him. I sat down in the comparative comfort of the cab and tried to "unlax." This place was a beehive of activity. Jeeps and weapons carriers kept darting in picking up ammo or rations and leaving a cargo of wounded on the station platform for the next train. Dirty, ragged, fatigued men walked through the area in a half daze, going about some business or another. In the immediate area of my jeep, greasy men were working on other vehicles and pieces of vehicles. And there was the ever present boom, boom, boom, from the mountains to the west, a constant reminder of the necessity for haste. The men worked on mechanically. I thought about the trip before us, over the same roads we had traveled the day before yesterday in our race from the north to plug up this gap in the bottom of our bag. It must be thirty miles back east and south to Masan and then south and west to Chingdong-ni. Already it was getting dark. How long would it take?

Wake up, Lieutenant! The jeep is ready! I shook once or twice and staggered out of the cab. It was now quite dark and the firing on the hill had assumed a furious pace. I was happy to be on my way out. I gave the men in the truck instructions about keeping the prisoner blindfolded and warned the driver about falling too far behind me. The straggler jumped in the jeep with me and we pulled out of Haman and ground for Masan with lights blazing (other vehicles also had their lights on, so I rationalized that it was safe).

The road was full of refugees and there was a good deal of military traffic. This helped our feeling of security. I pushed the jeep as much as I dared and trusted to luck and the alertness of the refugees that I would not hit anyone. The two-and-a-half stayed right on our tail, and as we flew over the treacherous mountain roads I could not help but think that we were undoubtedly setting a new speed record for the stretch, and wondered how rough a court-martial I might receive for such speed. My desire for all possible haste persisted, however, as a strong and overpowering sense of urgency took a tighter hold around the canned peaches in my stomach. The road seemed familiar but at times seemed utterly foreign, setting off fears that we might have made a wrong turn or perhaps had overlooked a sign. The moon was smothered by clouds and the air was heavy on our shoulders. There was not a hint of breeze and the dust from the road made a ten-foot-tall caterpillar of warm red dirt and air that stretched the length of the road. We plowed through this blindly, as if we were gophers. Under these conditions, each mile seemed ten, each minute an hour.

Other than our discomfort, the trip as far as Masan was uneventful. The city was electric with rear-echelon activity. Ammo trucks hustled in and out of town, and wire teams fretted feverishly over

111

the spider-web tangle that carried the business of war. Everywhere civilians searched for a place to get in off the streets in compliance with the curfew. Over all was a thick coat of red dust. We wondered how dirty a place could get.

After some thirty minutes of searching, we found the road south to Chingdong-ni. The road seemed familiar due to its hazards that had impressed us so much the day before. We wound south and west along the narrow ledge that was the road and felt as though the journey was near its end. I slumped in the seat as confidence began to creep back into my body, and I noticed that my companion had done likewise. The air was cooler here near the ocean and the dust had settled back on the road. This thought brought me up with a jerk. No dust, no trucks — no trucks, no GIs. What if we had pulled out of Chingdong-ni! I felt the peaches take a quick turn in my stomach and started to worry all over again. Would anything ever be certain in this war or would we continue to bungle on, always unsure, lost, guessing as to the situation? I spit out a mouthful of dirt and drove on.

We careened dizzily around the mountains, the headlights building forbidding shadows on the cliffs that made a wall on our right and searching futilely into the nothingness that was the left side of the road. The quiet was oppressive. We felt the stillness crushing us over the sound of the engine as it labored over the mountains. We reached the crest of a ridge and started coasting dizzily downhill. A flicker of light appeared on the road below us and then all was black. I hit the brakes and the boys in the two-and-a-half came to a screeching halt at our rear bumper. I cut the lights and we listened. Several hundred yards down the road we could hear motors and occasionally see a faint light. Then there were more lights, blackout lights, and we could identify trucks coming our way up the steep grade. I turned on our blackouts and pulled as far to the side of the road as I dared.

As the first truck came abreast we received a flood of oaths aimed at the "stupid son of a bitch" who would drive up a sniper-infested road with his lights on. We sat in silence and let the trucks pass. I thought of asking if the 27th was still set up at Chingdong-ni, but it would have been impossible above the roar of the motors anyway. The rattle of pots and pans and the tarps of the trucks identified them as mess trucks, so I felt reasonably certain the regiment was still set up because mess trucks had to feed somebody. As the last truck squeezed by we cranked up and started edging our way down the mountain, this time in blackout. It was not easy and I relied more on the sense of feel than sight. Our eyes were becoming more accustomed to the dark, the road began to level off, and we felt the salt breeze from the sea. This meant we were nearing the end of our trek. I became a little bolder with the jeep now and I tromped impatiently on the gas.

It seemed that it would be only a matter of seconds before we would reach the turn that would deliver us to the schoolhouse when — boom, boom, boom! We came to another screeching halt. The explosions we had heard had come from the spot where we expected the schoolhouse to be. I could identify most of the sounds of this dirty war, but this stumped me. The report was too great to be a 105 or a 4.5 outgoing and therefore it could be, and probably was, incoming mail of an unknown variety. We waited for a repeat performance, but none came.

I cranked up and we crept around the last curve, which would deliver us in front of the schoolhouse. To our relief we found a battery of 155s set up in the yard. These were the first mediums we had seen and I was delighted to have them in our support. We ground our way through the foot-deep dust that had been pulverized into fine silt by the many vehicles that had been operating here the past few hours.

I pulled up in front of the steps and had the boy with me unload the mess of NKPA papers, maps, and satchels, from which I hoped a wealth of G-2 information might be gleaned. The birds in the truck parked and trotted the prisoner over to the steps. I stuck my .45 in his back and marched him into the building with the other men following, loaded with all the paraphernalia we had liberated from the enemy. There were a couple of guards in the corridor, but they did not challenge us, so we continued on down the dark hall until we reached a lighted door. I pushed it open and stumbled in behind my blindfolded prisoner who had tripped on the doorsill after an energetic little nudge from the .45. The prisoner stayed on the floor as the remainder of my dust-coated crew stumbled into the room and stood blinking beside me in the brilliant light of a mantle lantern. I rubbed the dust out of my eyes and made a hasty survey of the situation.

Colonel Michaelis was standing with his back to a situation map staring at me, trying to decide if I were capable of speech and, if so, what language it would be in. Marguerite Higgins, the renowned Pulitzer Prize-winning correspondent for the *New York Herald-Tribune*, was staring at us, aghast, making an unsuccessful effort to look only at my party and not at the naked soldier on the floor. There was an AP photographer who stood limply by waiting for someone to say something, and Captain Freeman, the artillery liaison officer who had known me for months in Japan, only gaped in silence. There were other officers about, but none of them seemed important or made an impression.

Up to this point it had not dawned on me exactly what I would say or report, but now I began to think about this in earnest. My thoughts were interrupted by voices from the sea of faces staring at us making such original and witty statements as, "Goddamn, I'll be a sad bastard, who the hell are these hoods?" I walked over to the colonel and blurted out my story. He grabbed my hand, and started pumping it and exclaiming as to his happiness over my safety and the successful evacuation of the wounded. It seemed some knucklehead had reported us missing hours before. I looked around to find all the strange clean faces smiling at me. I asked about the situation and received a real "jolter." We had hit the center division of a three-division NK drive and had plowed a twenty-two-mile hole into the enemy position.

The flank divisions had sealed off the route of withdrawal in a matter of hours and the 2d Battalion had failed in its effort to reinforce our battalion. In other words, what we had thought to be a roadblock was in reality two NKPA divisions. With the route of withdrawal, reinforcement, and supply out and with the odds about twenty to one, the colonel had ordered a fighting withdrawal of the 1st Battalion. In fact, they had started the return trip only a few minutes after I had left that afternoon. The 155mm battery (A Battery, 90th Field Artillery) in the schoolyard and B Battery of the 8th Field Artillery were firing a preparation on the road in front of the battalion as it fought its way east and out of the trap. I gulped and wondered why I had been selected as the lucky one to evacuate the wounded and the G-2 poop.

The colonel dismissed me and I stumbled my way out to the jeep. The fatigue that I had been fighting for so long took a firm hold on me now, and I leaned dizzily on the warm hood of the jeep. I felt myself slipping down into the dust and knew that I was going to sleep, but I could not fight it.

The next sensation I felt was that of a boot (about size twelve) in the small of my back. "Get up, you lazy rascal before some hood runs over you." This voice I identified as Captain Beard's. The battalion was back. I struggled to my feet, grinned at the captain, and listened groggily to his invitation to sleep under a shed with his party where I would not be as prone to be run over. I mumbled something about *wanting* to be run over so I could go home as I stumbled after Captain Beard to the shed where his crew had already sacked out. This was some kind of a loading platform for rice with old rice bags scattered around that made luxurious beds. I flopped down on a couple of bags, heard the captain say something about getting all the tanks back, and listened to his voice lapse into a confusion of snores. I listened only for a short time, however, for it seemed mere minutes before someone was shaking me. I opened my eyes to find the sun shining brightly and to hear the staccato of small-arms fire crackling merrily on the hills just above and behind the schoolhouse.

I said something uncouth to the uncouth character who had awakened me about not getting his ass in an uproar and rolled over, trying hard to overlook the firefight that was taking place. This subterfuge would have probably worked if some inconsiderate hood had not set up a .50 at one end of the shed and started firing over the top of the schoolhouse and raking the top of the hill. The racket was unbearable. I sat up and looked around.

There were GIs behind all the vehicles scattered around the schoolyard, and little splashes in the dust around them confirmed their cause for alarm. A few rounds rattled through the tin roof overhead and I decided definitely not to sleep late. I put on my cartridge belt and .45 and picked up my carbine. It was evident that some enemy soldiers had to be killed before a man could get any sleep around this place.

I started walking over toward the school but ended up in a most undignified dash for its cover. By this time I was mad. The NKPA had wasted a good fifty rounds on me and had scared me half out of my jeans. I climbed through a window in the school and found a bunch of hoods lying on the floor shaking like hound dogs shitting peach seeds. Some major whom I had never seen before was screaming over a telephone for artillery, and some overly brave sergeant was sticking his .45 out of the window on the opposite side of the room and firing into the air. I asked a kid what the score was and he screamed something about millions of North Koreans on the hills behind the school and the colonel trying to get the 1st Battalion up on high ground. I looked nonchalant (I had been practicing), walked out into the hall, and then ran toward the side door on the west side of the building.

I peeked out the door and found Colonels Michaelis and Check rallying the troops in an effort to kick off an attack up the hill that began right behind the school. We had some men up there but they were hard pressed, and the North Koreans were already outflanking them on the left and right. I saw a platoon, or what was supposed to be a platoon, of Able start up the hill on the left flank (the west side) and I went after them, stopping at the open case of hand grenades to pick up a few. I reasoned that my job was with Able even though I had no communication to the field artillery. I yelled to one of the men of the weapons platoon, who was setting up the 60s with the other mortarmen in a little gully, and told him to run some wire to me as quickly as possible. I rushed up the hill, most of the time on all fours. It was only a short haul to the crest.

I found four or five men, led by Sergeant Matthews, fighting like hell to hold the crest. Scattered about were six or seven dead. To the right the enemy had already obtained the crest and were pouring a murderous fire into the schoolhouse and the remainder of the 1st Battalion, which was trying to mount a counterattack up the hill. Something came sailing through the air, dropped a few feet below me on the hill, and started rolling down. I identified it as a potato masher grenade before it ever hit the ground and made a dive in the other direction. I flattened myself against the ground and waited — one-two-three Crack. The explosion lifted me off the ground and started that uncomfortable ringing in my ears, but no damage. It was a concussion grenade and unless they went off over your head or in your hole, little damage was done.

A new burst of coordinated fire started from the crest just above me and I knew that the NKPAs were following up the grenade. One of the men was hit and Sergeant Matthews and the others started scooting down my way backward. The first Red came over the crest and somebody dropped him. Then four more popped over the top to our left. Another man was hit. I fired an eight-round clip and got one of them and Sergeant Matthews got another one. The other two jumped back over the hill. I started pulling pins and pitching grenades (only ten yards over the top of the hill). After four grenades, one of which came back but passed over our heads before going off, we edged back to the crest. Lucky for us we did, because several potato mashers came whistling over our heads to land where we had just vacated. This time we were ready. I had put the thirty-round clip in my carbine and the other men had full clips in their M1s. This time they came over in a rush, at least ten of them. We let them have it at point-blank range. I had my carbine on full automatic and simply sprayed as the enemy came over the crest all bunched up in a fanatical dive into our field of fire. At seven and eight yards we couldn't miss. We had the advantage because we knew where they were coming up and had our weapons trained on the spot, but they had to get over the top and then look for us. With this kind of a drop on them we lucked out. About half of them dropped on our side of the hill, and the others disappeared back over the crest. I pulled the pin from my remaining hand grenade, waited a moment, then let her rip, hoping to get an air burst over the little bastards' heads. A Korean lying in front of us was only half dead and I watched while one of the kids finished him off with his bayonet. I slipped my remaining loaded clip, an eight-round one, into my carbine and began loading my other two clips. The other men were doing likewise. (M1 clips of eight rounds came loaded and were disposable. Carbine clips had to be loaded and were reuseable.)

Someone called from down the hill a few yards; it was Sergeant Burris bringing up a wire and phone. With him was a man with a case of hand grenades. Good old Burris always came through. While he set up the phone, the rest of us took on a load of grenades. Two more men came puffing up and brought with them a bunch of M1 ammo in bandoliers. This made me feel a little better. They also informed us that we were to stay on the stinking hill at all costs and give the rest of the battalion supporting fire as they tried to mount the hill on the right. Two potato masher grenades came over now and one got one of the men who had just come up with the ammo.

We responded with a barrage of grenades that must have really jarred their asses. Each of us had at least a half-dozen grenades from the new case and we wasted no time in letting them fly. After I had thrown my last pineapple I eased up to the crest and peered over. There were at least fifteen dead or wounded Reds right below us on the other side of the hill. Ten or twelve others were working around to the left, however. I took a few pot shots at them and yelled at the men to move up on the left and make ready for the enemy.

I looked down our side of the hill and saw three more men with M1s coming up to our aid. The boys on the left opened up now and a brisk little firefight was developing. The hostiles still had grenades and they had a better position on us. One of the fresh kids bounced down beside me and asked blandly what was up. I shot him a look that should have frozen him to the spot and asked him if he had any grenades. He gave me one that I slung toward the NK soldiers working around the hill on the left, but I was far short. The new kid got the idea and tiptoed along the hill until he was just opposite where the enemy was last seen, and started pitching grenades like a big leaguer. With this kid's grenades plus the rifle fire from the others, the NKPA started back around the hill and into my field of fire from the crest. They were moving back slowly carrying their wounded. I cut down on them and the new kid dropped a grenade in their midst. At this, those who were able took off down the hill and dived into the rice paddy below with a hail of fire from us for company. As they disappeared into the green of the paddy we turned our attention to other matters.

There was a wounded man who was crying, out of his head, and Matthews was getting two men to evacuate the poor devil. Burris yelled that his wire was through and he soon had 60mm mortar rounds bursting all over the hill to the left, which was still in enemy hands. The remainder of the battalion had started their attack up the hill, and Dog Company's 81s were getting into operation. The men under Matthews dispersed along the ridge and set up a base of flanking fire for the attacking battalion. The main body of the enemy was only about two hundred yards to our left and in easy M1 range. In a matter of minutes, three men came blowing up the hill with a light .30. This made me feel as if we were going to stay. They set up for business in short order and began adding to the woes of our enemy on the ridge to the left.

I sat down in a little dip in the hill and began a search of the terrain to our front (north) with the glasses. I felt reasonably secure now and it had become SOP with me to always survey the landscape whenever I got a blow after a firefight. A lull simply meant that the enemy was regrouping. If I could spot them regrouping in an assembly area we could lower the boom on them with the artillery. I had started a slow sweep of a village about a thousand yards out with the glasses when I heard my name spoken. I turned around to find Burgess, one of Captain Beard's wiremen, kneeling beside me with an EE8 and a wire to Captain Beard who had contact with the batteries. We connected the phone and made a wire check. The captain was hanging on the other end and was loaded with exclamations concerning his relief over my healthy physical state. He also said that the colonel wanted me to get some fire on the ridge to the right in support of the battalion.

I gave a roger and out and took an azimuthal reading to the hill on the right. The azimuth was 1100. I could see the enemy plainly. I checked the map coordinates and gave the fire mission to Burgess who relayed it over the phone. "Fire Mission — Azimuth 1100 — Coordinates 63.5–34.2 — Enemy infantry concentration — Center platoon one round WP — Will adjust." We waited for only a few seconds before we got an "On the way" over the wire.

We heard the guns go off close at hand in the village on the bay and listened as the rounds whistled overhead. There were two muffled explosions and then, after a brief pause, two parallel columns of white smoke rose out of a little draw at least 800 yards on the other side of the target, but on the OT line (the observer-target line, in this case on azimuth 1100). I gave my correction, Drop 800. Burgess relayed on the telephone and shortly thereafter an "On the way" followed by the reports, the whistle over our heads, and two mushrooms of white smoke a little over the target.

My next command was "Drop 100 — Battery three rounds — Fire for effect." (Normally you get a bracket on your target, an over and short round, before firing for effect, but due to the proximity of our own troops this procedure would be entirely too dangerous so I simply brought the adjusting rounds up to the rear of the target and then edged in with a small range drop.) We got an "On the way" from the guns and hit the dirt as the rounds started screaming overhead like freight trains gone mad. I put the glasses to my eyes and watched the eighteen rounds (six howitzers firing three rounds each) go in. The effect was good but not as telling as it might have been with a little finer adjustment.

I gave Burgess a "Right 50 — Drop 100 — Battery three rounds HE." Shortly we got "On the way" and the rounds were again rushing overhead. This time all eighteen rounds were right where I wanted them, strung out along the ridge and a little bit beyond its crest on the enemy's side. Before the last round had hit, I gave a "Repeat range, Repeat fire for effect." The first thirty-six rounds had shaken the NKPAs up a bit, but they had not run them off the hill and that was our mission. The "On the way" came back over the wire and the rounds once again were rushing over us to do their bit for the cause. The effect was excellent. All eighteen rounds were right in there and the casualties were beginning to pile up for our antagonists. Besides, the artillery fire — the 81s, the 4.2s, the 60s — and the kids with the light .30s up here with me were taking their toll. I glanced down the hill to my left and saw the rest of the battalion galloping up with bayonets fixed. I called back for a "Repeat range — Battery three rounds WP." I reasoned a little hot phosphorous and smoke might confuse the issue somewhat for the enemy. We got an "On the way" and giggled in childish glee as the hot phosphorous engulfed the ridgeline.

This was all the encouragement the battalion needed. They clawed their way up the hill firing from the hip. I identified Lieutenant Young, the CO of Baker Company, as one of the first men to reach the crest of the enemy-infested ridge. Soon he was backed up by the rest of the battalion, throwing grenades, firing their weapons until they were empty, and clubbing and bayoneting like wild men. The Reds had started a fighting withdrawal, but as our attack gained momentum they fought less and bugged more. I gave the battery a command of "Left 50 — Add 200 — Battery three rounds HE." Soon we heard the rounds on their way and watched fiendishly as they crashed around the fleeing enemy soldiers.

The NKPAs were moving fast now, and I had to make a bold shift to catch any number. They seemed to be making for a draw that ran east and west up a large ridge about a thousand yards out to our right front. I made one more hundred-yard shift and after the rounds were complete I began an adjustment on the draw that appeared to be their assembly point. While I made the adjustment the ridge was secured by the remainder of the battalion. The enemy had disappeared altogether now. I got a bracket on the draw and began pumping HE and WP mixed into it. After about ninety rounds I ceased fire and asked the battery to mark the concentration.

The small-arms fire had all but stopped now, and other than the litter-bearers carrying the wounded down to the schoolhouse, there was no activity. Everyone on our little rise slumped over in an exhausted stupor. I took off my helmet and stretched out on my back. The sun was almost directly overhead; I looked at my watch, 1125 — this damn fracas had taken up the whole bloody morning. Men began dribbling up to reinforce us and some thoughtful soul had lugged along a No. 10 can of that wonderful staple, fruit cocktail. Burgess asked me for my canteen cup and volunteered to mooch some fruit cocktail for me. I readily went along with this and watched impatiently as Burgess walked over to the place where the can of fruit was greedily being divided. Shortly he returned with my canteen cup reasonably full of fruit. We got our plastic spoons that we had saved from C ration boxes and began shoveling down the moist sweet fruit from the same cup. It was gone far too soon and we both felt an awful let down when the spoons scraped the bottom of the cup. I put the canteen cup back in its place and rolled over on my side to look over the area to our front.

I knew that I should be searching for areas where the NKPA would be most likely to concentrate for the buildup that would most certainly follow, but I was entirely too spent to even hold the field glasses to my eyes. This morning had taken a lot out of me and I began to feel it. The area to our direct front was along a narrow valley with a road running up the left side and a creek running down the right. Between the creek and the road were rice paddies. To our right front was a tall file of forbidding mountains that formed the eastern rim of the valley and from which the enemy had swept down on us this morning. The left (west) side of the valley was another confusion of steep mountains. Across the road, which passed to the left of our little hill, and the paddies to our left front at about a thousand yards, was a village, tucked close to the foot of the mountains. Farther up the road at perhaps three thousand yards was another village and then still at a greater distance up the valley was another village, which was not quite distinguishable to the naked eye.

We were sitting on a little half-assed hill that jutted out from the major hills on the left and formed a finger that ran out into the mouth of the valley as far as the road. The road curled around our hill and ran past the schoolhouse, which was tucked in behind and below us. Past the schoolhouse the road junctured with the Masan road that ran northwest along the coast. Across the crossroads was Chingdong-ni. The little mud-and-stick town was squeezed tightly against the bay on the south by the space-starved rice paddies that ran the length of the valley and formed a delta at its entrance.

The bay was sky blue and the water was as calm as that in pictures of Lake Placid. Scattered about the bay, which was large, perhaps twenty to thirty miles in diameter, were irregular little islands. There were easily twenty of these islands, green and cool-looking, with terraced cultivated fields, thick canebrakes, and rusty-colored thatched roofs sprinkled about them. The islands all reached high out of the water. From our perch they appeared most inviting and I began selecting the one I would try to swim to if we got kicked into the water.

More men began to take up positions around us, and to the south troops started appearing with ammo. I began to notice the dead GIs lying about, most of them had been hit before I ever reached the hill. Matthews came up beside me and sat down. I asked him who the casualties were and he began by naming them slowly. I listened unbelieving as he mentioned Sergeant Miller. Miller had been one of my best friends and he was the best soldier I had ever known. He had seemed untouchable in this dirty little war. Here was a man who had fought through four years of war in the ETO and who had been wounded twice. A master sergeant who had spent his entire adult life in the army. A man who knew the answers and was not afraid. I listened to the other names as Matthews continued, but I could not get my mind off Miller. He was from Louisiana and had a pretty brunette wife and twins (a boy and a girl) about two years old. I had seen their pictures a week ago when we had shared the same hole at Wangang during the rear guard fighting back at Heartbreak Highway. Matthews commented that he got the son of a bitch that drilled Miller, but this didn't make me feel any better.

As our little post became more crowded we picked up enough scraps of information to give a fairly clear picture of what had happened. The NKPA that had hit us this morning were part of the three-division force we had tangled with yesterday. They had slipped west on a secondary trail and they now held the high ground west of Masan, cutting us off on our little peninsula south of Masan. The little raiding party that hit us this morning was evidently after the 155 battery that was sitting in front of the school. They were probably laboring under the supposition that we were still at the Sachon pass or dead. Fortunately, we had returned or the battery and the regimental headquarters would have been past history. I hardly think the enemy could have been any more surprised to find us on this spot this morning than we were to see them. The fact was clear, however, we had won. The enemy had not knocked out the regimental CP and had not taken our artillery. They had lost one hell of a lot of people and a good many small arms and machine guns. Perhaps our combined action of yesterday and this morning had upset their whole damn timetable.

This was by no means a cheap firefight for us, however. Our casualties had been high initially when the NKPA first ran us off the bloody ridge. We lost a large number of men in the school when the enemy got their machine guns operating on it and the cost of the attack back up the damn hill had not been light. Tales of outstanding bravery were on everyone's lips. There was Captain Weston, "the

Fighting Parson," famous in World War II in the China-Burma-India theater. He was an ordained minister who entered the army as a private and won a battlefield commission. He had come from the 7th Division with me and was given command of Able Company. He was wounded in our T34 battle and had rejoined the company this morning after a month of recuperating from his first wound. Today he was hit once in the leg, received first aid at the aid station, and returned to the hill and the attack. He was firing an M1 just like any other doughfoot when he was hit again. He was taken back to the aid station against his will and while receiving plasma had begged to return to the fight.

Then there was a sergeant from the I&R Platoon who was one of the first to realize what had happened this morning. He had picked up a light .30, charged up the hill, and commenced firing, minus the tripod. There were sixteen enemy dead around him when our forces reached his position. The sergeant had more than twenty slugs in him.

A little Mexican kid in Charlie Company, after running out of ammo, had used his M1 as a club, knocking NKPAs down and then bayoneting them. The colonel had directed the operation, fighting along with the men.

The fight had been a glorious exhibit of courage and bravery by the entire battalion, but the price of this victory had run high. Someone ventured to guess that we had only forty men in Able now. Lieutenant Buckley was the only officer —

Lieutenant Braum was hit yesterday, and Lieutenant Font, this morning. Perhaps there were 200 left in the battalion, counting all attachments. What would happen when there were only ten in the company? Who would be the last to be hit? Who would there be to evacuate you if you were among the last to get hit? How long would it be before we were all either hit or dead? I looked at the little islands in the bay and wished that the marines would hurry up and land.

I put the glasses to my eyes and began a search of the terrain. All appeared quiet and blissful. There was a gentle breeze off the water that set the rice below to rolling in long graceful waves. The little dikes that separated the paddies were lush with grass and scrawny brown cattle grazed greedily over them. Ordinarily the cattle are not allowed to graze freely. The Koreans cut the grass from the dikes with hand scythes and carry it to the cattle who put in a full day's work plowing, pulling a cart, or providing power for a mill. There was an occasional white-clothed figure who would show himself in the nearby village across the paddies to the left, but he did not arouse my suspicions as I searched the otherwise tranquil landscape. The NKPA had pulled a very successful disappearing act. Normally, we would have pursued them until contact was lost, but due to our limited numbers and lack of information as to their strength this was impossible. The best we could hope for was to maintain a strong perimeter that would hold against overwhelming odds until help arrived. The marines were to arrive any day, or so rumor had it, and they were to relieve us. If only rumors were right.

There were two scrubby little trees on our hill and I crawled over to a shady spot made by the sparse leaves. I gave Burgess my glasses and asked him to keep a keen watch out. He said that he would, and scooted over to a place where he would have a good view and some shade. I stretched out on my back and watched the vultures commence assembling in the sky overhead. Every inch of me felt raw and I could not throw off an acute feeling of tenseness that had taken a firm grip of me. The men around me were digging in and a crew of men with a recoilless .75 were coming up the hill. With all these reinforcements, we could hold out for some time. I looked along the ridge to our right and noted with a great feeling of relief that the remainder of the battalion was also digging in. A platoon of Baker had moved to the extreme height of the most extended ridge to the right and they were in a position to foil any attempt at that flank. Wire entanglements were being emplaced, and out in front about a hundred yards groups of men were setting up trip flares.

I rolled over on my side and closed my eyes when Burgess sounded off, "Lieutenant, come over here and take a gander. Looks like those little bastards are up to something in that village over yonder." I took the glasses and trained them on the village that was directly across the paddies to our left front. The

Reds were working their way around from the hills and into the village from the west. They were setting up machine guns, and it appeared that the bunch that were coming in were carrying mortars. I picked up the phone and called for a fire mission. I put the glasses to my eyes again. No doubt about it, they were setting up mortars in the doorways of the little mud houses. Ammo bearers were passing ammo to their comrades through the windows. Riflemen were working around the walls that formed little courtyards for the houses.

The telephone crackled and I got an "On the way" from the battery. The rounds whooshed through the air to our left and crashed into the side of the hill to the left and above the village. I gave a correction of "Right 100 — Drop 200 — Battery three rounds HE." Before the rounds were on the way the enemy mortars let go with a volley that went crashing into Chingdong-ni. I got an "On the way" from the battery and the duel was on. All of my rounds looked good, but they had not knocked out the enemy mortars. I thought the adjustment was good so I ordered a battery six rounds (thirty-six rounds) HE and WP mixed. Before they could be fired, the mortars started a barrage that sent rounds thundering into Chingdong-ni at a terrific rate. (My battery was in Chingdong-ni.) I held my breath while waiting for the "On the way." If the mortars got our battery before we got them, we had had it. The 155 battery was in the schoolyard, too close a range to fire at the mortars, and the 81s and 4.2s for some reason were not firing on the enemy position. They must have pumped a hundred rounds into the town before I got the "On the way," and watched as the rounds crashed into the village where the mortars were set up.

The effect was good. Several of the walls were knocked down by the HE, and the WP started a couple of terrific fires. I saw three men run out from under the shed that had been hit by a WP round and start rolling in the dust in a vain effort to put out the phosphorous that was toasting their hides. I ordered the battery to repeat range, repeat fire for effect. This time there was no delay and the rounds thundered into the target. I could see casualties occurring in the village and I saw two of the houses harboring the mortar positions receive direct hits with HE. When the rounds were complete there was only one mortar that continued to fire.

I screamed over the phone for the battery to repeat range, battery eight rounds WP. I figured forty-eight rounds of white-hot phosphorous ought to chill their asses for good. In a second or two the WP started taking its toll. This set the entire village into a flaming furnace and the rice in the paddies nearby turned brown immediately from the heat.

The Reds started fleeing up the hill to the north of the village and around the hill to the west. I gave a shift of left 50 — add 200 — battery three rounds HE. I reasoned the best target was the group withdrawing up the hill. I wanted the rounds to land

135

on those soldiers in the lead so that those behind and below would get the full effect of the falling rocks that were always the end products of HE on a steep rocky hill such as this, and that was always the case anywhere in Korea. The rounds exploded into the side of the hill, a little to the rear of the most advanced fleeing men, with good effect and a rock slide developed that was downright beautiful. I saw a good many of the soldiers carried down the hill by the rock and earth slide. I knew that I had not gotten all of those on the hill, but I thought that the NKPA bugging out around the hill to the left needed some attention, too. I gave a shift of left 200 — add 200 — battery three rounds HE. As I waited for the battery to get the rounds on the way, I noted with disappointment that the enemy were fast disappearing. The rounds crashed into the ravine that wound around the left of the hill. There was brush there and I could not see what effect the rounds had made, although they saturated the area I had shot at, where there were bound to be Reds. There was no more movement anywhere in the area now. I called cease fire, end of mission into the phone.

I turned the glasses over to Burgess and asked him to stay on the lookout. Three or four of the kids close by enthusiastically complimented me on the splendid fire in the village. I smiled and crawled back to the shady spot, which had shifted now very near Sergeant Miller's body. I stretched out on my back and stared into the blue sky — several vultures began to circle overhead. I watched them. The flies began to buzz greedily over the dead. The air was thick and rested hot on my body. I would sleep.

CHAPTER
SIX

Our Allies

It was around 1500 when I opened my eyes and squinted into the brilliant sun that was shining unmercifully into my face, the shade having moved on. My mouth had that dry, dirty-sock taste in it and every inch of my body felt cramped and sore, especially my back. The hill was in peaceful order now. Everyone was well dug in and most of the men were contentedly snoring away with their helmets cocked heavily over their eyes. I struggled to my feet and walked a short distance down the hill to answer Mother Nature's call. The schoolyard below lay hot and still in the dust. I walked back to the crest of the hill where Burgess lay asleep. I picked up my glasses and began a methodical search of the terrain from west to east. There was no activity. I put the glasses in their case and stared absently into the hot paddies.

Around the hill to my left came a patrol of South Korean marines. They formed a column of ducks and passed on up the road into the valley. The phone rang — the battalion switchboard operator had a message for me: an ROK patrol was going to be operating up the valley and I was not to fire upon them. They would be back down the road at 1900. Also, I was to have a detail of men bring all of our dead to the east end of the schoolhouse immediately. After that, we were to take the NKPA dead in our area to the edge of the rice paddy on the west side of the schoolhouse. I listened to this with dread, gave the kid a "wilco," and hung up.

I searched among the sleeping men until I found Sergeant Matthews. He was awake immediately. I gave him the story and asked him to make up a detail. He put on his boots and began waking up the listless men for the task. I went back to where Burgess was sleeping and watched the ROK patrol as it worked up the road, in an attempt to keep from being too conscious of what was taking place around me. I had been squeamish about fiddling with the dead from the start of this campaign, and I had always tried not to look at them. I put the glasses on the patrol and began to observe their progress carefully. They looked as though they had found something out in the rice paddies because several squads had left the road for the paddy and were encircling a large area of rice as if trying to flush something. It did not take long for the quarry to flush, either. Up popped two NKPA soldiers with their hands high above their heads. The ROKs quickly hustled them to the road and tied their hands to their rifles, which were placed across the shoulders behind the head, an effective way to curtail a prisoner's activity and at the same time force him to carry his own weapon.

While these prisoners were being tied and questioned, a squad of men threaded their way across the paths that ran through the paddies to the village that was still burning briskly from my fire mission this morning. They disappeared into the smoke and after a few minutes reappeared loaded with small arms, presumably taken from the dead left in the village. The major portion of the patrol had resumed its cautious passage up the road. After advancing about half a mile farther they stopped at what seemed to be a culvert under the road. The officer in command drew his sword and commenced jabbing vigorously in one end of the culvert that ran under the road. Out the other end popped three Reds, one clearly wounded in the hindquarter. While these new prisoners were being tied, the squad that had reconnoitered the village caught up with the main body. A detail started back in our direction with the prisoners and the captured weapons. The others continued up the road, extended a little more than they had been, which was wise considering that they were now out of range of most of our supporting fire in case they hit some resistance. I could still give them artillery support, however.

My attention was now attracted by the commotion going on behind me on the hill. I heard a couple of kids yell out "Mule Train" in an attempt to imitate Frankie Laine. I looked around to see them, each with a dead Red tied to the end of a machine-gun belt that they were using to drag them down the hill. (There were two reasons why machine-gun belts were used to move the enemy dead: [1] We had had experiences in the past where the dying had pulled the pin on a grenade and had died lying on it; when they were moved they exploded, causing casualties to those who moved them. With a used machine-gun belt, it was possible to slip a loop around an appendage, move off to a safe distance, and jerk. If the body was booby-trapped no harm was done. [2] The bodies were so filthy and germ-infested that no American GI could stand to touch them.)

I watched as the bodies bounced down the hill behind the "Mule Train" — singing kids. That was the fortunate thing about seventeen-, eighteen-, and nineteen-year-old soldiers. It made little difference how much hell they went through or saw, they would spring back like a green sapling in short order. I turned around completely and watched as other members of the burial detail dragged more Reds down the hill to the edge of the paddy on the west side of the schoolhouse. Most of the others were performing their task with less gusto.

All of the GI dead had been evacuated. The men were now busying themselves with the unpleasant job of putting the dead enemy in the ground. A platoon from the engineer company was setting charges in the rice paddy, preparing to blow holes that would be graves for the NKPA soldiers. The men who were charged with the task of bringing the corpses off the hill were assembling them in a most unmilitary manner along the edge of the paddy. There now must have been at least fifty enemy dead awaiting burial down below, but the men were still dragging down more. They had cleared our area, but on the ridge to the left there was still much work to be done.

Below, everyone cleared away from the paddy in order to save themselves the discomfort of a shower with rice-paddy muck when the charges were blown. After a few minutes of checking and screaming orders that no one paid any attention to, the engineers blew the charge. Black muck and green rice flew high into the air and yawning black holes were left in the paddy. The dead were black with the muck that had been blown over them. After the dirt had settled the men started to pull the corpses into their resting place. Because the Reds wore no dog tags and had no identification there was no point in separate graves and it had become SOP to bury them in groups of thirty-five to fifty. While the burial was taking place, other members of the detail continued to drag bodies off the ridge to the left.

Gunfire chattered up the valley. I shifted around and began searching for its source through my field glasses. I picked up the ROK patrol on the edge of the second village on the road at a range of some three thousand yards. They had deployed about the mud village and were pouring the fire to it. After a few minutes more, all was quiet, and they began a cautious advance into the village. Shortly all the members of the patrol had gone into the village and all was quiet. Occasionally a figure could be seen passing among the tight little group of houses, but it was impossible to determine just what was going on. The ROKs operated just like the North Koreans and they always kept you guessing. Burgess and I sat impatiently waiting to see what the outcome of this firefight would be.

A figure appeared on the road and soon a column of figures filed out behind him. I picked them up in the glasses and identified them as prisoners, tied together, each with his hands tied to his weapon behind his neck. There must have been ten or twelve of them. The patrol assembled on the road outside the village and about half of its members were loaded with captured weapons. Evidently they had left a good many dead enemy in the village. Probably it had been an assembly point for the wounded and they were waiting until night to be evacuated. The ROKs evidently had wiped them out except for those who had surrendered. From the number of weapons the ROKs were carrying, there must have been a good many casualties in that village. The main body of the patrol now started back, leaving a squad dispersed along the road on the other side of the village as a rear guard. As the main body advanced down the road toward us we could see that several of the captured were walking wounded. The ROKs were literally loaded with captured rifles and burp guns, each man with two or three plus his own weapon. That was one thing that could be said in praise of the ROKs. They always brought back any enemy equipment they could get their hands on, while our troops were doing well to hang on to their own gear. When the main body was a few hundred yards in front of us the squad that had been left behind assembled on the road and started after their company.

In the schoolyard to our rear there were still a few men dragging dead Reds down the ridge on the left. Most of the bodies had been cleared from the area where the large part of the battalion was dug in. There were still many dead in front of our positions, but they would probably remain there because it would be a risky business to advance several hundred yards in the open to drag in the enemy dead. Just because the ROK patrol had gone up the road several thousand yards without drawing fire from the hills did not mean that the enemy was not about. It simply meant that they chose not to give away their positions by firing.

I began to think about my empty stomach. It was 1840 hours now and the activity of the day plus the lack of nourishing or filling food was beginning to make my insides do flip-flops as they rubbed against each other. I drank the last of the hot, chlorinated water that had been in my canteen since yesterday. I gave Burgess the empty canteen and asked him to take it along with his to the bottom of the hill and get some water. I asked him also to check up on the chow situation and to bring up a blanket from the jeep. He took off eagerly, happy to be off the hill and impatient to get to the cool well water that he would take a bath in. As he went down the slope I thought that being on the hill was one of the worst disadvantages of being an FO. You were never able to get off the hill, for as sure as you would the enemy would start something.

I sat there and thought of the bath Burgess was going to get and decided to take off my boots and air my feet as a substitute. Damn, it would be nice to brush my teeth. I unlaced my boots and took off my socks. I lay back and put my head on my helmet and looked out into the placid bay. The water was still and the little islands had a golden glow around them as the late afternoon sun filtered over them and was reflected in the water. A few small fishing boats crept through the water and smoke could be seen snaking its way skyward out of the mud-and-stick houses. The evening "gohung" (rice) was in the pot. I closed my eyes, thinking I might catch a few winks when the phone began to ring. I grabbed it to hear Lieutenant Buckley on the other end make some fool remark about it being a nice afternoon for a funeral. I replied that it was, without too much enthusiasm, and asked about some chow. He said that a jeep had just come in from Masan with a trailer full of C rations and that I was to send a detail down to pick them up for the 2d Platoon and the attachments we had on the hill. I agreed readily to this and hung up.

I asked Sergeant Matthews to send a two-man detail down to the company CP to pick up the food and to take everyone's canteens and fill them while down there. As the men were on their way I lay back to relax and wiggle my bare feet in the air. I closed my eyes and felt that I was sure to catch a few winks before the chow arrived.

My rest was abruptly disturbed by the grating ring of the EE8. I reached for it and mumbled "Fox Oboe Able" (my telephone call sign). It was the executive office of A Battery, 90th Field Artillery Battalion, the 155 outfit that was set up on the south end of the schoolyard. The battery had laid on a compass of 2700, due west, in order to support the 1st Battalion's withdrawal and the 2nd Battalion's perimeter, which was set up a few miles west of Chingdong-ni. After the attack from the north this morning, it had been decided to supplement the fire of A Battery of the Field Artillery. This was laid on 3600 (north), which I had fired earlier in the day, with two sections of the 155 battery. The howitzers had already been laid on 3600 and they were ready for me to register on something up the valley.

I told him that I would be ready to register in a few minutes and to hold the wire. I called Burris over to act as my phone operator and then sat down on the forward slope of the hill just below the crest. I looked over the map and hastily decided that the most suitable registration target was the village down the road that the ROK patrol had visited earlier (village #2 on the battle map), it was in the center of the sector and something easily identifiable on the map and on the ground, both essential in a precision registration. I checked the map coordinates, took the azimuth (3100), and gave the fire commands to Burris, who relayed them over the phone. In a few minutes we got the "On the way" from the battery and heard the report of the piece to our rear.

The round steamed through the air over our heads and I put the glasses to my eyes and waited for the burst out front (in registration you use only one gun). There was a wild explosion short and to the left of the village. Rice, water, and mud flew crazily into the air and after a moment the deep *Boom!* floated down the valley to us. This was the first time we had had 155s and I was amazed and tickled at the extreme difference in the effect of the gun in comparison with the 105s that had been our only artillery up until this time. This 155 was really an ass chiller from way back. I gave my command to Burris — right 200 — add 400. Soon the round passed overhead and burst about 100 yards beyond the village and a little to the right. I made an adjustment of left 50 — drop 200. This gave me a burst short of the village but on line. I split my bracket once and then split it again and went into fire for effect (six adjusting rounds at the same deflection and elevation). After the registration we had a time adjustment on the same target. We now felt that we could hit anything in the valley, the battery using the "K" (mathmatical constant) from the adjustment in firing any fire missions to follow. The 105s had pumped enough shells into the village across the paddy on the left to have a satisfactory adjustment so I felt confident that we would have adequate and accurate artillery support when the sun went down.

Already the sun was below the horizon and it would not be long before the light would be no more. I decided to have some light up the valley and that the best torch would be the village we had just fired on. Not only would it burn all night giving light that would silhouette any troops between it and us, but it would also prevent the enemy from using it as an assembly point. Also, it would clearly light the road so that no tanks or self-propelled guns could sneak up on us.

I called the 105s, because they had not fired on this target as yet and I wanted them to make a good adjustment on it before dark. I fired the center platoon one round first. The bursts were a little short and to the right and left. I made an adjustment and got the burst smack in the center of the village. I fired battery two rounds (twelve) of WP, and as the rounds rushed overhead I put the glasses on the village and waited for the white burst. They crashed into the village unmercifully and fires burst out everywhere among the houses. The straw roofs were like tinder and the WP set them to blazing instantly. I gave the battery a cease fire, end of mission, and put the field glasses back into their case, feeling confident in the knowledge that we would have a huge fire blazing in front of us all night to light the valley and give away the movement of the enemy. The fire in the village to the left across the paddies was still going briskly from this noon's barrage.

I went back to the place where the phone was secured below the crest on the back side of the hill and found that the detail had arrived with the C rations. There was a box for every two men and Burris had drawn a box to share with me. We sat down and dug into the cans greedily. We shared a can of beans and frankfurters and each had a can of fruit. There were biscuits and we pooled the packets of powdered coffee to cook a boiling black inky canteen cup of it over chips of Sterno that Burris had managed to stash away for such an occasion. The fruit, as always, was the best of all and I was let down after it was all gone.

I gave Burris the entire pack of cigarettes that was in the box (I don't smoke, anyway) and he let me have all of the piece of chocolate, an agreeable trade for both of us. When the coffee was ready, Burris poured off the top half of the fluid into my canteen cup and we settled down to nurse along the steaming coffee and muse and brood over the nasty little war and the comforts of the garrison life in Japan.

We both confessed that we kind of enjoyed the parades and that there was a great deal of satisfaction in putting on a crisp set of khakis with polished brass and shoes that would reflect your face. Then we talked about clean crisp sheets and the actual comfort there was in an army cot. Sergeant Burris noted that it was Sunday and that if we had been back in Japan we would have had fried chicken today. I thought about fried chicken and he replied eagerly that he had the best recipe in the world. He began to enlighten me as to the Ozark method of frying chicken. I listened politely, thinking about the way I fried it and after Burris had finished, I launched into a scholarly dissertation on my method of doing it that was a mixture of old Georgian, Floridian, and Navajo technique. He listened respectfully.

The coffee was gone now and all light had left our dirty little corner of the world. Sergeant Matthews came down to our spot of comfort and said that everyone was settled for the night. The men were in two-man foxholes, as were the ROKs, and one would be awake at all times until four in the morning, at which point all the men would be awake. I told Matthews that this suited me to a *T*. He sat down with us and we slipped into the topic of uplift brassieres. Matthews was a little better versed on the subject than either Burris or myself, but we made up for our lack of knowledge with lies.

We heard a few rocks tumble down the hill and then huffing and puffing as somebody labored up the hill. After a while a black figure appeared below and as it got close it developed into Burgess. He struggled up to us and sat down. After catching his breath he reported that Headquarters Company had B rations and that he had stayed over for chow. He gave me my canteen, which he had filled, and began deluging us with the rumors that were current down around battalion headquarters. He swore that there was a good possibility that the mess truck would come to the schoolyard tomorrow and we were going to have B rations, too; a sergeant had given him the straight word that the marines were landing in Pusan at this minute. Seems this sergeant had been to Masan and had talked with an ambulance driver who had been in Pusan this morning. We all perked up at this news and agreed that the ambulance driver probably knew what he was talking about. With the marines here we would have damn near four divisions on this stinking little peninsula. Too bad they were only at three-quarters strength.

Burgess had some more rumors about food, casualties, and conditions in the States. He said that he had seen a *Stars and Stripes* down at the schoolyard and that in it he had read Harry (Truman) was roughing it on the yacht *Williamsburg*. We all were delighted to hear that he was enjoying himself and that he was able to beat the Washington heat. The *Stars and Stripes* had also said that the 1st Cavalry was winning the war in Korea and this morsel of information brought hope to our hearts for we had been under the impression that the 1st Cav was on the Yankee side, especially since their artillery had continually shot at us all the time we

151

were fighting the rear guard down Heartbreak Highway. In fact, we were practically sure, for hadn't the 5th Regiment of the 1st Cav left all of their equipment on the road behind us so that our fighting withdrawal would be more difficult? No, it couldn't be true that they were on our side. But, Burgess swore that they were and that they were winning the war for us. After all, he had seen it in the paper. We were much encouraged by this revelation.

Sergeant Matthews said something about checking to see that the men were alert and walked off. Burris said he needed sleep and simply fell back and started snoring. I told Burgess to stay by the phone and went over to the .75-recoilless position to check up on things. The crew was alert and the weapon was well dug in. I gave them one of the packs of cigarettes I always managed to have on supply and sat down on the edge of their hole. They passed the cigarettes and took turns getting down under a shelter half in the bottom of the hole to light them (to hide the light that would give away our position). I asked about ammo supply and they reported that they had plenty. One of the crew made a comment about the fires in the villages and I gazed at them contentedly. Great orange and red tongues of fire licked up into the sky and the land was lighted for a mile or so around the fires up the valley. The fire across the paddies had lost much of its vigor, but it still gave off a good deal of light and made it hot enough that the enemy would not be likely to use it as an assembly point or mortar position again.

I took out my field glasses and examined the burning villages carefully. There was no sign of life. I got up, told the .75 crew to stay on their toes, and felt my way over to the heavy .30 position. The crew was asleep, except for one man. I asked him if everything was in fighting shape and he replied *jo toe* (Japanese for just swell). I stopped at a few rifle positions and in each case one man was awake and alert, as had been ordered. I checked the light .30 position and then started back to the phone and Burgess, satisfied that my perimeter was in good shape and alert.

As I walked back to the telephone position that was developing into my CP, I became acutely aware of the fact that I had not had a bowel movement all day. The hot coffee that I drank with Burris was making any thought of procrastination out of the question. I pushed by Burgess, picked up my entrenching tool, and started for a level spot a short distance down the hill. I arrived on the ledge in a state of near panic and went frantically to the task of digging a cat hole and taking down my britches at the same time. It was only superior skill and long and continual practice that enabled me to accomplish this feat without major catastrophe.

I finished this painful operation with some splintery C ration toilet paper, scraped the dirt back into the hole with my shovel, and labored up the hill. Burgess was sound asleep by the phone. I picked up the receiver, cranked the handle, got the switchboard, made a wire check, and asked them to call us every two hours for a wire check. I put the receiver back into the canvas case, pulled the top up over the whole works so that the dew would stay off of it, and prepared to sack out. I found the blanket Burgess had brought from the jeep and began looking for a likely spot to collapse. I had overlooked the prospect of digging a hole and I decided that it was not time to start now (a bad practice for anyone and exceedingly so for an officer who must insist that his men dig holes). There was a little bank a few feet below the crest and I chose a spot under it as a bed. I stretched the blanket down and took off my cartridge belt and helmet. I leaned my carbine against the bank and dropped down on the blanket. I untied my boots (and didn't dare take them off) and settled back for some sack time, with half the dusty blanket under me and the other half over me. My eyes clamped shut and I knew that I would be asleep in a matter of seconds when I heard gunfire down the valley and then heard HE burst on the front side of the hill.

I lay still a few moments and there was more firing from guns about the size of 51s or 76s, probably antitank guns the NKPAs were using as nuisance pieces. This time the rounds went whistling overhead and out to sea behind us. I got up, took my compass from its case, and climbed into the hole with the men on the heavy .30. I asked them if they had seen the flashes when the pieces had fired. They hadn't, but all agreed that it was from the ridges on the east side of the valley that the fire had come from. We waited, but not for long. There were two reports and the rounds exploded into the hill to our left almost before the reports could reach us. I didn't see the flash and neither did anyone in the crew. I agreed with the others that the guns were on the ridges to the east of the valley, and I guessed the range at about 2,000 yards.

I determined to take the hills under fire even though I had not spotted the field pieces, and I called down to Burgess to get A Battery on the phone. He was a jump ahead of me and already had the 105s on the wire and awaiting fire commands. I called back the commands "Azimuth 200, from last concentration — Right 800 — Drop 1,000 — Center platoon one round, WP, enemy field pieces, will adjust." While I was waiting for Burgess to relay the message and for the battery to get the mission on the way, I glued my eyes to the spot where I expected the pieces to be. There were two more reports and this time I caught the flashes. They were smack on the crest of the ridge and at about 800 yards greater range than I had guessed. I called back to Burgess to change my commands, but it was too late. The battery barked behind us in Chingdong-ni, and we could hear the rounds rushing on their way over our heads. There were two yellow and white bursts on the ridge out front, short and to the left of the place where I had seen the flashes. I gave a correction of right 400 — add 800, and waited.

The Reds, figuring they had been spotted, began pouring in the rounds at full speed now. Most of the bursts were on the people to our left, but we caught a few too close for indifference in our perimeter, too. The guns sounded to our rear and the WP adjusting rounds were on their way. They crashed into the side of the ridge below and to the left of the flashes. I made a 100-yard adjustment to the right and raised the ST (sight altitude) 50 yards. All this time the enemy guns (two of them) were firing at maximum speed.

We got an "On the way" from the battery and the rounds screeched up the valley. I saw the white and yellow burst of the white phosphorous go off on the hill smack on the spot where I had seen flashes. I called for the battery to "Repeat range, battery three rounds HE." In short order, the rounds were bursting all over the area where the guns had been spotted. I waited for a moment for some sign of activity on the target area, but none followed. I gave the battery "Cease fire, end of mission, mark concentration." I could not be sure whether or not the guns had been knocked out, but it was evident that they had been "talked out" of shooting at us for a while and there was a good chance that we had caused some casualties among them. I waited a few minutes for some sign of retaliation from the enemy, but none came and I turned back to my blanket and some sleep. I called down to Burgess to record the concentration number of that last mission when the battery called back to give him its number; Burgess said that he would and I fell off to sleep.

The blanket felt warm and cozy and the rocky hill could not have felt better if it had been a feather bed. I slept soundly until gunfire, about 51mm, started coming in again; this time the impact area was Chingdong-ni. The EE8 was ringing and I heard Burgess drawl "Fox Oboe Able" into the receiver. Then he called me and said that the boys in artillery battalion headquarters were crying because they were being shot at and wanted to know why in the hell I had not taken that pesky gun under fire. I told Burgess to tell them I was trying to spot it now and for them to hold their jeans on for a minute and I would knock it out. I went up to the machine-gun emplacement and asked the man on watch if he had seen the flash. He shook his head. He said that it seemed to be on the ridge to the right front, as were the other guns earlier, but he could not spot it. I listened as the rounds continued to be pumped in at a rate of about two per minute. This time there appeared to be only one gun firing, of the elephant-gun variety, a flat-trajectory weapon with a high muzzle velocity. I searched the ridge and valley and listened intently. I could not spot the gun, but I agreed with the man on the machine gun that the thing was emplaced somewhere on the ridge on the right of the valley and at a range of from three to four thousand yards. This could possibly be one of the two guns that had fired on us earlier and had displaced after our counterbattery fire. Perhaps we had knocked out its partner.

Burgess called to me and said that the people in Chingdong-ni were crying for some counterfire and they wanted it now. I decided to shoot at the place where I thought the piece might be. Maybe I could scare the enemy into shutting up and it would pacify the people down there in Headquarters Battery who were getting shot at. I gave a shift from the concentration of the village and placed two rounds of WP on the top of the ridge. With two guns, I moved the bursts up the ridge in fifty-yard shifts, one gun firing HE and the other WP. I moved the fire up the ridge about 600 yards and then brought it back again. I gave the battery "cease fire" and awaited developments. The enemy gun was still firing, but not nearly as heavily, only about two rounds every five minutes. I hadn't hit them, but perhaps I had scared them. I scanned the ridge until my eyes were ready to pop out of my punkin head, but I could not find the flash of that gun. The people in headquarters began calling Burgess again and telling him that we did not hit the piece that was firing at them and asking what the hell I thought I was paid for. I told Burgess to tell them they must be mistaken, that I had completely knocked out their antagonist. I went back to searching for the possible hiding place for that pesky little field piece when it stopped firing of its own accord. I waited a full ten minutes and then decided on some sack time. I went back to my blanket and cuddled up for some real sound dreaming. It was swell.

"It's 0400, sir," said Sergeant Burris.

I pretended that I was dead but it was no use. "Sir, it's 0400, time for the alert," Burris insisted. I sat up, looked at his black figure in the dark, and glanced to the east. There was no sign of light. The dew was heavy on everything and I felt cold and dirty. The moisture had turned the dust on my face to mud and when I rubbed my eyes I simply smeared the mess over my face. I put on my helmet and remained sitting on my blanket. Matthews came up and reported that all the men were awake and alert. I said, "Swell."

Boom, boom, boom; the 155s began sounding off down in the schoolyard. It was the platoon that was facing 2700 (west) firing in support of the 2d Battalion. Evidently the enemy were making their main effort this morning in the 2d's sector. I asked Burgess to make a wire check and report that we were all awake and alert. He did. I took out the glasses and began wiping the lenses with a scrap of lens paper I had been hoarding in the binocular case. The dampness ate its way into my bones and I shivered and clamped my jaws together tightly to stop my teeth from chattering. I wrapped the blanket around my shoulders and got up.

I gave the glasses to Burgess and asked him to make a thorough terrain survey as soon as there was enough light. I walked over to the .75 position and then to the machine-gun positions. I stooped over and jarred a rifleman who had gone back to sleep, and went down the hill to the level ledge that was becoming our latrine. I accomplished the act of kidney elimination with much shivering. As I turned to go back to the top, I stepped in some of the slipperiest shit I had ever encountered, and it was only through the help of God and a superior sense of balance that I managed to keep from landing right in the middle of it. As it was, I fell on the edge of the mess, which was certainly catastrophic enough. I screamed wildly at the lowly son of a bitch who didn't have the decency to cover up his own droppings and swore that I would rub his nose in the goddamn mess if I ever found out who the lowlife bastard was.

I walked up the hill to a relatively grassy place, sat down, and scooted myself over it, in the fashion of a dog with an itching behind, in an effort to rub the spot off the rump of my fatigues. This procedure eradicated most of the feces, but thoroughly saturated my britches with dew. Swell! I was cold enough before the catastrophe, now with a wet fanny I was like an iceberg. I struggled back up the hill and asked Burgess when the hell the sun was coming up. He replied that he didn't know and asked some asinine question about the state of our latrine area. I walked on past him and sat down next to one of the machine gunners who had a dry shelter half spread out on the ground.

The false dawn was at its end so the real thing could not be far off. If we were to get an attack this morning it would come in the next thirty minutes. The Reds did not like to attack after the sun was well up if they could help it. They had too much respect for our firepower when we were well dug in and waiting for them. They much preferred to hit us between four and five in the morning so that they could get in close before being discovered. This way they could best employ their burp guns, hand grenades, and superior numbers. If we were not hit early in the morning, we could usually relax until 1630 or 1700. At this time the NKPA would start their patrols operating, searching for a soft spot. After dark they would attack, if one was coming. At any rate, this was the way we had the enemy figured. They always seemed to sleep in the middle of the day. From dark until midnight and from 0400 until light seemed to be the most critical hours.

Neither Burris nor the men on the machine gun took this piece of information with even a particle of humor. *The dumb hoods probably don't get it*, I thought. We sat there in silence, waiting for the sun to peek over the mountains or the enemy to attack, or both. Behind us we could hear the people in the schoolyard rattling around equipment and generally showing signs of life. The 155s began to sound off again, firing west, and shortly the 105s in Chingdong-ni began to fire west also, in support of the 2d Battalion. Soon the 4.2s were adding to the din. In the distance we could hear the chatter of small arms and the crack of the recoilless rifles as the firefight developed on our west flank. The 2d

Battalion was on the forward slope of the hills to the west of the valley and Chingdong-ni so we could not see the scrap, but to hear it satisfied most curiosities. We secretly enjoyed knowing that someone else was getting hit because it always meant that there were fewer chances of our being attacked simultaneously and there would be fewer North Koreans for us to cope with after the fight.

The commotion on the left continued to grow in ferocity and, as the sun appeared, four Mustangs came winging out of it in support of the 2d Battalion. The planes swooped down over the hills to the west, making a dry run. They disappeared below the hills and then came up to circle around. They disappeared again and we heard the rattle of .50s leak through the hills. In a moment the planes had made a rocket run and we heard the rockets "crack" into the target area. There were more rockets and then more strafing with the .50s and the "fly boys" went home. The artillery commenced a coordinated barrage now and the noise developed into a continuous roar. We sat smugly on our little hill and listened.

The sun crept steadily higher and the fighting roared on. Burris and I had coffee and spaghetti and meatballs (a C ration delicacy) for breakfast. The men took turns going down to the well and I also began to consider the prospect of leaving the hill for a short bath. After all, Burris could fire a mission as well as I could and the NKs weren't likely to try any tricks this late in the morning, especially after making such a large effort on the left. The firing in the 2d Battalion's sector had fallen off to sporadic machine-gun bursts now, anyway. With this rationalization, I decided definitely to leave the hill and get a bath and some clean socks and underclothes. I called Burris, who had just come back from the schoolhouse, and told him to take over for awhile. He could call me over the wire if something began to pop. I picked up my carbine and began picking my way down the steep hill.

My first stop was the well. I threw the cold muddy water over my face and filled my canteen, dropping two halazone tablets into it. I then walked around to the front of the school where the jeep was parked and rummaged through the crap in the back looking for a gas mask bag in which I had some clean socks and underclothes. I found them along with my razor and toothbrush. There was a piece of GI soap lying on the back of a mess truck, which I liberated as I proceeded back to the well. I took off my clothes and spent thirty wonderful minutes washing, shaving, brushing my teeth, and washing the socks and underclothes I took off. When I ran out of things to wash, I simply dumped water over my head with my helmet. This was sheer luxury. I would have probably continued this all day if there had not been a huge group of men waiting to get to the well. I put on my clothes and left the well reluctantly.

When I reached the jeep Burgess was there. He watched silently as I put my wet clothes over the hood to dry and then with a sly grin, he produced a No. 10 can of fruit cocktail.

After a few minutes of shooting the bull I got up and walked into the school. I found the room in which the CP was located, and moseyed in. Captain Beard greeted me warmly and beckoned me over to a chair. I sat down and we exchanged rumors. Colonel Check entered the room and came over to slap me on the back and say howdy. Captain Hickman (the S-3) arrived shortly after the colonel and sat down next to Captain Beard and me to exchange the bull. Hickman said that he expected the marines to relieve us at any minute. He said that they had definitely landed and that it was a sure bet that they would be committed right away. Beard and I both agreed with this logic. I asked about the regimental headquarters and was told that they had moved out last night. The Reds undoubtedly had known its position, so they had taken the precaution of moving just in case the enemy tried a repeat performance at the school. The location of the new regimental CP was not for publication. As it was, the battalion was quite comfortable with the school all to itself.

I had stayed in the cool schoolroom as long as I dared so I reluctantly rose and started cautioning Captain Beard to hang on to his Confederate money. He said that he would. He also told me that I could keep Burgess until we were relieved and I could get some replacements from the batteries. I thanked him and went out the back door of the school. I stopped at the well and heaved some cold water on my face and head. I put my helmet on and trudged back up the damn hill.

When I reached the top I was ringing wet from perspiration and hot as a firecracker. The sun was beating down unmercifully. The members of my little perimeter were settled in their holes trying to sleep. The men on the light .30 were busy cleaning their weapons. I flopped down just over the crest and inspected the terrain. There was no sign of movement. I looked at my watch, 1140. I went back to the worn place where we had the telephone. Burgess was sound asleep beside it. I sat down and gazed out into the bay. To my surprise, I saw two ships on the water, about ten miles out. I took out the field glasses and examined them.

They seemed to be destroyers and were coming toward the shore. I could see that they were flying a flag, but I could not make it out, although I felt certain that it must be ours. I picked up the EE8 and called battalion to give them the word. After a moment's pause, the operator told me that the colonel said the ships were South Korean gunboats that had been ordered into the bay to give us fire support. I hung up and thought of the novelty of firing ships for a change. It also entered my head that these two boats just might be the thing to swim to in case the enemy really did kick us into the water. I put the glasses to my eyes and watched the two ships approach, happy to have the diversion.

165

Burris appeared from somewhere and suggested that the sun might drive us crazy. I went along with this and asked him how long he thought it would take. He refused to make an estimate, but suggested that we put up a shelter half to protect us from the sun and dew. This idea struck me as being long overdue. With the help of some bamboo poles that were on the hill, a little assault wire, and a few rocks, we were able to have the shelter half up in a matter of minutes. Because it was pitched on the back side of the hill, there was no danger of giving away our position. Of course, the enemy probably knew where each man was dug in anyway.

We spread my blanket on the ground beneath the suspended shelter half and settled down for some relaxation. No sooner had we stretched out than Burgess came up and sat down, making his play for some of our shade. Soon Matthews joined us, squirming under for a square foot of shade. It was not long before three of the other hoods had come down to our palace for its luxury. By this time it was as hot under the shelter half as out, with all those people crammed together. I gave up and walked to the crest to look over the situation and to cool off.

I sat down next to a little kid from Dog Company who was attached to us with the heavy .30. He asked me if I noticed anything different out there. I took a quick gander and didn't. He smiled, pleased at his superior sense of observation, and asked me to look for the enemy dead that had been scattered all over the hills in front of us yesterday. I took another quick gander, and they were all gone. The hostiles had come within a hundred yards of our positions last night to get their dead. This was the kind of thing that made a man worry.

I put my glasses to my eyes and began a systematic search of everything in the valley. The Reds were there if I could only find them. The villages were still smoldering, and the stray cattle were still grazing in the paddies, but there was no human activity anywhere. I checked the ridge positions where the elephant guns had been emplaced last night, but this gave me no clues either. Where did the stinking little bastards hide? After a few more minutes of futile search I went back to our shelter half and told Burris to call battalion and tell the S-2 that the enemy came after their dead last night and pulled them all away.

"I'll be goddamn; look at that bastard with the busted leg; they are mean little bastards. Did you see him kick that son of a bitch?"

I sat up to find half the men on the hill standing around on the back side looking down into the schoolyard where the ROK marines were marching off the prisoners they had captured yesterday. Matthews said he had heard that the ROKs had come up to the CP this afternoon and demanded their prisoners. The ROKs said they had only turned the prisoners over to us for interrogation and that they now wanted them back. We had no choice but to give them to the ROKs and now they were taking them to their own CP, which was a large house with a big wall around it, on the road into Chingdong-ni.

The reason for all the spectators was the method by which the prisoners were being marched. The ROKs had the prisoners' hands tied behind them and as they stumbled along, half of them wounded, the ROKs would jab them with bayonets or swing a rifle butt into their kidneys. I watched for just a moment and then turned away. I didn't like the North Koreans, but I'd be damned if I liked to see them treated this way. I went up to the little bank that ran along the crest of the hill and sat down. Shortly, Burris joined me. We sat there and talked about everything under the sun but the war, in an effort to pass the time. It was 1500.

Things had quieted down and I was about to go back to the shelter half for some more sack time when three extremely clean and white men appeared in front of us. It was the division public relations officer with an AP reporter and photographer. The reporter asked us to tell him about the Sachon attack the day before yesterday. We did, but not too much. The photographer took some pictures and they left. As they went down the hill I thought that they were probably the cleanest men I had ever seen. "Did you see those pressed fatigues?" we exclaimed.

After the visitors had been thoroughly discussed, I went back to the shelter half and crawled under its shade. I decided that it would be a good idea to take off my boots, and as I went about this task four navy

Corsairs approached from the sea. They came in over our positions and circled Chingdong-ni. I had just taken off my left boot when: *boom*! The ground shook and the air was thick with dust. My ears had that awful ringing in them again.

In Chingdong-ni there was nothing visible but the cloud of brown dust that engulfed it. In the air the planes continued to circle. The men on the hill had all dived for their holes and it was only the most courageous who now dared to poke out their heads and have a look. As the dust began to clear it was surprising to see how much was still standing after that terrific explosion. It was evident that one of the planes had dropped a bomb, but it was the size of it that was shocking. It was speculated that it had been a 2,000-pounder. I had fully expected to see Chingdong-ni flattened when the dust cleared. To my surprise, most of the buildings were still standing, however, there was a large section in the center of town that had been completely demolished. Everything was covered with a thick coat of dust and the thatched roofs of the houses near the impact area had all been blown off. The planes flew off, evidently realizing their mistake. The people on the hill began to mill around again, uttering such remarks as "Goddamn, Jesus Christ, I'll be a sad bastard," and the like.

The tragic thing was that the town was so damn crowded. There were two batteries of artillery, artillery battalion headquarters, a platoon of 4.2 mortars, and the regimental CP in that stinking

169

little town, and that's what the navy picked to bomb. I called the battalion to see if they had any report on the damage and learned that the wire was out between the 1st Battalion and Chingdong-ni. They didn't know any more than we did, but said they'd fill us in when they got a report. We sat on the hill and watched the ambulances go into the town from the clearing station. This was the kind of thing that really hurt morale.

The phone rang and Burgess said Buckley wanted to speak to me. I picked up the phone and got a most pleasant surprise. A replacement lieutenant had arrived and was being assigned to our company. Buckley was giving him the 2d and 3d Platoons. He was on his way up the hill now.

This was something I hadn't counted on. He was our first replacement. I gave the phone back to Burgess and called Matthews who had long been holding a weight of responsibility too heavy for his rank as a tech sergeant. We sat down on the bank and waited for the new lieutenant.

His name was Bropolawski, he was about thirty-five, tall and slender, dark, with searching brown eyes. We liked him immediately. After a few minutes of getting acquainted, Matthews took him around to meet the men of his command and to acquaint him with our situation. I went over to our shelter half and took off my boots. Shortly, Matthews and Bropolawski were back. They sat down and we launched a bull session. Just four days before, our replacement had been on recruiting duty in Chattanooga, Tennessee. He had been flown directly to Tokyo by commercial airline and there given a suit of fatigues, a pair of combat boots, and a carbine. He was flown to Pusan this morning and had traveled by jeep from there. His home was Topeka, Kansas; he was married and had six children. We decided to call him "Pop" for short.

When it was time for chow Burris came forth with the same old tired box of C rations we had been working on for two days. There was no fruit now and the appeal of a can of chicken and vegetables was not too strong. Burris went about lighting the Sterno with as much gusto as ever in an effort to stimulate our appetites. Pop had a full box of C rations that he offered to pass around but we refused, knowing full well that he would need the rations for himself. We did accept some of his coffee, however.

While the food and coffee were being prepared, I pumped Pop for rumors. He said the marines were in Pusan and believed they were really going to relieve us. This was heartening news. I asked about things in the States — Harry was still steadfastly supporting the secretary of defense, Louis Johnson, the man who had "not cut an ounce of muscle." We who had begun this "police action" with two-thirds strength and now fought at one-half strength were puzzled by this, but it was "not for us to reason why." We talked on for several hours, mainly about things at home. Most of us had not been home for at least a year — some had spent three years in the

171

Far East. Pop was full of all kinds of timely information such as the skirt length currently in style, the latest hairdos, the new car characteristics, and politics. This helped the tasteless rations go down and the time flew by. Soon it was night.

Matthews explained the SOP on night watch, Pop went along with it, and they took off to check positions. Burgess had already curled around the EE8 and was sleeping soundly. I walked down to the latrine, came back, wrapped myself in my blanket, and soon fell asleep.

It was only about 2100 when Burgess shook me and said that the 90th Field Artillery wanted me on the wire. I learned that the 155s had some star shells (illuminating shells that explode about a thousand feet in the air ejecting a flare with a parachute attached; as the flare floats to earth it lights the surrounding countryside). The 90th had received them during the day and wanted to know if I wished to shoot some up the valley so that we could take a gander. I said I would be delighted. I gave them an azimuth up the center of the valley and a range. Burgess took over the phone and I went up to the crest to take a look. Soon the round passed over us and there was a muffled explosion in the air about four thousand yards up the valley. The flare ignited and began floating down on its parachute.

The valley was beautiful in this eerie light. The road was like a silver ribbon and we could see it for several miles. There was no enemy, however. The valley was as deserted as it had been during the day. I called the battery and told them how pretty the flare had been, and informed them of the absence of North Koreans. I asked if they could fire a flare every hour during the night. They said they could. I hung up and told Burgess to pass the word about the flares. The men were to be extra alert and report any movement they observed. I went back to sleep.

The following morning was bright and shining. Pop was sitting next to me putting on his cartridge belt. "Boy, you are some sack artist!" he exclaimed. "Didn't you even hear the skirmish up the ridge on the right?" I shook my head and asked what he had reference to. A Red patrol had worked in close and the boys next door had lowered the boom on them. I was happy that I had slept through it. This had been the first full night's sleep I had enjoyed since I had been on the hill, and it was wonderful. Pop said the mess truck had come in from Masan and that hot breakfast was being served in the schoolyard. Although this didn't seem out of the ordinary to him, it was headline news for the rest of us. It had been almost two weeks since the mess truck had been able to bring up hot chow. The situation must be loosening up. Pop asked Matthews to start sending the men down in any method he saw fit, just so two-thirds of the men were on the hill all the time. This was easy, and in a matter of seconds the first group started down the hill. As was SOP, I waited until all the men had gone to the mess and returned before I went down. Pop did likewise.

As we waited the men came back with tales of fried chicken. Of course, being an old soldier, I was not about to fall for this story, but just about everyone insisted that they had eaten fried chicken, and I began to wonder if I had committed some outrageous sin to get the entire outfit indignant enough to plot this mass conspiracy. When the last man returned from chow, Pop and I made our way down the hill and into the schoolyard. We located the mess truck and there I received a terrific shock. We *did* have fried chicken! It wasn't ten o'clock but it really made little difference to us if chicken was not the customary diet for breakfast. We were hungry and it was good and that was all that really mattered.

Pop and I each got a cup of coffee, a hunk of GI bread, a canteen cup of fruit, and a helmet full of chicken. I made up my mind when I first saw the chicken that I was not going to stuff myself, but after the first bite I knew that I was doomed for a stomachache that afternoon. The stuff tasted so good I knew that I would not stop when I had had enough, but only when I could hold no more.

We were sitting on the shady side of a two-and-a-half-ton truck gorging ourselves. Two or three hoods had collected about us and we were attempting to carry on a conversation and eat at the same time. Somewhere toward town we could hear moaning and occasionally a scream. I didn't pay any attention to this having been in Korea long enough to expect some misery around every corner, and being callous enough not to be interested.

Finally, Pop could not sit still any longer and he asked one of the men what in the hell that racket was. A kid sitting on the fender of the truck leaned over and replied, "Don't worry about that, sir. It's only the damn gooks getting tortured." Pop looked surprised and turned to me questioningly. Another man piped up, "Oh, it's not our people who are doing the dirty work, sir. It's those dirty little ROK marines. Jesus, they are mean little bastards." Suddenly there was a blood-curdling scream from down the road that made everyone shiver, in spite of the heat.

"What in God's name are they doing to them?" asked Pop.

"Oh, there are lots of good tortures," answered the kid on the truck, "but you should see the one they give with two EE8s. They connect a pair of telephones together with about six feet of wire. They strip all the insulation off the damn wire and wrap it around the prick and balls of one of those gooks. An ROK turns the crank on each of the two phones sending electricity all through the yellow bastard's nuts. Goddamn," the kid laughed, "you should see those bastards dance when the juice starts through 'em."

Pop looked at me unbelieving. I shook my head and told him that it was the way of the Orient and there was nothing we could do about it.

Another man sounded off. "Shit, Lieutenant, that's nothing. You should see what they are doing now. They got long bamboo slivers and they have shoved them about three feet up the ass of them prisoners. The hollering you hear now is caused when them ROKs tie them north gooks' hands behind their backs and to their ankles. It causes that bamboo to cut their guts out when it's bent thata way."

"Yep, them ROKs are mean little bastards all right," someone else was moved to say.

I was through eating now and I could see that Pop was, too, although half of his food was untouched. We washed out our canteen cups and went behind the schoolhouse to the well. We washed and brushed our teeth. Pop didn't have much to say. Neither did I for that matter.

We checked in at the battalion CP and found things quiet. There were no choice rumors floating around. Pop stopped to look at a pile of NK weapons we had captured that were in the corner of the CP. We went past the well and back up the damn hill. It was quiet everywhere. The men were asleep in their holes when we reached the crest. I took a look out front. Nothing was stirring. Pop sat down and stared into the bay. I went to the latrine.

CHAPTER
SEVEN

R&R Troops in a Pea Patch

That afternoon the marines relieved us. There was no interservice friction here. There was not a man among us who wouldn't have kissed these marines. They were entirely welcome. The morale on our hill increased tremendously when we saw the first marine trucks come nosing down the road. They swarmed all over our positions. They were big healthy kids with rosy cheeks and pressed fatigues. Their equipment was new and their weapons were sparkling clean. There was no sign of uneasiness, and everywhere there was a spirit that ran at flood tide. These men were ready to fight.

When the marine FO came up to relieve me, I was amazed. He had a sergeant and five men other than himself in his crew. Their equipment was brand new and they were loaded with it. When he saw me and my borrowed man (Burgess) he was startled, too. The thing that bothered the marines most, however, was that they had so many men and so much equipment that there was not enough room for them on the hill. When we left they were still fretting over this problem.

At the foot of the hill the rest of the battalion had already formed a convoy on the road to Masan and the men were loading into quartermaster trucks. I got into the jeep and Burgess piled in on the other side. I got it started after much coaxing. We pulled out of the schoolyard, found our place in the column behind Captain Beard's jeep, and soon were on our way. Along the Masan road there were signs of combat everywhere. The NKPA had evidently tried to hold a few roadblocks all the time we were in the schoolyard. There were shot-up trucks here and there and I saw two light tanks that had hit mines and thrown treads. There were ROK road guards every two or three hundred yards and on all commanding ground there was either a light tank or a half track. The enemy was high in the hills above the road, watching.

We rode back to Masan without incident. We proceeded through the town and turned left on the Pusan road. After traveling three or four miles, we pulled off the road into a large pea patch; this was to be our rest camp. Able Company was given an area about the size of two football fields in which to set up shop. The men were given sections of the area by platoons, and then everyone started making themselves comfortable. The mess truck was already there and set up for business. We had only been in the patch about an hour when chow was served. The rations were class B and everyone thoroughly stuffed himself. After chow Burgess suggested that he report back to Captain Beard because he was only to stay with me as long as we were on the line. I agreed and decided that I would also look up the captain.

Burgess and I had one hell of a time in the dark stumbling over the troops that had already sacked out on the ground between us and Headquarters Company. We found Captain Beard drinking coffee under the kitchen fly that had been pitched by the mess people. I flopped down, had a cup of coffee, and listened delightedly as the captain predicted that we would probably remain in this pea patch for several days. He invited me down to the headquarters area to bunk with him and I readily accepted, since I had no duties with the company now that we were off the line. I stumbled back to Able's area, told Buckley where he could find me, and picked my way to the jeep. I got my blanket and toilet articles and carried them back to Captain Beard's jeep. Without too much ado, we pitched his mosquito bar (one net large enough for both of us) and went to sleep. This was to be one night that I would sleep twelve hours, and I did.

I woke up to find the sun shining brightly on the dew. Coffee was boiling away in the mess about thirty feet away. Captain Beard was awake and washing in his helmet, which he had propped on the bumper of the jeep. I sat up and just wiggled my toes in the fresh air for a full five minutes. How nice it was to wake up in the morning and have your boots off. I reluctantly put on my socks and boots and drew a helmet full of water out of the battalion water trailer parked nearby. I washed my face and hands, shaved leisurely, and brushed my teeth. This rest camp life was something. Captain Beard and I sauntered over to the mess and sat down under the fly to a breakfast of cereal, eggs, bacon, fruit juice, biscuits, and coffee. It was sheer luxury.

After breakfast there was a command meeting. Nothing of importance was said, although it was a rather pleasant gathering. After this we simply sat down in the shade and waited for lunch. Captain Beard and I both agreed that we should write our wives, then decided that we were entirely too tired, but promised ourselves that we would write letters in the afternoon. I asked the captain what he wanted me to do about the jeep, which was in sorry shape after being shot up at Sachon, and about my total lack of personnel. He came up with a rather ingenious answer, "Go find the damn artillery battalion this afternoon and steal a jeep and Shanghai some men." He added, "It's for damn sure no one's going to volunteer to go with you." The captain was a practical man.

We had a lovely lunch, B rations again, and after a short nap I reluctantly crawled into my battered jeep and took off toward Masan in an effort to find the 8th Field Artillery. I had heard that they were somewhere in town, but I had no clue as to which part. I made the perfectly normal mistake of asking an MP, who was directing traffic, where they were.

Naturally he gave me the wrong directions and sent me on a wild goose chase all over the suburbs of the city. Masan is a long narrow city built along the bay with streets that twist and turn in a most unreasonable manner. Consequently, it is easy to get hopelessly lost. While lost, I ran across a quartermaster portable-laundry unit and shower. There was nothing for me to do but stop and take a shower. This consumed a most pleasant hour. Afterward, I received clean clothes. It was really a nice arrangement, you simply turned your old dirty clothes in to the laundry people and they would give you clean ones. Someone else would get your clothes after they had been laundered.

When I started back to my jeep to continue the search for the 8th, I noticed a truck go by with the outfit's markings on its bumper. I hopped in the jeep and followed it. After about a thirty-minute ride the truck turned into a side street and then into a walled courtyard of a factory, which turned out to be a cotton mill. There the entire battalion was comfortably bivouacked in the factory buildings. I found the CP and parked outside. There were the usual greetings that always reminded me of a college homecoming. I arrived just at supper time so before any business was accomplished we hustled off to chow.

After chow I went around to the area where A Battery was bivouacked and found the CP group comfortably set up in a maze of antiquated spinning looms. I sat down to have a good old-fashioned bore ass with Captain Hull and Lieutenant Plummer, who had been newly assigned to the battery as executive officer. I put in my request for a jeep and replacements. I was given a different jeep and two new men, Privates Minor and Kelly. The replacements reported. Both were eighteen. I told them where my old jeep was parked and instructed them to take it around to the motor sergeant and make the trade. I told them that we would pull out at about 2000 and for them to have their gear in the jeep and ready to roll by that time.

They took off and I turned back to the bore ass. Talk was running high as to when we would go on the offensive. The 7th Division in Japan was rumored to be beefed up with fillers from the States and there were choice stories of the 82d and 11th Airborne Divisions being in Japan. Captain Hull reported that he had received some replacements who swore that the stories about the 82d and 11th were true. One kid had said that the advance parties for these outfits were in Camp Drake (outside of Tokyo).

All of this was music to our ears. We were plenty tired of running and it was clear to most of us that we couldn't do any chasing until we had some reinforcements. From these rumors it looked as though the long-expected help was at hand. Everyone agreed that we would win the war in short order once we gained the initiative. We expected that we would run through the North Koreans like a dose of salts once the hard crust was broken. They could not hold up long under concentrated artillery and armor supported thrust along the main arteries back up to the 38th Parallel. We agreed that they would collapse in short order after a few decisive defeats. As to whether we would cross the 38th, no one would venture a guess. We had some coffee and Plummer and I talked about the good old days at Jinmachi. When we were there we had complained constantly, and often compared our dinky little post to one of Custer's. Now, Jinmachi, Japan, seemed like a paradise.

All too soon the soldiers who had just been assigned to me reported and I noted with disgust that it was 2000 hours. I got up and Plummer walked out to the jeep with me. He slipped me a new mosquito bar and told me to be sure and drop back in the following day. I said I would try and thanked him for the net. I asked Minor to drive and we bounced out of the factory yard and onto the dusty road. It was almost dark and I had Minor turn on the blackout lights. We made our way to the Pusan road and soon covered the few miles to the pea patch. We pulled up next to Captain Beard's jeep. He was sitting in the seat smoking. He looked around and smiled, "Guess what, Hood? We are going to a picture show." I hesitated a moment, not wanting to be too gullible and fall for a hoax, but the prospect was so inviting. "When? Where?" I asked trying to seem indifferent. "It will be across the road in about fifteen minutes. Let's go." I jumped out of the jeep and took off after Captain

Beard. I called back to Minor and Kelly and told them to secure the jeep and go to the movies.

The screen was set up on the back of a two-and-a-half-ton truck and the projector was on a three-quarter-ton. Everyone sat on their helmets on the ground. It's really a neat trick. In between reels you turn your helmet over to prevent the uncomfortable effect of a helmet-molded behind. The picture was good — a comedy with Abbott and Costello. We were just getting into the third reel when we heard a plane motor. There were two explosions to the west toward Masan. The North Koreans had bombed us? What a low blow. The picture was stopped and we were told to go back to our area. There would be no more pictures. I was furious. When morning came it was learned that the enemy had killed two pigs. There were no other casualties.

We rose around 0800. After a helmet bath we had a breakfast of Canadian bacon and eggs. This rest camp life was really *jo toe*. The quartermaster had set up a portable shower unit about a mile down the road and a schedule was made whereby each company in the regiment would be taken to the showers by truck for a good soaking. A shipment of socks and drawers arrived and things generally began to look up. We took our weapons, which were in poor repair or in need of parts, to the division ordnance outfit in Masan, and received replacement weapons along with extra parts that had been critically needed throughout the last month's fighting (particularly gas cylinders for BARs).

The unbelievable also occurred — we got a few replacements. I guess our battalion got about thirty men, all fresh from the States. Our company received nine of these new men. There was an overall feeling of well-being among the troops, and that whipped expression that had been so prominent on so many faces disappeared. There was a lot of talk about the "victory parade" in Seoul and the occupation duty in Pyongyang. The men slept twelve to fourteen hours each day and, except for those few in any outfit who always seem to get some whiskey, the camp was quiet and orderly.

Late in the afternoon there was a mail call. I received eight letters — five from my wife, two from my mother, and one from my aunt. Like any other soldier, these letters meant a lot. I read and reread them. I noted with extreme interest my wife's accounts of our son's progress and growth. He was now seven months old. I carefully put the letters in my pocket. Captain Beard had also received a bunch of letters and we both confided a feeling of guilt over not writing while we had been in the pea patch. We made a solemn vow that we would write letters all morning the following day.

That night we went to another picture show in the field across the road. This time we were not interrupted by any sneak air raids. After the show we were passing by the CP, when Captain Hickman called us in for a surprise, ice-cold Coca-Cola. We sat around the CP tent for about an hour in a congenial bore ass. Everyone was in the best of spirits. Around 2230 I decided that it was sack time and Captain Beard agreed. It was only a matter of minutes before I was peacefully snoring under my mosquito bar.

It was some time in the middle of the night when one of the men in the headquarters group began shaking me. "Wake up, sir, we're moving out." This was the news we had all expected and dreaded. I brushed aside the mosquito bar and soberly began putting on my socks and boots while the dampness ate into my bones. All over the area men began to stir and the night was filled with those noises that can be made only by fighting men and their equipment. I buckled on my combat boots and checked on Minor and Kelly. They were both awake and nervous as wet hens. I took my helmet over to the water trailer and drew the water for what might be my last shave and tooth brushing for some time. The water was uncomfortably cold and the dull razor bit unmercifully at my face. I finished shaving and felt my way through the dark to our jeep. I put on my field jacket and checked on Captain Beard. He was up and ready for chow. We walked over to the mess and settled down to enjoy this last hot breakfast. As we ate I felt an unusual fear grip me and felt like I had that first morning of combat. I wondered if it would be like this every time we went back to slaughter after a rest. The men were unusually quiet, too, and I rationalized that they probably felt as I did.

We got the order to move out at about 0400. I had Minor drive and I wrapped up in a blanket in the front seat while Kelly burrowed under equipment in the back. We pulled into column with Able and proceeded west into Masan. Speculation ran high that there had been a breakthrough at Chingdong-ni and that we were going back to that bloody schoolhouse but when we reached the road junction, we turned north instead of south. This could mean anything. We could continue on to Taegu or stop anywhere along the route. One thing we all felt sure of, there had been a breakthrough somewhere on the line and we were going to put out the fire. This was always the way. We would ride long enough for everyone to get good and cramped and then we would stop and fight like hell. After we had licked the North Koreans, some other outfit would come in and take over the quiet sector and we would be moved to another fire. Was there no justice?

I fell asleep in the midst of this mental bitching and woke up as I was nearly thrown out of the jeep when it cut hard to the left. We were going west now and the sun was peeking over the mountains in our rear. It seemed to me that we must be on the road to Haman. After another fifteen minutes I recognized enough landmarks to be sure of the road. I settled back, believing that I at least knew where we were going, when we turned off at a fork

187

to the right. The road went to the north of a schoolhouse where we had stopped for gas when the regiment first came south. I pulled out my map and tried to read it in the bouncing vehicle.

As near as I could see, the road continued in a westward direction, bearing a little to the north. It crossed the Naktong River about ten miles west of our present location. As we continued on I saw a platoon of half-tracks parked around what looked like a CP. Later we passed a company of engineers. Wire was tangled thickly in the ditches and the tracks on the road and stream beds all added up to the fact that the actual fighting was not far off. Soon the infantry dismounted and the quartermaster trucks sped past us on their way back to Masan.

I pulled up to Buckley's jeep to see if he had any clues. He had none, but suggested I stick close by. The troops disappeared in the ditches along the road and we waited for orders. After a few minutes I got a call on my radio to proceed to the front of the column for a command-group parley. Buckley got his message at about the same time and he jumped in my jeep as we pulled out. It was only a few hundred yards to the head of the troops and we pulled up to find Colonels Check and Michaelis along with the 1st Battalion's staff, Captain Beard, and the other company commanders. In a nutshell we got the story.

The enemy had shifted its forces north along the Naktong after the bloody nose we had given them in the south. They were trying to slide around the right flank of the 24th Division where they were separated by about twenty miles from the 1st Cavalry. The 35th Regiment had been trying to hold this sector, but the North Koreans were outnumbering them a hundred to one. We were to get tank support and advance up the road and across the Naktong, if the bridge was still up, as it was last reported to be. Captain Beard gave me a map of the area we were to operate in and dropped a warning about not sticking my neck out this trip. Fortunately, Baker was leading the reconnaissance in force this time, Able was following at an interval of a hundred yards, and Charlie was to follow us. While this info was being passed out, eight Pershing tanks ground up the road and stopped just past us, waiting for their passengers.

The command group split up and Buckley and I went back to Able. The jeeps were to go along on the attack so I had little to worry about. Minor turned the jeep around and I noticed that Kelly was not saying too much, but I didn't attach any importance to it. He was probably just a quiet kid. I felt steady myself, having recovered completely from the early morning shakes. I guessed that it was the cold and dampness that had earlier caused the nervousness on my part. I crawled back in the jeep and made some stupid remark about there being open season on Reds today. This remark was designed to create confidence and to get a rise out of Kelly, but to no avail.

Soon the column moved out with the troops in a column of ducks, the tanks with Baker aboard leading the way. We proceeded up the road, crossed the Naktong, and engaged the enemy in strength about a mile the other side of the river. We had a hot little firefight that proved indecisive after several hours. We broke off the engagement, withdrew across the river, and dug in on the high ground on the east bank for the night. What followed was five days of extremely heavy patrolling at night and artillery duels throughout the days. The bridge was charged but never blown.

As I look back upon these days the outstanding incident was Kelly's "crack-up." The war had gotten into his guts and he could not get it out. He took three black nights on the OP with me and then all self-control left him. At dusk of the fourth night he slipped into a soft, high-pitched sobbing that gathered force as the thick black night engulfed our nest, which sat damply on the top of a bare-assed cliff.

At first I chose to ignore his condition thinking that he might conquer his fear, but as it grew dark I could see that he was losing ground. There was not another foxhole for a hundred yards (thousand-yard company front) and I was afraid that if I tried to send him to the rear he would be shot by friendly troops (it was SOP that we were to stay in our foxholes at all times during the night hours; if anything moved, it was shot). My efforts to comfort him were a total flop and as he grew more frantic my chief concern was keeping him in the hole with me. He pleaded to be allowed to go to the rear and failed to comprehend when I attempted to explain the impossibility of such a move at night. His sobbing gave way to wailing by 2200 and I was afraid he was going to bolt on me. I put my arm around his shoulder and got a firm grip on his suspenders. He leaned against me and rocked gently back and forth with each long high-pitched wail. He whispered "Mother" over and over again, his teeth chattered violently. His body began to shiver and perspiration broke out all over him. He called for his mother repeatedly and choked frequently over his emotion. I urged him to drink some water and pleaded with him to try to sleep, but he ignored me completely as if he were on the hill all alone.

Out in front all was quiet. The slow muddy river moved silently out to sea and the armies that were poised on its banks were deathly still. This was misleading, however, for patrols were probably wading in the river at several different places at this minute, and all night there would be North Koreans with burp guns and grenades sneaking around our positions dealing death to those who exposed themselves and meeting death themselves if they were seen first. On the other side of that dirty stream our patrols were working, seeking information, taking prisoners, killing, and being killed. Yet — all was quiet except for the sobbing of the man next to me. A man? A boy. A normal healthy boy. The kind who at this minute were tinkering with

Model As back in the States. Boys like this one were having dates, drinking Cokes, working on farms, playing golf, working at soda fountains, stealing watermelons, going to summer school, cutting grass — at home. Why was this boy over here? Why was I here? Were we engaged in a worthwhile enterprise? Was this a worthy cause for which we fought?

A machine gun chattered downstream and then it was quiet. Kelly looked into my face searchingly. "They are coming over tonight. They will get us for sure tonight, Lieutenant. Let's bug, Lieutenant! We will die! How can you sit there?" he screamed.

"I am going to leave," he whispered after a moment of heavy breathing. "I don't care if I get court-martialed, I'm going to leave. I ain't gonna sit here and get killed!"

At this he jerked away from me and jumped out of the hole. I lunged for him and caught the leg of his fatigues. He struggled frantically and screamed for me to let go. After a moment of struggling, I managed to pull him back into the hole. He fought frantically for a brief minute and then threw himself across my lap and cried pitifully. I put my arms across his shoulders where I could prevent another attempt at flight and tried to comfort him. He relaxed somewhat and simply lay across my lap sobbing gently, completely whipped.

It twisted my heart out to see what this dirty war had done to him. We spent the long dark night this way, the boy lying across my lap sobbing. The circulation left my legs from his weight and they

192

went to sleep. I sat there in the muddy hole staring into the darkness, listening for a rolling stone, a rifle bolt, a whisper, or some other clue that would warn me of the presence of an enemy patrol. I listened, searched, nodded, listened, waited, shivered, waited, listened — the black turned to gray — there were a few rifle rounds fired somewhere in the haze up the river, the gray diappeared, and the sun rose red and warm out of the mist in the rear. The night had passed.

The boy sat up and looked into my face with red eyes, round and pleading, his skin was gray. "It's day now, sir. Can I go?" I nodded my head. He pulled himself out of the hole and stumbled over the crest and back to the rear.

I picked up the phone and turned the crank vigorously. I listened but there was no answer. I turned the crank again, thinking that perhaps the men at the CP were asleep, but after several attempts it was obvious that there would be no answer. My wire had been cut during the night. If Kelly were here he could have run the wire back and found the break, but he was not here. I had to do it. If I checked it, who would man the position? Damn it, I should have never let Kelly go, no matter how wide he had cracked. I had planned on calling the CP to tell them that he was coming back and for them to send up Minor, but now without communication I was lost. There was no telling what Kelly would say, if anything, and with Minor being new, he probably would not know that he was

193

to come up on the OP with me. I fretted and worried for half an hour, then decided to check the wire myself and continue on to the CP after I had spliced the break. I got out of the hole, stretched, then walked the hundred yards it was to another position. I found two riflemen to the left and below. I told one of them to man my hole while I ran my wire back. I told him that I would call him from the CP after I had spliced the wire.

I trudged off after the wire. I had to follow it only about three hundred yards to the place where it had been cut. There were tennis-shoe prints in the wet sandy soil where the North Korean patrol had passed. I sat down, stripped the insulation off the two ends, and spliced the wire. After wrapping friction tape around the splice, I wandered down the back side of the hill to the village where Able had set up its CP. I found Buckley and the CP group holed up in a shed. I walked in and asked if everyone was happy. All replied in the affirmative and asked if I was in the pink. I answered that I was simply "tickled pink with the world."

After this bit of foolishness, I sat down and accepted a cup of coffee someone offered me and asked for Minor, who I had instructed to stay close by. No one knew his whereabouts, but all agreed that he had not gone far. I called over to the switchboard operator and asked him to ring my wire. He did, and called to me that the wire was in.

Buckley gave me a look and walked out in the yard. I got up and followed him.

"Don't bother with going back to the OP," he advised me in a whisper. "I have it on excellent authority that we are going to pull out of here this morning."

I looked at him unbelieving.

"It's true Add, I just talked with Hickman down at the battalion and he said that we will move before noon."

This really was music to my ears. I started screaming for Minor at the top of my lungs and he came out of a house half asleep, blinking. "Go up to the OP and stay there until I come up or call you," I ordered and turned back to Buckley.

"Let's go take a bath. I'm the dirtiest man in the army."

Buck agreed with me and we strode off to the center of the village where a well was located. After a cold bath and a shave I felt like a new man and I am certain that I smelled like one. When we returned to the CP a man had arrived from the battalion with C rations. Buckley sent a case to each of the platoons and we dove into the case that was left for the CP group with much gusto. After chow I lay down on the porch of one of the houses and immediately fell asleep. The next three hours were spent in sound slumber.

At 1310 one of the new replacements we had received at the pea patch shook me gently and said that we were moving out. I sat up reluctantly and blinked at the bright sun. I adjusted my cartridge belt and walked back to the CP, which was now alive with activity. The men were getting their gear ready to move and the company's jeeps had backed up into the courtyard for loading. The switchboard had been taken down and the wires from the platoons and the OP were all stuck in one EE8.

I cranked the phone and called for Minor. He answered along with everyone else on the wire. I gave him the word and told him to pull out with all equipment on the OP (the EE8 and my map board). I hung up and walked back to the well to throw some more of that wonderful cold water over my head and face. I was soon joined by several GIs, eager to get at least the top layer of dirt off before the move. The question on everyone's lips was, "Where are we going?" I couldn't guess, but I thoroughly enjoyed listening to the guesses of the others. They ran all the way from an advance to Pyongyang to a withdrawal to Japan. One thing was certain, wherever we went there would probably be excitement and casualties. The Wolfhounds seemed to always draw the bulk of the action. This last conclusion, everyone agreed with. We just couldn't be left alone on a quiet sector.

I picked up my helmet and strolled back to the company CP. It was 1400 now and the platoons were beginning to drop in from the hills. Minor had just arrived. I told him to go to the jeep and wait for me. Back in the CP the line from battalion was ringing. A young soldier called Buckley to the phone and after a brief conversation Buckley hung up and told the first sergeant to get the company on the road. He came over to me and said that we were moving east to a road junction where trucks were to pick up the regiment. I asked if he had any idea as to what our final destination might be and he asked me if I knew when the war was going to end. After this exchange of silly questions, Buck said something about the 35th Regiment (or the "Triple Nickel" as we later came to call it) coming into this sector. I told Buck that I would meet him at the crossroads and took off.

I found Minor sitting in the jeep at the side of the road. Beside him was Kelly. He was still as dirty as he had been when he left me on the hill early in the morning. His eyes still had that frightened look in them and he stared blankly straight ahead. I asked him how he felt and he whispered stiffly, "All right, sir." Minor asked, "What the hell is wrong with him?"

"He's all right," I assured Minor. "He just doesn't feel well."

Kelly got over into the back seat to make room for me. I sat down next to Minor and announced that we were going east. I instructed Minor to pull up to some poplar trees where there was some shade and told him that we would wait there until the battalion was ready to move. The 35th was all over the area now. Trucks were running back and forth on the road and rifle companies could be seen toiling up the hills that overlooked the road, bridge, and river. The 35th seemed well equipped and at far greater strength than ourselves. We sat there and watched them go into position quietly, happy that we were not staying and frightened as to where we might be going.

After an hour, the battalion was all on the road and the column moved out. I fell in behind the supply jeep of Able and we crept along in pace with the doughfeet. It was 1700 when we reached the crossroads. We had a chow break there. The trucks were about an hour late arriving so the men got a pretty good break. Most of them slept. When the trucks pulled up the men were piled in in short order and we got under way. We traveled east for about an hour and arrived at the main north-south road from Taegu to Masan. To everyone's relief, we turned right (south) and proceeded on to Masan. There we turned east again and moved on to our pea patch. This was unbelievable. We were going to get another rest! I slept soundly and comfortably that night in the same hole I had had the time before.

The following morning I awoke to find that Captain Beard had joined me. He was sacking away when I heard someone call "Chow." I jumped out of the sack, woke the captain, and scurried over to the headquarters' mess, simply famished. Captain Beard joined me shortly. This was indeed the way to fight a war.

During the day we had baths, ate fresh peaches, slept, wrote letters, and took more baths. I also took Kelly into the battalion headquarters (8th Field Artillery) and requested that he be transferred into

Service Battery. This was done to his great relief and I received in return a man from the division headquarters who had requested action with a line outfit. He was of middle height and heavy set. He had his hair shaved completely off and he wore glasses. His voice was warm and cultured, and his English was perfect. I liked him immediately, but I was a little leery of his sticking qualities. I don't remember his name.

I took the new man and his gear back to the pea patch after stopping by at the cotton mill where the firing batteries were bivouacked. I found Hood Plummer and we had a wonderful thirty minutes talking. Seeing Plummer was my chief recreation and he never failed to cheer me. Reluctantly, the new man and I shoved off about 1700 and reached the pea patch in time for hot chow. Captain Beard, Hickman, two new lieutenants, and I engaged in a lengthy bore ass after chow. It was quite a leisurely evening. I went to bed about 2100.

It was 0430 when someone shook me. "Wake up, sir, we are moving out!"

CHAPTER
EIGHT

Taegu, ROKs, Mortars

As all the mornings had been the last few days, this one was damp and gray. The moisture hung to everything and the dampness penetrated to the very bone. I rolled up the mosquito bar and blanket and threw them into the jeep. Minor and the new man were still sacking away and I kicked at their mosquito bar causing it to fall on them. They awoke with a start and I gave them the word. They were up in short order making ready to move. I drew a helmet of water from the water trailer and shaved and washed. I brushed my teeth, put on clean socks and drawers, and felt pretty near human. I was thankful that I had had the foresight to wash my spare clothes yesterday. Now I was at least starting out with a clean set of drawers.

I walked through the wet grass to the mess fly and found most of the other officers sitting around on boxes drinking coffee and eating fruit. I picked up a cup from the officers' mess kit and was served a cup of the black liquid that we showed the courtesy of calling coffee. I took my canteen cup over to some open cans of fruit and helped myself. I found a crate to sit on near Captain Beard. I asked him for some hot rumors and as was SOP he told me we were going to China. I thanked him for the information. I had just finished my second cup of coffee when the order to move out was given. We walked back to our vehicles and waited for the column to get rolling. I found Minor and the new man nursing half-finished canteen cups of coffee and cussing because this damn army couldn't ever move in the daylight. I looked at my watch; it was 0515. A hell of an hour to be going anywhere.

I crawled into the jeep beside Minor. "We are to go with Able as usual and they will be the last company out of the patch," I told Minor. He said that was okay with him and went on about his coffee drinking. He asked me if we were to draw any C rations for the trip. I said that we had not been told about it if we were. He smiled and motioned to the floor in the back of the jeep. The new man triumphantly raised a blanket and there were two whole boxes of C rations. I smiled approvingly and thanked them for their thoughtfulness. Minor realized the important things in this dirty war.

The column moved by and we pulled in behind Able. To everyone's surprise we hit the road and turned east toward Pusan. This was really a tricky maneuver. No one could guess why in the hell we would be going back to Pusan. I decided not to worry about it and settled back to try to relax. I felt as though I might have a case of the GIs coming on, and as we rode on I became certain of it. I managed to control myself until the first break about 0645, and then I began a long yellow trail that could be followed all the way to Pusan and from there to Taegu, our destination. We arrived at an apple orchard east of Taegu at about 1800 and we bivouacked there, adjacent to two regiments of the newly arrived 2d Division. We were told to make ourselves comfortable, that we might be there for some time. This didn't fool anybody. I was called to the CP by Captain Beard and told that I should be prepared to go on a reconnaissance at any time and to sleep near the CP. I had planned on that anyway due to the headquarters mess. I went by the aid station, which was also close, and got some medicine for my diarrhea.

I returned to the jeep to find that Minor and the other man had already set up a shelter half and had located a well at a house a short distance down the road. I got out my toilet articles and proceeded down the road after them. After a bath and a tooth brushing we all felt much better. When we reached the jeep again, they started calling mess at the kitchen truck. Captain Beard called for me to hurry and accompany him. Minor and the other men took off on the double. We ate and then slept. It had been a long hard day and we were all thankful for this night of rest before being committed.

At dawn I awoke to find things rather quiet in the area. This surprised me for I had fully expected someone to have awakened me in the night and informed me that we were moving out. I got up without waking the other two and went down to the well to wash. When I returned, the mess truck was collecting a group of hungry men, so I sauntered over to find that breakfast was ready. A few other officers showed up but there was not enough activity to indicate that we were moving that day. After breakfast I returned to the jeep and began writing a letter to my wife. Minor and the new fellow had gone to chow. I could see that the colonel was up and Captain Beard was also stirring. By 0715 everything was functioning smoothly, and I began to wonder just what the hell was up. I finished the letter and walked over to the CP tent to give it to the clerk for mailing. A sergeant told me that the colonel wanted to see me. I gave the letter to the clerk and walked around to the side of the tent where the colonel and his staff had congregated. He said good morning as I approached and asked me to sit down. It was here that the story came out.

The NKPA had got a bloody nose from the offensive to the south. They had tried to outflank us and they had failed. Now, G-2 reports indicated that the enemy was building up for another major effort to run us into the sea — this time down the north-south roads, through Taegu, and on to Pusan. That was why we were in the north of the perimeter again. We were to help stop them. I listened quietly, telling myself that I might have guessed that we would be out of the frying pan and into the fire. Damn if they would leave us on a quiet front. The colonel instructed us to be prepared to make a reconnaissance with him within an hour. That was it in a nutshell.

About 1030 we set out. There were three jeeps with the colonel in the lead. After a thirty-minute ride we entered Taegu. We got directions from an MP and proceeded to Eighth Army Headquarters. We waited in the courtyard while the colonel went inside. The Eighth Army was in a Korean university. The buildings were frame and painted gray, the only painted buildings I ever saw in Korea. There was a tall fence around the area and it was heavily guarded by MPs. From the roof of the center building there were tall aerials and from a small building to the rear we could hear the loud steady throb of electric generators.

After thirty minutes the colonel reappeared with a major. He came over to the jeeps and announced that we were to stay for chow. We jumped out of the vehicles and followed the colonel and his friend to what appeared to be the rear of the campus. There, in a rectangular building, was the officers' mess. We entered through the screened doors into a clean mess hall complete with tables, chairs, and canned music. It was luxurious. We were served an excellent meal with all the iced tea we could drink. Just as I was preparing to leave, Major Williams, the executive officer of my old outfit in the 7th Division, came into the room. I rushed over to greet him. He was glad to see me and insisted that I come up to his quarters for a drink. I was forced to decline but took a rain check, seriously. Major Williams was in Eighth Army artillery under General Ferral. He was in a position to know what the big picture really was, but he declined to comment, even after the most persistent begging. All too soon the colonel was ready to move out. We walked back to the jeeps and pulled out of the courtyard, the colonel equipped with a bunch of new maps and with a guide.

We proceeded out of the city to the north on the main highway to Sangju and Andong. We crossed several large bridges over almost dry rivers. In the river beds were more tanks than I even dreamed were in the Far East. This sight of armor began to send thoughts of an offensive running through my hot head. What if we were brought up north to make a breakout? Was it possible that even the colonel was not told? The answer to this question was, of course, no, but I did not stop to rationalize.

The road we traversed was a good wide dirt road and it wound north up a valley as all Korean roads do. Here, near Taegu, the valley was quite broad, but as we proceeded north it narrowed just as all the valleys in this stinking country did. When we were only ten miles out of town we passed an ROK artillery battery beside the road on the left. It was firing furiously up the valley. We went through the small town and then through some fields of cotton and peppers. We entered a village just north of a creek and turned into a schoolyard. Everywhere were ROKs. This was an ROK division headquarters and we had come up to effect a liaison. It turned out that the commanding officer was not in. We were asked to wait.

I sat down on the steps of the school and watched the activity of the South Korean soldiers. There were at least two hundred recruits dressed in white civilian clothes in the yard armed with bamboo spears. They were divided into platoon-sized units, and what I presumed to be noncoms were giving them close order drill. This was their basic training and they were receiving it between their own artillery and the line.

Two new GMC two-and-a-half-ton trucks pulled into the yard with much crunching of gears and dust. They were immediately surrounded by screaming ROKs. A few men who seemed to be loaded with authority rushed out of the school and out to the trucks. They clubbed a few unfortunates who got in their way, with the butts of their carbines, and climbed up on the trucks to shout orders to the noisy mob. In short order the men were organized into squads and those who had climbed on the trucks passed out two cases of the truck's cargo to each of the squad leaders. The cases were quickly opened and the contents passed out to the waiting men. We watched as they savagely tore open the boxes and greedily grabbed for their contents. It was food of some kind. The men squatted in the dust and commenced stuffing their faces. Soon the entire yard was still except for the smacking and slurping of the several hundred men eating.

My curiosity was aroused by this display. I could not imagine what in the world these men could be eating with such gusto. I strolled over to the trucks where there were hundreds of wrappers from boxes of American products. The ROKs were having a feast of graham crackers and grits. They were sitting contentedly on their haunches eating uncooked, dry grits with enjoyment. I was amazed.

I returned to the steps and told the others what the ROK menu had been, and settled down to wait for the Korean commander to show up. It was not a long wait. A 1932, four-door, convertible Ford buzzed into the yard. In the back seat, riding like a king, was the T-shirted division commander wearing a hat that must have had ten pounds of gold braid adorning it. He stepped out of the car, swagger stick and all, after the door had been opened by a sentinel at the school door. He was ushered into the school by about ten lackeys who had rushed out to meet him.

The colonel, who was already inside the school with an interpreter, reappeared after about fifteen minutes with the Korean general. He gave us the order to mount up and hopped into his jeep. We followed him out of the schoolyard and north on the road. After about a mile our column pulled to a stop at the side of the road. We dismounted and went up to the colonel's jeep. There, we got the story.

He identified our position on the map and pointed out the ROK positions, which were only a few hundred yards to our front, running east and west. We were to bring up the regiment at dark and set up behind the ROKs in a reinforcing position. The 2d Battalion was to be on the right side of the road and we (the 1st Battalion) were to be on the high ground to the left (west). The colonel pointed out approximately where each company would go and located the site of his CP. We were to return to a riverbed about six miles down the road and wait for the outfit to come up from the bivouac area.

We got back to the riverbed at about 1630 and after a short wait the battalion arrived in QM trucks. The troops were told to stay put, and in a few minutes we were moving back up the road leading both battalions. Able and Baker Batteries of the 8th Field Artillery were left in the riverbed, in anticipation of another move before going into position. The trucks turned around at the school we had visited earlier and the troops dismounted and formed a column of ducks. Buckley went ahead of the company to the area pointed out as his sector by Colonel Check. I drove my jeep to the place where the troops would leave the road. When they arrived I gave Able its directions. I remained there for some time not knowing just what to do. Buckley had said nothing about wanting me to set up an OP, anticipating another move, and I knew that I could do no firing with the ROKs to my front.

I made a decision to take my party back to Able Battery for one more hot meal. It was only a short trip and this might be the last time we would get a hot meal for some time. I also considered the stream of water that trickled down the center of the otherwise dry riverbed and when I considered this in relationship to the thick coat of dust that we had collected on the roads in the course of the day, my mind was made up. I told Minor to turn around and go back to the battery position. I called to Sergeant O'Leary, the supply sergeant of Able, who was sitting nearby with the company's three jeeps, and told him that I would be back in an hour and to inform Buckley. Then we were off, Minor giving the jeep its head and the new man and I enjoying the cool breeze that the speed made. After we had covered a mile or so we got tied up in ROK traffic. There were vehicles of all sizes and descriptions going both ways, with Korean drivers yapping back and forth at each other like Chicago taxi drivers.

Our progress was slowed to a walk, and as night dropped down around us I began to wonder if I had done the right thing. I had fully intended to be back with the company by dark and here we were creeping along at 1920 hours with the battery still a couple of miles ahead of us. Suddenly a familiar "whoosh" passed over us, followed by an explosion, and then many more explosions. We were in the center of an enemy mortar barrage. The jeep shot ahead as an opening appeared in the traffic. I looked at Minor. He was white as a sheet and bent over the steering wheel as if he were Barney Oldfield (a famous race car driver). I thought at first we should stop and take to the ditch as most of the others had done, but then I thought that maybe we could outrun the barrage. This was poor rationalization.

I sat back and put my feet up on the hood of the speeding vehicle and screamed over the roar of the bursting shells for them not to get their asses in an uproar, just as a round hit in front of our left front wheel. Minor gave the wheel a jerk to the right and the next thing I knew the jeep was on its side, propped up against one of the poplar trees that lined the road. I felt an excruciating pain in my left leg. I opened my eyes to find that I was pinned halfway in and halfway out of the jeep by the tree that had my leg in a vice-like grip.

Minor and the new man were in the ditch, apparently all right, and the mortar rounds were still coming in thick and heavy. I lay there and prayed frantically for the mortars to stop. Soon my prayers were answered. Minor and the new man came out of the ditch and began pushing on the jeep in an effort to free me. They managed only to shake the jeep slightly, which made my leg hurt all the more. I was sure that my leg was broken and I could feel the shock take hold of me. Soon two or three ROKs came up and the combined efforts of the group righted the jeep. The jar nearly jerked my leg off, or at least it felt as though it had. They sat me on the ground on the shoulder of the road and Minor took off my left boot. An MP appeared out of the dark, asked me some simple questions, and announced officially that my leg was broken. He disappeared and soon returned with two men carrying a litter on which they placed me and in a wink I was on an aid jeep. I took off my .45, field glasses, cartridge belt, and so forth, handed them to Minor, and told him to give them to Plummer. Then I was on my way to Taegu and a clearing station, the 15th MASH, I believe.

I was carried into a large building that must have been an auditorium and put on the floor under several bright lights. The room was full of wounded men and smelled of blood and antiseptics. A doctor came over and read the tag the medic had put on me when he had picked me up. Someone else ripped open my pant leg and I was given a pill. Another doctor arrived and looked at my leg, then twisted it a little. I winced. He twisted it again and asked me if it hurt. I replied that it did most emphatically. The doctors talked and wrote something else on the tag. They called to two litter-bearers and told them to take me out. As I was being picked up I asked the doctor if my leg was broken. He shook his head. I had been so certain that it was broken and that it meant the end of the war for me. I was embarrassed at my own disappointment and I hoped that no one had noticed it.

211

I was carried out of the building and into a large wall tent in the yard. There was a lantern in one end that provided a dim light. A medic directed the litter-bearers to place me in a vacant place near the door. He took the tag off my chest and carried it over to the lantern to read it. After a moment he returned with a pan of water and washed my leg. Then he covered the injured area with methiolate and, after putting on a dressing, wrapped my leg from the knee down with an Ace bandage. A Korean came in and put a blanket over me and that was all I remember.

I opened my eyes to find the sun shining brightly through the doorway of the tent. I looked around and after a few minutes of rubbing I called to a young Korean who appeared to be an orderly and asked him for a "duck" (urinal) and a pan of water to wash in. He understood and was back in a few minutes with what I had asked for. I sat up on the litter and took off my fatigue jacket. While I was washing, the boy picked up my filthy jacket and said "washie-washie"?

I went along with this readily and when he left with the pan of water he also took my fatigue jacket and pants. This left me with one pair of dirty drawers and a right boot and sock as my sole uniform. I sat there on the litter, among twenty to thirty other men, and looked at my bandaged leg and felt pretty sorry for myself. Here I had hurt my leg something awful and yet it wasn't broken. This was just my luck. I imagined the next few weeks as pure torment in this damn tent. A medic came by and asked me if I could walk. I told him that I didn't think so, but I got up to make an effort anyway. The pain was acute, but I found to my surprise that the leg would hold my weight even though it hurt. The medic wrote something on a clipboard and left. I sat down on the litter again and began to wonder if I was going to get any breakfast. Then the young Korean bounced in with a quart can of grapefruit juice. He gave it to me and said, "Chop-chop."

I replied *domo* (Japanese for thank-you) and put the can to my lips. The juice was cool, just the thing I needed. I felt its effect almost immediately. I drank the whole quart of juice, then dropped back on the litter and fell asleep.

When I awoke there was a sergeant standing in the middle of the aisle in the tent calling out names. As a man's name was called he would get up and walk out of the tent carrying all of his belongings with him. As I listened I glanced at my watch and saw that it was 1100. Then my name was called. I gave a start and asked what it was for. The sergeant gave me a dirty look and growled, "Get up and get on that goddamn truck, soldier. You can ask questions later." For a moment I thought that I would bicker with the sergeant and tell him that I was an officer, but I decided against that. I put my right boot on, it being the only item I owned other than the drawers I had on at the time, and limped painfully out of the tent. Nearby was the aforementioned truck.

I walked over to its shady side and thought that I would rest before hopping on. This was a mistake. The "mean sergeant" came out of the tent and yelled to the driver that he had all of them now. Then he looked at me. "Get the hell on the truck," he screamed. I made several unsuccessful efforts, and then the sergeant came to my assistance with a boost that sent me sprawling on the red-hot steel bed of the truck. The tailgate was slammed shut and we were rolling.

The GI riding on the seat on the left looked at me in sympathy and said, "That son-of-a-bitching sergeant is almost as mean as the goddamn officers." I nodded in agreement and accepted his arm as he helped me up on the seat, which ran the length of the truck bed.

I sat there in silence as we bumped along the dusty streets of Taegu, mentally kicking myself for not telling the sergeant that I was a lieutenant when he first sounded off in the tent. This was certainly no way to treat a wounded man. I made up my mind then and there that a sergeant in the medics was nearly as bad as a rear-echelon MP.

After a fifteen-minute trip we pulled up to a gate in a brick wall. ROK policemen opened the gate and we rode in. We stopped before some old Quonset huts and were told to dismount. The tailgate was let down and we climbed out, the same GI helping me down. A sergeant told us to sit down and take it easy. This would have been all right with me if I had had some pants on like the others, but attired only in loose-fitting drawers I did not relish the idea of sitting in the dust and rocks. On the other hand, it hurt me to stand.

In due course a major appeared and addressed the group. It was here that I got the shocker. His opening statement was, "Welcome to the 15th Replacement Company." Hospital, Hell! I was headed back to the line. He gave a fifteen- to twenty-minute speech that I didn't listen to and as he finished asked if there were any officers in the crowd. I raised my hand. He did a double-take, not believing his own eyes. The other men looked at me, too, and the GI who had sympathized with me had a picture of complete horror on his face. I guess that I was a bit untidy looking. The major finally said, "Come with me" and disappeared into one of the Quonset huts. I followed him as fast as I could on my bad leg.

When I reached the door I heard the major telling someone about the dirtiest, ugliest, most bedraggled, naked officer he had ever seen in the army. As I entered he turned to a lieutenant and said, "Help this man get clean and give him the best clothes we have."

The lieutenant looked at me and grinned and I grinned back. I liked him.

The lieutenant asked me if I would like a shower, I said yes, and the next thing I knew I was sitting in a wheelbarrow and a Korean was pushing me over to the extreme end of the walled yard. The lieutenant was walking alongside talking merrily and carrying a completely new set of clothes. There was a QM shower set up and the young Korean boy pushed me right up under a sprinkler. The lieutenant climbed up on the machinery that made the thing work and soon I had clear cold water falling all over me. It was now that I noticed that I had failed to take off my boot and drawers. This I now did with much laughing from the lieutenant and the young Korean. I was handed a bar of Life Buoy soap and I scoured myself completely. After the shower I put on the new clothes, including boots. The expression, "clothes make the man" flashed through my mind and I thought, *how true*.

I was taken back to a Quonset hut and assigned a cot, complete with a mosquito bar. The young Korean then asked me, "Chop-chop"? I nodded and he was off. I sat down on the cot and the other men present introduced themselves. There was a lieutenant colonel, a captain, and two lieutenants quartered in that portion of the hut with me. I can't remember anyone's name with the exception of Lt. Charles Sever, who was from my home town, Macon, Georgia. Immediately we were engaged in a bore ass. The young Korean brought in a plate of chow and a cup of iced tea. I thanked him and turned to the task of stuffing my face and talking.

I spent the afternoon talking and writing letters to my wife and mother. I found out through the conversation that I would be allowed to rest here for several days before going back to the outfit. This made my leg feel better and by suppertime I was surprised at the way I got around on it. Although it had turned a deep blue and was swollen to about double its original size, it was evidently all right. I had gotten over the first disappointment of not having a broken leg and I was now reconciled to going back to the outfit in a couple of days, but the initial shock this morning had been sharp. We had a good evening meal and I went to bed at about 2000 hours.

It was raining when I opened my eyes the following morning. I lay there, comfortable in the mosquito bar, and listened to the rain on the tin roof. It was pleasant, I thought, to lie on a comfortable cot, nice and dry, and listen to the rain. After several minutes of this, I noticed that the others in the room were stirring and that someone outside was yelling, "Chow."

I sat up, threw back the mosquito bar, and commenced dressing. The bandage, which had gotten wet in the shower and lost a lot of its adhesive qualities, had come halfway off during the night. I decided to rip it the rest of the way off. This I did and I was shocked to see how small the actual break in the skin was. The entire leg from the hip to the knee was a deep blue, however. I put on the rest of my clothes and hobbled out with the other officers to the mess. The rain had nearly stopped.

The food was good and the other men were cheerful company. I felt like a new man after the

217

night's sleep on a cot and the swelling in my leg and ankle had gone down a little. After breakfast, I wrote another letter to my wife and read some back issues of *Stars and Stripes* that were left in the hut. Sever had a copy of the *Reader's Digest* that he had read and he gave it to me. I read it from cover to cover. Late in the afternoon we all had showers. After supper cold beer was passed around. This repel center was really plush. I felt better every minute. That night I fell off to a sound sleep with that comfortable stuffed feeling in my stomach.

The following morning the blow fell. I was on the roster to return to the line. Because I was in the 1st Cavalry's sector, there was no transportation back to the outfit. The trucks that came to pick up the others who were returning were going to one of the cavalry regiments. I guess that I was the only body in the place from the 27th. The reason for this was that we had come up to reinforce the 1st Cav and the ROKs. There were no other elements of the 25th Division in the sector. I told my story to the lieutenant who had helped me when I first arrived and he assured me that transportation was at hand. I was surprised when I heard him use my pet expression, "Don't get your ass in an uproar." I took his advice and went back to the hut. I slept a little bit and read some in an old *Saturday Evening Post* that had found its way into the hut. After the noon meal the lieutenant asked if I was ready to shove off. I said that I was and followed him around to the supply room. He asked if I needed any more equipment and before I could answer gave me some more socks and drawers. I inquired about a weapon (I had left mine with Minor) and he gave me an M1 with a bandolier of ammo. Could I think of anything else? I asked for a paperback book from the Quonset hut and selected a worn copy of Hemingway's *Across the River and into the Trees*.

We got into a jeep and were off. He said that he had spotted a service battery of the 8th Field Artillery in town and that he would take me there. They could get me up to the front. We buzzed through the streets of Taegu dodging civilians and traffic as if playing a game. When I looked over at the lieutenant's face I could see that he was playing a game. There was a silly childish grin on his face as he steered us in and out of the traffic at a speed that was downright dangerous. After some twenty minutes of this we pulled into a large courtyard on the outskirts of town. There was a sign at the entrance that said SERVICE BATTERY 8TH FIELD ARTILLERY. I slipped out of the jeep and thanked the lieutenant for the ride. He grinned, waved, and was off with a screech of gears and a cloud of dust.

I looked around to find that the Service Battery was located in what formerly must have been a large bus garage. There were sheds with paved floors in the area and in the center of the yard was a building that had evidently been the office. As I limped over to it I was greeted by Haeger who came out of the door to meet me. His first words were, "What the hell you doing with that crummy gold bar on your collar? You made first two weeks ago and the orders just caught up with us yesterday." I grinned and noticed the silver bar on his collar. He had made it, too.

We walked into the building together and I was greeted by everyone from Colonel Terry on down. I was told that a jeep was going up to Able Battery after supper and that I could ride up then. I could pick up my jeep and party at the battery and then get to the infantry under my own power. Haeger and I went out to one of the sheds and sat down on a truck to catch up on events.

The outfit had had a rough go of it. A 120 mortar round had landed in the center of the battalion CP tent and killed the executive officer, the assistant S-3, and the liaison officer for the 2d Battalion, along with half of the FDC (fire direction center) personnel — the heart of a field artillery battalion. This was why the colonel, Haeger, and the other HQ people were back in Service Battery. The FDC for the battalion had been moved to Able Battery and Plummer was running the show. I asked Haeger if Plummer had made captain. Haeger shook his head. We both thought that Plummer should have made it. He had been a first lieutenant for eight years.

Supper was over. I got into the jeep with Able Battery's first sergeant, who had come in after the mail. We bounced out of the yard and were soon speeding along the road north out of Taegu to Sangju and Andong. That was the road where we had made contact with the ROKs; the road the regiment had moved up a few days before; the road the mortars had plastered; the place where I had been hurt; and the road that tomorrow would be made famous as the "Bowling Alley." We crossed over the bridges and passed the place where I had last seen the battery; passed the place where the mortars had come in; whirled by the schoolhouse that was the ROK CP; and passed the place where the infantry had turned off the road for the high ground on either flank. From here on it was new territory for me. A mile farther on we made a big right turn and there in the bend was the battery in position. The jeep turned on a little rut of a road and came to a stop near the mess truck. After exchanging greetings with the men I followed the sergeant through a group of trees to a house that was the center of the battery position, behind which the CP was dug in. Plummer greeted me with open arms and we sat right down on the porch and shot the breeze. Plummer convinced me in short order that I could not get up to the infantry before dark (it was 1930 then) and I decided to spend the night with the battery. Word was sent back to the motor park for Minor to come up to the CP. Plummer said that the GI who had been with me was sent forward to replace a casualty in one of the other OF parties.

Soon, Minor came up and nearly dropped his jaw when he saw me. He had been certain that I had had a broken leg. I told him to get the jeep and equipment ready to roll first thing in the morning.

221

Plummer went into the dugout and came back with my cartridge belt complete with all my old equipment on it. Minor produced a Korean leather shoulder holster for my .45 from somewhere and handed over my carbine, which he had cleaned to perfection. This display of affection touched me to the quick. I thanked him and gave him the new M1 I had brought up from Taegu in exchange.

I slept well that night, waking only once or twice when the battery had a fire mission. The next morning, Plummer presented me with a new man to make up for the one I had lost. His name was Roberts. He was a big six-foot-three, seventeen-year-old Texan who had volunteered to go up on an OF party. He had the M1 I had given Minor slung over his shoulder, and from the way his pockets sagged he must have had fifteen hand grenades in his pockets. He suited me just swell. We got into the jeep and took off like a bunch of wild Indians.

We passed through several villages that were packed with ROKs. We turned left past several ROK antitank guns and proceeded up a narrow valley. On each side were tall hills that went up at a 50 to 70 degree angle. We saw a few parked vehicles and stopped to ask some questions. We learned that the 1st Battalion's CP was located on the left (west) of the road at the base of the hills. I left Minor and Roberts in the jeep and took off on foot for the CP.

I found the group, dug in in an erosion ditch just where I had been told they were. Everyone greeted me as if I were a long-lost brother. I made a few inquiries as to the situation and announced that I would take off for Able Company. At this, Captain Beard changed my plans. Colonel Terry had called and said that I was to go over to the 2d Battalion. Lieutenant Parker was their only OF, and because their positions were nearer to the road than the 1st Battalion's, he thought that I would be needed more over there, at least for the rest of this engagement. Upon hearing this, Colonel Check made a strong protest that flattered my ego considerably. I didn't like the idea much, either. I had grown attached to the 1st Battalion and to Able Company and I didn't want to leave them, but the assurance that the move was to be temporary made the switch a little easier.

I walked back to the jeep and drove to 2d Battalion's CP. I found the liaison officer, a lieutenant in place of the captain who had been killed, who told me to run up to Fox Company. The wire was already in, so I just took an EE8 to tie into it. I had given up on the radio working early in the campaign. Roberts said that he wanted to go to the OP with me and Minor had happily agreed to stay in the CP area with the jeep. Roberts and I picked up our weapons and took off for the company.

We found the company after what seemed like hours of climbing straight up. My leg really began to hurt after the exertion and I cussed the damn medic for sending me back before the leg was well.

The company commander received us warmly and showed us where the last OF had had his hole. The wire was still in and the shrapnel-shattered

EE8 was still connected. I took it off the wire and tied on our phone. After giving the crank a twirl the switchboard at the battalion CP soon answered. This was a relief to me. I didn't want to have to worry about fighting that hill again or putting down another wire.

The company CO left us and Roberts and I made ourselves comfortable. We cleaned the debris out of the old hole and put some fresh bushes around the position for camouflage. I located my position on my map and took azimuthal readings to prominent landmarks. Out in front was the valley. I sat on a high ridge on its right, or east. The enemy was north. About 4,000 yards out the valley split, as did the road — east to Andong, west to Sangju. There were the remains of a village smoldering about 2,000 yards away and on the road, three or four burned-out T34 tanks. To our right was a tangle of higher mountains occupied by the ROKs, to our right rear (just arrived from Okinawa) was the newly acquired 3d Battalion in the "walled city" of Kasan.

I had Roberts make one more wire check and then settled back to relax. That climb had exhausted me. All was quiet. I looked at my watch. It was noon.

CHAPTER
NINE

The Bowling Alley

We spent a quiet afternoon snoozing and daydreaming. Out in front there was not a thing stirring. About 1700 a sergeant came into our position and said that he had C rations for us. I said swell and sent Roberts back after them. The sergeant sat down beside me and made some comment about what a good guy the OF who had been killed was. I said, "Yeah," and looked over the harmless-appearing real estate out front. Soon Roberts came back with the box of C rations and the sergeant left. We devoured the rations eagerly, feeling the full effect of not having a noon meal.

The sun dropped low over the hills to the west and I decided that it was a good time to send Roberts after water. There was a five-gallon can full of the stuff at the company CP. We had been told to help ourselves to it when we first came up. Roberts disappeared in the bushes and I sat down on the edge of the hole absentmindedly. There was something spooky about the position that I didn't like. I did not know what it was, but I felt uneasy. There were knee-high bushes all over the place and they were plenty thick enough for someone to crawl right up on you before he could be seen. For another thing, I didn't like being in a dead man's hole. I wasn't superstitious, but it was sound reasoning that if the North Koreans could hit this spot once they could do it again. I guess a lot of my uneasiness came from the fact that I had been out of the scrap for a few days and I knew from experience that it was always hard when you first came back.

The telephone rang. The lieutenant who was the liaison officer was calling to tell me that G-2 was expecting something tonight and that I should be on my toes. He also mentioned that the batteries had star shells on hand. I was to call for them whenever my suspicions were aroused and I wanted to light up the valley for a look. He said that the batteries had already registered and could hit about anything in the valley from coordinates. With this he hung up.

Roberts reappeared with the canteens of water and in a few minutes we had settled down with nothing to do but swat mosquitoes and talk. "Those goddamn people really stuck us out here by ourselves, Lieutenant," Roberts was moved to say. I agreed with him but tried not to show any concern.

"That's good," I lied, "Those damn machine guns and BARs draw fire. We are lucky that they aren't anywhere around."

"Never thought of that angle," replied Roberts. "I guess you are right. We sho' as hell won't draw any fire here."

I began to wonder who was kidding who now. We sat there talking and the sun dropped behind the hills. In a flash it was dark and the air became cool. I buttoned the top of my fatigue jacket and turned up the collar. So did Roberts. We talked on. Roberts told me about his home in east Texas, about his younger brother, and how the two of them used to hunt and fish together. He said that their favorite sport was fox and coon hunting. He had six hound dogs back in Texas that he swore could outrun anything with four or two legs and hair on its back. I believed every word he said. He said that those dogs could smell a coon five miles away and that they would never lose a trail once they had picked it up. I sat there listening to Roberts talk feeling that he was enjoying it as much as I.

By 2300 he had exhausted the hunting topic and had entered fishing, which had promise of lasting all night. About this time the phone rang. The liaison officer. He had a report that motors were heard on the road. He got a call from Lieutenant Parker who was with Easy Company. He said that he had heard motors, too, and wanted an illuminating round out there, hiokko. I gave the phone to Roberts and turned my attention to the road and waited for the round to go out. I listened intently for motors, but because of my altitude I couldn't hear any. There was a report from the rear. The round whooshed above us and burst high over the valley a thousand yards out. There was a splendid silver spray of light and as the parachute opened and the flare burned to maximum efficiency, the entire valley was illuminated.

I stared below, shocked and frightened. There were tanks and self-propelled guns cluttering the road, bumper to bumper, scrambling toward our positions. Around these armored pieces were hundreds of NKPA infantrymen. I grabbed for the telephone and screamed for a fire mission. The FOS must have done the same thing because I could hear the switchboard operator answering other calls along with mine. I yelled for him to tell the others to adjust on the rear and center of the column and that I would get the leading elements. I gave my fire mission, hurriedly calling for battery three rounds to start off with. While I waited for the "On the way" I hoped that the batteries were really as well registered as I had been told they were because there was no time for an adjustment now. I heard the rounds leave the howitzers in the rear and watched eagerly for them to burst.

While my rounds were still in the air I heard another battery sound off in the rear, which meant that the fire for the rear of the column was also on its way. There were big red flashes and explosions on the road to my left front now, and as I watched the eighteen rounds go in I gave a real old rebel yell because I got a direct hit on a tank and it started to burn. I yelled over the phone to repeat range and repeat fire for effect (battery three rounds). I looked farther down the column and gave another yell as I saw the rounds that Lieutenant Parker had fired crashing all over the enemy armor, starting several fires. In the meantime, the 60mm, 81mm, and 4.2-inch mortars had gone to work on the column and somebody had the sense to keep shooting star shells over the area. The din from all the shooting had reached a constant roar now and I couldn't identify my rounds, but I saw them go in, all right. They hit the front of the column with a wide enough spread to saturate the rice paddies on either side of the road, which was thick with Reds.

I called for a rolling barrage now (in this case a shift of fifty yards in range with each three rounds) with HE and WP mixed. Farther up the valley I could see that some of the other FOs had already started using WP on the enemy. In the meantime, the Reds, seeing that they were discovered, started pouring the lead in our direction. The tanks and self-propelled guns on the road opened up on us, and the elephant guns and 120 mortars started firing at the battery positions to our rear. The sound of the artillery going back and forth through the air was hair-raising, and the awful explosions of the bursting shells was accentuated by the manner in which the sound waves were funneled up and down the valley. It was this sound of artillery shells rushing through the smoke-filled air and exploding with a terrible crash that prompted one GI to refer to the valley as the "Bowling Alley" when speaking of it to a correspondent the following day.

My eyes were glued to the road and rice paddies below, and in the strange silver light of bursting artillery, oil fires, and star shells, I could see the hostiles coming out of their tanks like rats from a burning ship. Roberts was yelling at the top of his voice and beating on my back in wild excitement. His war whoops would have made most any Indian run in terror.

The recoilless rifles that were emplaced all along the hills on both sides of the road were slicing into the enemy and taking their toll, and backflashes down close betrayed the presence of bazooka teams. Our tanks had rolled up to point blank range from their place of concealment behind a little rise. The Pershings opened up with their big guns, and their .50s and heavy .30s were cutting across the valley in a withering crossfire. The barrage of the mortars was now accelerated to a deafening roar, and the bursting rounds were falling like water being poured out of a pitcher. Here was U.S. firepower at its best. We were cutting them to pieces.

But it was not a one-sided engagement. Above the screaming roar of battle could clearly be heard the shrieks of our own wounded, and enough heavy stuff fell around our position to give both of us a shower of dirt and rocks several times. It was not going to be easy for us by any means, but from the first few rounds I knew that we were going to win.

The maddening duel went on for two hours and then seemed to gradually slow down. It appeared to me that all the vehicles had either been hit or crippled and there seemed to be no Reds about them. The telephone rang and I answered it to find the battalion executive officer wanting to know what the hell was going on out front. I gave him the picture as I saw it and suggested that we keep a battery of 105s firing up and down the dead column all night, just for good measure. It seemed that all the targets of opportunity either were hit or gone. Evidently, after talking with some of the other FOs, this course of action was taken, for the firing appeared to stop soon afterward, except for one battery.

As the heavier pieces were silenced I became aware of a terrific small-arms firefight to our right rear. It was in the area where the ROKs were and where the 3d Battalion was holed up in the old walled city of Kasan. I listened for a while and grew increasingly concerned. The NKPA had evidently pushed its armor and some infantry down the road, and pushed its larger force of foot troops over the high ground to our flank, as was customary. I had thought at the time that there was something fishy about the NKPA making a frontal attack without controlling the high ground, too. As I listened it became clear that most of their artillery had been diverted to the targets on our right flank, and from the constant booming in that direction it seemed that they were really pouring in. After thinking all this over for several minutes it dawned on me that Roberts and I had been stuck way out on the right flank of the company. And if the ROKs had pulled back as the fire indicated, there was nothing between us and the enemy on the right. Most of the action was actually taking place to our right rear and on higher ground than we occupied. This was bad. I cranked the telephone and called for the liaison officer. I told him what was going on and asked that something be done about securing the right flank. I had no contact with the company CP (negligence on my part, although it's normally SOP for the OF to be included in the company wire net by the company wire corporal) so it was up to the battalion to let the company know about their exposure on the flank.

Roberts became concerned after hearing my conversation with the battalion and he fingered his M1 nervously. I checked my carbine several times myself. We sat there quietly and listened to the racket to the right. I put a couple of grenades on the edge of the hole for immediate use, as did Roberts. The mortar and gun fire increased. It was evident that the enemy was making a major effort to kick this attack into Taegu. They wouldn't shoot up mortar and artillery rounds in such quantity unless they really had the power to go in behind it. I fretted and worried for another hour, listening to the fight pass farther and farther to our rear. If the Reds decided to slide off the high ground they had taken from the ROKs, we really would have had it.

Roberts and I would be the first resistance they would hit. I looked over the terrain to the north in an effort to see the flash from the guns that were pumping in the support fire for the assault that was taking place to the right and rear, but the search was futile. The NKs were past masters at concealment, and they always had their fieldpieces well camouflaged and in a defilade.

It dawned on me that there were probably thousands of NKPAs running along the ridge on the right, eager to gush through the hole that had been poked in the ROK lines by the assault troops. Once enough of the troops poured through for a buildup, they would undoubtedly flank us from the rear. I decided to bridge the crest of the north-south ridge to our right with fire in an effort to at least slow up this flow of NK infantry. I called for a fire mission and learned from the operator that all the batteries were now firing in support of the 1st and 3d Battalions, which were hard pressed. I listened for a moment and from the booming in the rear I knew he was right. I had forgotten all about the 1st Battalion across the valley. A glance in that direction bore out the statement that they were hard pressed. I could see tracers burning north and south along the ridge. The North Koreans were advancing along the high ground on both sides of the valley. If we were caught on the low ground in the middle of this squeeze, we would be finished. It now seemed even more imperative that I get fire on the right to slow up, if not halt, the enemy reinforcement of the advantages they had already gained. I asked if I could have the 4.2s. The operator was gone for a moment and then answered that they had a mission now, but that he would call me as soon as they were available. I told him to hurry and hung up.

Roberts and I sat there and nervously bit our lips, waiting. Roberts swore that he heard rifle bolts clicking nearby. I was not sure whether I heard them or just was afraid that I might. With the thick brush we feared that the enemy would be on top of us before we could get our share.

The operator called back. In a second we were connected with the 4.2 FDC. The mortar operator told me that they were out of HE but were loaded with WP. That suited me swell and I gave the fire mission. Soon the rounds whistled over and burst just beyond the crest to the right. I made an adjustment and got good distribution along the ridge. I ordered a battery three rounds and then turned back to the ridge to wait for the "On the way." The WP from the first adjusting rounds had started a few small fires, and I thought I saw black figures running, silhouetted against the red light. The rounds were "On the way" and I grinned with satisfaction as they crashed into the ridge. More fires were started, and, as the small fires came together, they became large fires. In a matter of minutes the whole damn ridge was a mass of yellow and red flame. Roberts and I could see little black figures running through the flames. There were explosions from ammo that had evidently been stashed away on the ridge or had been on some unfortunate ammo bearer's back. I called the mortars and shifted the fire two hundred yards south down the ridge, toward our lines. I fired into the area and started another good fire in the brush. I was about to shift again when the operator called and said that the mortars were being taken away from me for a higher priority target. I complained but there was nothing I could do. I hung up. Roberts and I contented ourselves with watching the enemy run through the burning bushes in an attempt to reinforce those that had gone before.

The small-arms fire traveled farther to the rear. It was apparent that the ROKs had pulled back several thousand yards. The NKPA mortars continued to pound away at something to our right rear, but the artillery had stopped. Our guns were going full blast but the targets were all in the 1st or 3d Battalion's sectors. To our front all was quiet, and down the road the Red tanks and self-propelled guns burned merrily.

I began to notice that I could see things better, that the prevailing color had changed from black to gray. In the sky to the east was a hint of yellow light, and the morning mist was accumulating in the low places in the valley below. It was already dawn. I suddenly felt tired. I looked over at Roberts and he had fallen into a deep sleep, sitting upright in the hole with his legs curled under him, Oriental fashion. I decided to let him sleep for an hour and then wake him so I could get some sack time.

I sat up on the edge of the hole and opened my eyes wide to fight off my weariness. I stretched out my legs across the hole and listened. I looked into the thick bushes that grew in a tangle right to the edge of our hole. I watched the fires burn on the enemy ridge and hoped that the ROKs and 3d Battalion would hold the enemy back at the walled city of Kasan. I thought about the possibility of the NKPA flanking us from the rear and of them sneaking back into our own lines, as often was the case coming back on Heartbreak Highway. I thought about my injured leg and wondered how it would endure a long withdrawal through the hills. I worried, swatted mosquitoes, cussed, dozed, and snapped out of it, for one long terrible hour. I looked at my watch. It was 0640. I shook Roberts, and he snapped up with a start, his hands searching for his M1. He was surprised and ashamed that he had gone to sleep on me, but I assured him that it was okay and that I intended to get some sack time now while he stood watch.

I told him to let me sleep two hours and then give me a shake. He was to wake me at 0840. I dropped down into the bottom of the hole and stuck my feet over the side at the end. Sleep came immediately.

When I opened my eyes the light was bright, and above me, lying across the hole, were bushes shading my face from the rays of the sun. I looked at my watch. It was 1150. I sat up with a start and looked around for Roberts, flinging aside the foliage over the hole.

"Howdy, Lieutenant," he drawled. "I figured that you needed a little more than two hours' sleep so I just thought that I would let you get it. That all right, sir?"

I grinned and said that it was, but for him to wake me up at the time I requested from here on out. *He was a good kid*, I thought, and felt an unusual attachment to him even though he had only been with me two days. He handed me an open can of peaches from the C rations and asked if I thought he should go after some more water. I drained the last drop out of my canteen and gave it to him. He took it along with his, and was gone.

I ate the peaches and looked over the landscape. There was not a round being fired anywhere and there was no sign of life. The fires I had started on the ridge had gone out. On the road the Red tanks were burning mighty feebly. The rice paddies on both sides of the road were brown and black from the HE and WP that had poured in during the night. Throughout the area were lumps of blackish brown that last night had been men with the fire of world revolution burning in their hearts. The only things that burned now were their destroyed tanks that had made the long journey across the Siberian railway only to be clobbered by some such as me. I felt proud as I looked down upon the desolate mess, but not cocky. There was no room for cockiness in this dirty war. We were in bad shape, and unless help were to reach us soon we would be hard pressed to keep our narrow footing on this small beachhead.

I thought of the defeat of the North Koreans. Then what? Would we have to keep four or five divisions over here to see that the same thing didn't happen again? Would China and Russia stand by and watch us move into North Korea? What if the USSR decided to send the Chinese into the war? Would we go to war with China? If so, why? What would we have accomplished after we had beaten China? Wouldn't our real enemy still be menacingly poised with overpowering numerical strength? What if the Chinese came into the war and we failed to go all-out against them and the war could not be won by either side? Would the American people close their eyes to the casualties that we would pile up in a year or two of a holding action? Would the voters sit idly by and let their young men be killed or maimed in a "police action" that had backfired without demanding that Far Eastern policy be revamped? Would the people at home let us fight on and on over here for a principle that had no meaning for those of us fighting the war? If it was true that we were buying time for the Western Europeans, why didn't they cooperate with us in our efforts to build a European defense?

I stopped thinking now; I had already thought too much. In the past, our armies knew what they were fighting for, or at least the individual soldier thought he knew what he was fighting for. In this case it was different. No one knew why we were here and, although the policy makers in Washington had published statements of policy that might be acceptable to the party supporters at home, I knew that the same statements would sound mighty hollow in this valley where the smell of death was so heavy. I wondered how many GIs would accept Washington's explanation of the war as adequate justification for the price they individually were paying over here in the filth.

After about two hours I started reading Hemingway's *Across the River and into the Trees*. It provided a complete escape. I remember lying in the hole on my back, reading with my feet propped up on the edge of the hole. There was a distant rifle discharge, and I heard the branches on the brush surrounding the hole snap. Some damn sniper was shooting at me. Hell, I was busy reading. The sniper fired only three or four times.

Roberts burst through the bushes. He was puffing and blowing from his climb. He gave me my canteen full of cool water and asked if I had become too attached to this position. I told him I hadn't. He said that we were to go down to the company CP. Rumor had it that we were moving over to Easy Company for a while. Colonel Terry had ordered us to relieve Lieutenant Parker, who had been on the hill for several days and had drawn quite a little fire last night.

This change suited me fine, especially when I considered the open right flank. We took our EE8, our weapons and mapboard, and started back to the CP, which was about half a mile straight down.

There we were met by a runner from Easy Company who was to direct us. I called the switchboard (something I should have done before pulling out) and told them that I was at Fox CP and headed toward Easy CP. Roberts, the runner, and I started off down a path that led us to the road, where we walked within a few yards of the first knocked-out Red tank. We turned right to climb up the front side of the hill that we had just come down. This route didn't make too much sense to me, but I went along with the runner figuring that he knew what he was doing. We approached a long narrow ditch in the hill. In this was located the company CP. I met the CO, a Lieutenant Norron (the spelling may be wrong), and we had a friendly chat before I left for the OP.

Roberts and I were given a fresh box of C rations and we took off up the practically vertical side of the hill. A path had been worn and there were bushes to hold on to so it was easier than the other route we had taken yesterday, but it did not make my bad leg feel too good. We found Lt. Dixie Parker snugly dug in with the 2d Platoon in a dugout, complete with roof. I was impressed and happy to move into such plush accommodations. The sergeant in command of the platoon was Johnson from South Carolina. He had been with the 7th Division in Japan, and he and I had sat next to each other on the train from Osaka to Fukuoka, on our way to this war.

After several minutes of back-slapping and cussing the enemy, Parker pointed out the areas of enemy activity on the ground and then on the map. He gave me his concentration numbers and assured me that the batteries were already well "fired in" on all the targets in the valley or ridges to the front (north). Parker and his man collected their equipment and took off down the hill. I tied our telephone into his wire and settled down to make myself comfortable. It was now 1600.

In about fifteen minutes the NKPA mortars opened up on the 3d Battalion to our right rear. At 1630, small arms began to crackle in that area, and by 1640 there was the damndest firefight to our rear and right that I had ever heard. All the time the enemy mortars continued to pump rounds into the area. Our mortars and artillery were replying in kind. Although we could hear all of this we could see nothing. The battle was taking place out of our sector. We were prevented from seeing any of the action by the shielding ridges and hills. We sat quietly and listened.

Roberts broke out the C rations at about 1800 and we ate a pretty heavy meal, each of us eating at least three cans of rations. After chow, I went off into the bushes and, naturally, as was the SOP, the phone rang and the call was for me alone. No one else could take the message. I went back to the phone cursing Alexander Graham Bell. It was that new liaison officer on the wire and he wanted to know how things were going in our sector. I told him. I asked what was up in the rear and his classic statement was, "The situation is confusing." With this the conversation was over and I went back to my business in the bushes.

A few minutes later a flight of B-26s came out of the blue and began one hell of a bombing, rocketing, and strafing mission to our right rear. The noise and smoke were all of the results available to us, but we later learned that these boys really saved the day. The defenses of the "walled city" in the mountains were crumbling and the ROKs were in full flight. It had been this assistance from the air force that had saved the day or at least saved it for a while, anyway. The firefight broke off after this air strike and the mortars slowed down. Overlooking the fact that it was disconcerting to see your own planes making a strike in your rear, it was encouraging to learn that the enemy had withdrawn to regroup. It meant that we had killed a few North Koreans.

Sergeant Johnson came over and sat down beside me. We began to talk about Southern fried chicken and how nice it would be to go home after the war was over. It got dark and the mosquitoes came in by the squadrons. We put on some repellent that the sergeant had and found that it helped a bit, but did not keep the most hungry insects away. I told Roberts to get some sleep and that I would wake him when I got sleepy. He stretched out and was out like a light. I sat there with Johnson and looked out into the black valley. A few of the dead tanks were still burning weakly. There was no more mortar fire now and our batteries were also quiet. In the 1st Battalion's area there were a few scattered rifle shots, but nothing else. We sat there and listened. I could hear men in the nearby foxholes talking in low tones, and somewhere out in the valley a cow bawled.

I stayed awake until 2400. I shook Roberts and told him to wake me at 0200 for certain. He nodded that he would and I stretched out.

It was 0200 and Roberts was shaking me. "Wake up sir, It's time for your watch." I rubbed my eyes and my back where I had been sleeping on some rocks and got up. Roberts stayed awake a minute to be sure that I was up for good and then he turned in. I sat down on the roof of the dugout and looked out into the valley. Everything was still quiet. I wondered if the NKPA were going to give up a breakthrough in this area and try somewhere else. I guess everyone else was wondering the same thing. I speculated over the rumors that the 82d or 101st Divisions were on their way to the Far East, and I wondered when the 7th, which had been brought up to strength in Japan, would be committed. I considered the possibility of an amphibious landing on our part as everyone I had talked to believed.

I sat there in the damp dark fighting the war. I guess all soldiers do the same thing. You sit in your hole or on the side of it and plan the campaign or fight over old engagements and figure out what you might do if you were in command. It is always refreshing for the individual man in his hole to look at the big picture for then there is always promise. The big picture always holds so much more than the dirty little sector you are personally concerned with. I was deep in thought when there were two flashes on the west side of the valley at about three thousand yards. A few seconds later I heard two sharp reports and the round whistled down the valley and crashed into the rear, about a thousand yards back.

I lunged for the telephone and put in a fire mission. It appeared to me that the pieces were emplaced on the left fork of the road that cut through the mountains to Sangju. I called for fire on that road and asked for a star shell to illuminate the area, which it did. There were two self-propelled guns pumping shells down the valley as fast as they could fire. I waited for several minutes. The rounds I had called for did not arrive. I got back on the phone and asked why. To my surprise, the operator told me that the guns had been given to another observer for a higher priority target. I started screaming into the phone that there could be no higher priority target than enemy self-propelled guns shooting into the middle of our perimeter, but the operator could only tell me that he was not the one who called the shoot off. I told him to call me the minute the guns were ready to fire my mission and added that I hoped the North Koreans didn't shoot his ass off before I was allowed to knock them out. He said, "Yes, sir, so do I," and hung up. I sat there mad as the devil and watched the muzzle blast of the enemy pieces flash down the valley. They were having a field day.

There was a booming in the rear, and I heard the rounds from one of our 105 batteries go over. I waited, then saw the burst, just short of the NKPA pieces. I was furious. I picked up the phone and cranked it savagely. The operator answered. Between my teeth I asked if the fire that had just gone over was the fire that had taken priority over mine. He said that it was. That's when I really blew my top. Somebody had delayed the fire mission for at least ten minutes, taking it away from me and giving it to someone else who was to fire at the same target. I hung up the EE8 and sat there furious, watching the rounds that were now being fired at the Reds land everywhere but on top of them.

The Reds, in the meantime, were pouring the shells down the valley. I could hear them crashing into something down the line and felt uneasy when I thought that their infantry was probably sneaking in close in the rear and on the right flank, shielded from this fire. Some happy Red bastard was probably sitting on the other end of the hill I was on, directing the fire. This went on for about twenty minutes, then the self-propelled cranked up and backed around the bend of the road, safe behind high banks. We had missed this chance to knock them out.

The phone rang. Again, the new liaison officer. He wanted to know if I had seen any NKPA fieldpieces out front. I told him that I had but that they were gone now. Then he had the guff to ask me why I had not taken them under fire. This was the last straw. I said I had been sleeping and that I only fired between 0800 and 1200. If he wanted me to fire I would be glad to do so during those hours. I overheard the switchboard operator snicker, and I have reason to believe that the man caught on. From then on my missions were to go through immediately, he informed me, and hung up. I felt better in a small way.

I turned around to find Roberts grinning at me in the dark. "You sho' did give that fellow the turd-eating word," he drawled. I grinned and agreed with him. I looked at my watch and it was 0500. I had let Roberts oversleep a little. Johnson came up and said that he had received a call from the company CP that we should be on full alert from now until light. We had a patrol out operating in the valley for a few hours and they had just come in reporting that the enemy were building up for something down there. We took this bit of news casually and decided to brew some coffee in the blacked out dugout. Sergeant Johnson had a squad burner that was just the equipment for the job. Roberts volunteered to be cook. He disappeared in the dugout with the burner and our canteen cups. We spread a raincoat over the entrance to keep the burner's light from escaping and settled down to wait for the coffee and anything the Reds might cook up. As it turned out, they never did a thing and we simply sat on top of the dugout and drank coffee and watched the sun come up. At 0800 I crawled into the dugout and went to sleep.

About 1030 I was aroused when the ants tried to pick me up and haul me off. I got out of the dugout, blinking in the bright sunlight. Everyone was sitting around in their holes and some were dozing. Roberts had crawled into the bushes and was sleeping like a lamb. I took off my helmet and scratched my head. Out front all was quiet and there was no sound of firing anywhere. I took out my glasses and looked over the terrain carefully. I spotted a patrol of three NKPAs way out, shuffling along through the paddies, and over near the spot where the self-propels had been there was a shack on fire. Other than that all was serene.

After a while Sergeant Johnson came up and sat with me. He said that a patrol of GIs and ROKs was to go up the road in a little while and that we were to support them with fire if they needed it. I agreed and took out my field glasses again so we could follow the progress of the patrol in detail.

The patrol passed out from under our hill on the left and started cautiously up the road. Their mission was to take a prisoner. We watched as they moved past the burned-out tanks and the scattered dead which, after two days in the sun were beginning to fill the whole area with their odor. The patrol moved up the road, watched by perhaps thousands of unseen eyes other than ours. It took them about thirty minutes to reach the fork in the road. They took the left-hand fork and approached a small bridge under which ran a small creek. Here the patrol deployed, and an element went around each flank of the bridge. A third element advanced cautiously over the bridge with their weapons at the ready. Then a surprising thing happened. A man came out from under the bridge with his hands up and he was soon followed by ten more. The patrol had accomplished their mission, if they could get back without incident.

We watched them as they hurried back down the road with the prisoners and began to speculate as to the fighting spirit of the Reds when we could get prisoners without a fight. The fact that the patrol had not been fired upon by the Reds was more than we could fathom. We knew most certainly that they had guns covering the road. It was all confusing. It was always difficult for us to try to understand the Reds, however. They just didn't think the way we did, and no matter how long you had been in Asia, you were always amazed at the reasoning of these people. Perhaps they had a perfectly good reason for not firing on our patrol. Perhaps the prisoners had been "planted." Only events would tell the story.

The patrol passed safely into our lines and we relaxed a bit. I crawled into the bushes where there was some shade and tried to sleep. The time of day was approaching when the whole front would sleep and I wanted to get a head start.

At 1400 Sergeant Johnson came over with the news that we were to get a hot meal. The company mess truck had arrived at the back side of the hill and they were feeding now. He had sent half of his platoon down and when they returned we were to go down with the other half. I woke Roberts who was still sacking away in the dugout and we prepared to go below. This also meant that we would have an opportunity to wash at the well which was at a nearby house. Roberts responded to my invitation to eat like gasoline to a match, and we were on our way down the hill in minutes. Due to the steepness of the hill, we traveled most of the distance on our fannies.

At the company CP we were motioned into a ditch and someone told us to keep real quiet. I asked what was up in a whisper, and the same individual told me to stay quiet and I would see. The road was only about twenty yards below the CP and riflemen were in position with their weapons trained on the road. Roberts and I also got our weapons ready, expecting to see at least a dozen Reds come into range. Soon into view marched a little runty NKPA officer, complete with hip boots. On his shoulders were huge red epaulets that extended several inches out from his body both to the front and rear. On the epaulets was every kind of gold braid, and he had bright gold buttons on his tunic, which fastened tightly around his neck. He was followed by a small bedraggled figure loaded with the officer's belongings, including his sword. The GIs sprang up and covered the two. They stopped and threw up their hands, the man in the

249

rear being forced to drop his load in the dust. The GIs ran down on the road and frisked them for weapons, then marched them up to the CP. Roberts and I sat there watching, very entertained. The NKPA officer said something to his aide who stopped dead in his tracks. Then he turned to the GIs and said that he wished to speak to the division commander in English. We were astonished. The company CO stepped forward saying that he would take the officer and his aide to the battalion CP. He took a couple of men as guards and marched the two down the road. Roberts and I followed, turning off at the mess truck that had run up behind our hill in a big gully.

After chow we went back to the company CP and stopped to get the story on the prisoners. We were told that the NKPA officer was a lieutenant colonel and that he was an artilleryman. That was all the information that anyone had. Later someone said that the colonel had not been questioned at battalion but was taken directly to regiment. This was the first field-grade prisoner that we had taken in the war, and speculation ran high that the enemy morale was about to crack, but the wiser old soldiers simply said, "Them gooks are crazy, it don't mean anything. There is still lots of fighting to do."

The story on the NKPA colonel was a good one. He said that he was a lieutenant colonel when the war started and that most of his colleagues who had been lieutenant colonels were now full colonels. He had been passed over when the promotions came out. Also, he had been living the "Russian way" for five years and he thought he liked the "American way" better. To show his sincerity he volunteered to pinpoint his artillery positions on the map for us. Our planes flew over the areas he had pinpointed and, damn, if the guns weren't there. They were subsequently blasted off the peninsula by our artillery. The colonel had at least known where his guns were. We all felt grateful that he "preferred our way of life." (We later learned he was Lt. Col. Chong Pong, CO of Arty Regt. N.K. 13th Div.)

Roberts and I climbed back up the hill and the rumors were flying that we would be pulling out of the place. An ROK division was reported to be moving in to replace us. By 1600 I had received a call from battalion confirming these rumors. The plan was for the ROKs to make a limited attack about two thousand yards to the front; our tanks were to make a feint up the road to cover their assault over the ridges to the right and left. I was to support the ROKs with fire. The attack was to kick off at 1630.

At the appointed time the tanks nosed out into the road with about a company of infantry screening for them. Soon I could see the ROKs working forward on the hill to the left and then on our right. They advanced cautiously without firing or drawing fire. They made the first thousand yards without incident, and the tank force stopped on the road about five hundred yards out, as was planned. Then the fireworks started, the tanks started to receive mortar and gun fire thick and heavy. I spotted the gun emplacements at the forks in the road and called for fire. While waiting for the rounds I was told by the operator that the 8th Field Artillery had moved out and that the 38th Field Artillery, a new battalion from the States, had moved in. This was all right with me, just so they would fire. I waited and there was no fire. I asked the operator what was up and he said that he would call the FDC and find out. I waited; there was no voice on the other end of the wire and the fire mission never did go out. In the interval, the enemy was plastering the hell out of the tanks and infantry that were on the road. I waited and cussed. After I cranked the phone nearly to pieces the operator finally answered. "What the hell are they waiting for?" I screamed.

"I don't know, sir," came the reply, "just a minute." Then, "Sir, they want to know the coordinates again." I gave them to him. Another long wait. I sat there and watched the enemy rounds landing on top of our troops. The tanks fired a few rounds in the direction of the enemy fieldpieces but they could not hit them with their flat-trajectory fire. Sergeant Johnson came up and asked what the hell was wrong, and after I told him, he helped me cuss out this new bunch of hoods in the 38th Field Artillery. Finally, I could stand the waiting no longer and I began cranking the phone again. The operator answered immediately and I asked to be connected with the S-3 of this new outfit that was supposed to be supporting us. In a few minutes I heard the voice of some major. I asked him what the delay was, after identifying myself, and he replied that the mission was unsafe to fire due to the fact that "friendly troops occupied the area of the coordinates I had given him." This was the crowning blow. I glanced at the map to make certain that I was not in error, and then I was insubordinate in the worst kind of way. The major hung up and I called for the liaison officer. I gave him the story and asked him to plead for the fire mission. He said that he would. The tanks and screening force stayed out in the road about ten more minutes and then withdrew, bringing their dead and wounded with them. Among the dead was Major Butler of the 2d Battalion who had gone out in command. The tanks were fortunately undamaged.

The 38th Field Artillery never did fire and I watched as the Reds pushed their guns back into prepared dugouts after firing.

The ROKs, by this time, had gained their objective and were digging in. The sun was dropping quickly behind the hills on the right, and the time for us to pull out was fast approaching. Roberts and I collected our gear and made ready to "bug." At 2000 the word came. We disconnected our EE8 and took off with the 2d Platoon of Easy, down the back side of the hill. We were the first platoon to pull out and when we reached the road there was a single Pershing tank standing guard. A company of ROKs was assembled against the base of the hill. I called to the tanker and asked for a lift, he said sure, and Roberts and I climbed aboard with our equipment. The tanker asked if we were the last off the hill and I assured him that we were. The tank lunged forward and we ground our way to the rear. We had to ford a creek where the bridge had been blown, and when we reached the road bed again we found Minor in the jeep waiting for us. The tank stopped and we thanked the tankers and hopped in our jeep. Minor had orders for us from Captain Beard. We were to proceed to Taegu and meet him at Service Battery. We would be with the first battalion from here on out.

Minor stepped on the gas and we buzzed on by the long lines of sweating troops that were making their way to the rear and a rest. About four miles farther we passed the trucks that had been assembled to transport the 2d Battalion. In a couple of hours we reached Taegu and the area where Service Battery had been. Now, all the batteries were there. I found Able, and Plummer had a sack all picked out for me on a litter underneath the FDC truck. We refought the engagement and then went to sleep.

CHAPTER
TEN

Haman

We remained in Taegu all of the next day and night. Then Captain Beard was ordered back to the infantry with his FOs. We found the regiment bivouacked in one of the riverbeds north of town. Here we spent another day and night. The following morning Able Company and its attachments were ordered up to another riverbed, about four miles north, to form a perimeter for a battalion of tanks that were in a marshaling area. We spent a day and a night there and caught up on our sleeping and letter writing. Then we moved out.

The 1st Battalion was loaded on trucks and we took off for the south. The 2d Battalion was to follow at a few hours' interval. The story, as we got it, was that we were going from Eighth Army control to division. Because the other two regiments of the division were on the southern end of the line it was only normal that we join them. This reasoning seemed sound to me, and as far as I know it was correct.

We reached Masan at dark and were bivouacked in an ordnance center that was set up in a school.

The area was south of town and might have been a campus. Our orders were to return to the line west of Chingdong-ni, the area we knew so well. The 35th Regiment was holding there now.

We arose at daybreak, with everyone excited as hell. What had happened? I was told the plans for us had been changed, and that we were pulling out immediately to fight somewhere. We were on the road by 0600 and headed north. The battalion was traveling alone. Where the rest of the regiment was, I never knew. We rushed through Masan, which was becoming an old stomping ground for us, and proceeded north over the road to Taegu. At the Haman road we turned left and made our way west toward Haman and the Naktong River. Five or six miles from the turnoff the column came to a halt near two artillery batteries situated across the road from each other. I think they were the 164th Field Artillery Battalion, in support of the 24th Regiment, or "Eleanor's Rifles" as we called the outfit. I got out of the jeep, went to the FDCs, and asked to see the executive officer. He came into the tent and asked what he could do for me. I explained that I was with the outfit on the road, and that I didn't know when our artillery would catch up with us. I asked him what radio channels he was working on and told him that I would operate on his radio channel until the 8th Field Artillery arrived (I had the crystals to put in my radio to get on his channel). The column began to move again and I had to run to get back in the jeep before we held up traffic.

About a mile farther on we turned left onto a new road, or a trail, really, and a few thousand yards beyond that we reached the 24th's regimental CP. This is an all-Negro regiment. I have never seen so many soldiers in a combat area as bunched up as they were. There was wire tangled everywhere, and the road was hopelessly jammed with all types of vehicles going in both directions from there forward.

We dismounted and the trucks were sent back to Masan. Captain Beard, Lieutenant Record (OF with Baker Company), and I sat around and watched the confusion in horror while Colonel Check made liaison in the CP. We opened up some C rations and wondered just how a breakthrough had occurred. Damn, if we didn't always have to run and put out the fires.

The colonel came down to the area where most of the command group had assembled and said we were going on a reconnaissance on foot. I yelled to Minor and Roberts to get our jeep with the vehicles of Able and bring them forward. The colonel had already started down the road and I hastened to follow. We walked about a mile, all straight up. The entire mile was jammed with troops of the 24th. We began to wonder who was manning the forward positions. The road ran perpendicular to the crest of a large ridge, then passed through a cut to the other side. As we approached the cut the congestion grew worse: a South Korean truck loaded with refugees stalled and blocked the road. We passed this, mounted the high bank on the left of the cut, went over the crest, and stopped to reconnoiter.

Before us lay the sorriest example of a military withdrawal that I had ever seen, and I had seen plenty in the last couple of months. Haman sat in the valley before us at a range of about five thousand yards. On this side of Haman a stream ran perpendicular to us. From the stream to our hill were lush green rice paddies. The road ran almost through the center of them, out of Haman, and up to the cut. This road, too, was jammed with vehicles, combined with a constant human stream, mostly weaponless, coming our way on foot.

In the rice paddies there were many little black dots (the size a human appeared to be at that range) struggling toward us. Occasionally a mortar round would land in the midst of the dots, and they would move quickly in another direction. When a round landed they would alter their course in a new direction. It was most disheartening to watch.

We were joined by the 24th regimental commander, who watched the mess silently. Colonel Check noticed shellfire on some tall peaks across the valley at a range of about five miles. He asked the colonel who was over there and was told that it was his 1st Battalion, which had been cut off for several days. Colonel Check also learned that the people on the road and in the paddies were the 2d and 3d Battalions of the 24th. The regimental colonel said something to Colonel Check that I did not understand and then took off.

Our little colonel stood there for a moment and then went into action. He ordered a lieutenant to get that ROK truck off the road and start the column moving to the rear. He wanted the road clear in an hour. He told each of the company commanders where he wanted their companies to go into position along the ridge. Able was to be on the high ground to the left of the road. He directed Captain Hickman to get the battalion up to the cut for deployment and asked me if I was ready to kill some North Koreans. I said that I was, and he ordered me to take Haman under fire and to keep it that way until he told me to lift it.

At this, he turned and went down the hill. The company commanders went to reconnoiter the positions assigned to them. I sat down to check the coordinates of Haman on the map and take an azimuth. Soon the company came up the hill, and with them, my party. They backed the jeep off the road about two hundred yards below and ran a wire up to me. I called back the fire mission; they relayed it on the radio, first to the outfit whose radio channel I had squeezed in, and later to the 8th Field Artillery that moved into position at about 1000 hours. Before long we had contact with Able Battery of the 90th Field Artillery (155s) and Haman was beginning to really get a bombardment.

At 1400 the artillery fire was lifted and the air force came in for a strike that was a beaut. At 1420 we got the order to move out and take the high ground on the other side of Haman, Able on the left, Baker in the center down the road, and Charlie on the right. This we did. In fact, we took the high ground the other side of Haman without losing a man, and then advanced about six thousand yards through another valley and on to the high ridges that the 24th had abandoned by dark. We had several firefights in this last advance and suffered a few casualties, but the cost had been light compared to the ground we had gained and the equipment we recovered, practically everything the 24th was issued. We occupied the old positions to find them littered with C ration cans and Korean beer bottles, and in my area, we found a wind-up Victrola. Boy! These guys had been fighting a tough war on the quiet end of the line. Everywhere were American weapons and ammo that had been left by "Eleanor's Rifles." There were bazookas, 81mm mortars, radios, BARs, heavy and light .30s, M1s by the dozen, and ammunition for all these weapons. The surprising thing was that there was no brass from expended ammunition that would indicate that a fight had been put up, and there were very few dead, mostly officers. The evidence pointed to a complete rout on the part of the 24th.

We had come back with one understrength battalion and recovered what a whole regiment had run off and left. Our people were not so much proud of their accomplishment as they were bitter toward the 24th for causing us the casualties that would have been avoided if they had done their share of the fighting.

We stayed on the hills west of Haman for four days, withstanding repeated counterattacks and killing several hundred NKPA with small arms alone. Baker and Charlie Companies received most of the casualties of these hard days, taking losses of about 30 percent of their number, and they had been at only one-half strength to start with. Able, being on the left flank, fared much better. For some reason the Reds didn't seem to want our positions.

Our main difficulty in the days west of Haman was communications. We were out of radio contact with the field artillery that did not displace after we had made our advance. The wire which Captain Beard's crew was laying was continually being cut. It had to run through Haman, across a stream, over a mile of rice paddies, up the road and through the cut, and back off the ridges to the FDC. What with constant troop and vehicle movement, plus the prowling of large NKPA patrols in the area, the wire was almost always out. My wire to the battalion CP and to Captain Beard stayed in, but it didn't do us much good if we couldn't reach the batteries. Of the four nights we were in the position, we had artillery support only one night, probably the night we needed it the most.

Plummer had sent the wire crew from Able Battery forward with a wire in hopes of laying a line directly to the 1st Battalion, rather than going through FDC. This proved to be the answer, because the line was laid directly across the hills and over a route that was not as heavily traversed as the route to the FDC. The line was through to Captain Beard at the battalion CP on the evening of the third night, and he tied the wire into mine through his switchboard.

My first knowledge of this was when our phone rang and the voice on the other end yelled, "Hi, Hood." It was Plummer and he wanted to know if I had any enemy soldiers to shoot. I told him not at the moment, but if the line would stay in for the night, I felt certain that I could oblige him with some activity. This turned out to be the case.

We had received a replacement lieutenant who had formerly been in command of the regimental ambulance train, but had been sent to us as platoon leader when things got tight up at the Bowling Alley. He had taken a reinforced squad of men out on a knoll that stuck out from the main ridge and was connected to it by a thin saddle. It was our most forward outpost. There were old holes on the knoll and lieutenant (a hell of a good man) and his few men had moved in. I had run a wire over to him during the afternoon and this was his only communication with us. He and his men had formed a tight perimeter around this little bare spot of real estate. They could control the low ground on either side of them with fire as well as the saddle that ran out to their front end up to a ridge some eight hundred yards to our front on which the enemy were holed up. It was an important piece of ground to hold, but a precarious perch for the men out there.

As soon as I learned of the line to Plummer, I called to the outpost and told them I had artillery support and could give them fire whenever they wanted it. This seemed to cheer them and the lieutenant who was operating the phone.

Early that night, at about 2100, a brisk firefight developed on the ridge to our right where Baker and Charlie were fighting along a 2,000-yard front. There were no mortars or artillery being used by the Reds, but the machine-gun fire was heavy and well employed. Our mortars and artillery were supporting Baker and Charlie up to a hundred yards from their position, and, in the dark, it often seemed to us that we were actually hitting our own troops with the supporting fire. This was never the case, however. We sat quietly in our holes in Able's sector and watched the tracers knife back and forth to our right. The engagement lasted for several hours, and the casualties suffered by the enemy were staggering, as the count of the dead in the morning proved. At about 0100, the Reds broke off the engagement and all was quiet. I assumed that the attack was off until 0400 or 0500, as was usually the case with the North Koreans. I began to relax; most of the men did likewise.

Instead of 100 percent alert, we went into 50 percent alert so that some of us could get some sleep. I was in a hole with Sergeant File (2d Platoon leader) and Roberts was in a hole nearby, that we had dug for the radio. But the radio failed and thus provided nothing more than extra cover for Roberts.

I had fallen asleep and Sergeant File was on watch. The phone rang and I was awake immediately. File passed the receiver to me. It was the lieutenant on the outpost. He talked in a whisper that I could barely hear. He said the Reds were pouring like water off the ridge to our front; that they were taking to the low ground to our left in an effort to flank us; that there were also a few close enough for him to hear rifle bolts clicking, but that he hadn't fired on them yet to keep from giving away his position. I told him that I would get fire on his saddle to his front and the low ground to his left. This I did. I ordered the center platoon one round in the adjustment. The rounds were on the way in a second, and as they came screaming over I thought certainly they would be short and would crash into our own positions. The rounds burst on the saddle in front of the outpost, and I asked over the phone if they were on the target. The lieutenant's muffled voice came back, "Move them over about fifty yards to the right and they will be perfect." I did. I gave the battery a shift of fifty right, and ordered the battery two rounds (twelve rounds) HE. We got the "On the way" and the rounds came screaming over, clearing our ridge by only a few yards. They crashed into the narrow saddle with the flank rounds dropping on the slope on either side of the saddle, which was at right angles with us.

I phoned and asked the lieutenant how those were. He whispered, "Perfect, but I'll be damned if I didn't think they were going to land in our hip pockets." I asked him if he wanted to shift into the valley on the left, he thought we should. He believed that there were a large number of NKs making their way around our flank by way of this low ground. I gave a shift of left 100 — and add 200. I told the lieutenant I would come down the draw with battery salvos at fifty-yard intervals, that he was to observe the rounds and let me know their effect. I gave the battery its orders and cuddled deep in the bottom of the hole as the rounds began to screech over, clearing our ridge by feet. Two of the rounds on the last salvo, which was at the lowest elevation, did hit the ridge we were on but far enough to the left so that no damage was done. After the rounds were complete the lieutenant told me of their effect. He said that we had gotten some of them because he could hear them yelling excited commands and could hear the groans of the wounded. I said I would repeat the fire, only this time I would move it up the draw instead of down. This I did.

In the meantime we heard some grenades go off at the outpost, followed by rifle fire and then machine-gun fire that was not ours. I heard the phone ring frantically.

"They are right on top of us" screamed the lieutenant. "Repeat the first mission that you fired before you fired on the draw."

I asked him to hold on. The operator was listening on the wire and had the battery in a second. Plummer answered.

"Get the battery on the first target you fired for me, Bill, and hurry," I yelled.

Plummer's reply was a cool, "Okay, Hood, coming right up." The artillery was quiet for a minute and the firefight at the outpost seemed to be picking up. The heavy .30, which was dug in nearby, began to open up on the base of the tracer fire that was streaming into the outpost. I heard the lieutenant yelling to his men to use grenades and not to fire at the enemy and give away their exact position. This was sound advice, for the grenades would roll down on the enemy and not reveal a thing, whereas a rifle or carbine would pinpoint a hole every time it was fired. Over the phone, I heard Plummer yell, "On the way," then the rounds were rushing overhead.

They crashed into the saddle and the slope on either side. The lieutenant was on the phone again. "Those rounds were right in there, but we are more worried about the North Koreans in close. Could you bring it any closer?"

I asked him if he thought it was safe to drop fifty yards. He thought it was and that his men would stay in the bottom of their holes when the stuff was coming in. I gave Plummer the word and told him to have the section chiefs check each piece before it was fired because a mistake could be costly firing this close to our troops. This was done and the rounds skimmed over the top of our ridge and dropped no more than twenty-five-yards in front of the knoll. The lieutenant approved and asked for more of it. At this I ordered the battery three rounds. This did the trick. Afterward, the lieutenant, breathing much easier now, yelled over the phone that he thought we had discouraged them, that we should fire in the draw to the left again, because his men swore they could hear NKs down there. Thus the night dragged on, the outpost being hard pressed nearly every hour and the enemy making a bid for passage to our flank in between. We kept the battery firing most of the night from the draw to the saddle, then back to the draw.

When morning dawned, the area around the knoll was littered with enemy dead. In the draw on the left we found fifty corpses. To everyone's surprise, there was not a casualty among the lieutenant's men. They had stayed in their holes, used hand grenades generously, and let the full weight of supporting artillery be felt by the enemy. This was the way to fight our adversaries. Keep the high ground and the real estate leading to it, stay in your hole at night, and let our supporting weapons take their toll while the enemy was in the open. Sometime during the fourth day the wire was cut and we never had communication with the artillery again at that position.

All was quiet on the line and most everyone slept in the middle of the day. The 24th Regiment was to come in and relieve us for duty elsewhere. But the outfit was so widely scattered and the stragglers had run so far to the rear that, on the third day after they had left the Haman sector in complete rout, only one company out of the entire regiment could be located intact. The MPs were busy picking up the rest of the outfit on the roads and a large percentage in Masan where some had shacked up. This is no exaggeration, and the facts may be had from anyone who was there.

Late in the afternoon of the fourth day a group of new officers came up to our area to reconnoiter. They had just come from the States and were assigned to the 24th Regiment as replacements. They said that the outfit, with fillers, would move in early that night to relieve us. No one envied those men.

The 24th came up at about 2300, and we retired. We went no farther than the cut where the road went over the ridge on the east of Haman (the same place we started the attack that was to take us to the old 24th position). Here we bedded down in a reinforcing position. It turned out to be wise. Some mortar rounds began to drop on Haman and on the low bluffs just the other side (between the town and the forward positions). Soon the road and paddies were cluttered with "Eleanor's Rifles" bugging out for all they were worth. By morning our area was full of "lost" GIs who swore that their company was "wiped out." No one knew what was going on, and the milling troops of the 24th had our men so damn riled up that we were seriously concerned over a firefight breaking out between the two.

Some tanks had come up with the 24th, and we put a reinforced company around two tanks and sent them into the valley and Haman. It turned out that Haman was completely deserted and that about 30 percent of the 24th was still in position in the old emplacements, two thousand yards the other side of Haman. Those who had bugged out were simply cowards who had run at the first few mortar rounds that landed near them. No casualties were reported.

When this news was passed around among the troops, our battalion's GIs hit the ceiling. The men who had bugged out were herded together and sent back down the road to Haman. There they were intercepted by the first sergeants of their companies and taken back to the positions where their braver comrades still held.

There were many brave men in the 24th Regiment and I do not want to discredit them. What I do want to point out is that the lack of discipline and backbone on the part of many of the men of this regiment caused the burden to be carried by a few rather than the group collectively. It also brought undue hardships and casualties to those other outfits that often had to do their fighting for them. My only hope was that the fiasco of Haman was not repeated.

It took until noon to get the 24th back into position, and our battalion had to remain in a reinforcing position until this was done in order to provide a blocking position in case of an attack.

There we noticed a good deal of fire about four or five miles to the north. We investigated and learned that the 2d Battalion had a pocket of Reds cut off in that area. This was the first we had heard from them since leaving Taegu. In reality they had been as hard pressed as we were. The 3d Battalion had still another pocket of NKPA cut off and surrounded farther to the rear toward Masan. The NKPA must have really been operating in force behind our lines.

At about 1300 it started to rain, adding to the misery of the dirty, tired men. We were ordered back to the regimental CP where the trucks were to pick up the infantry. We got there to find that the trucks had not yet arrived, I was wet and cold and so were Roberts and Minor, although we were more fortunate than the average doughfoot who had to walk to our present location. We had used the jeep. We found Captain Beard and his crew alongside Lieutenants Record and Anderson. We stood in the rain looking forlorn for a while when suddenly I had an idea. "What's wrong with us going on down the road until we find Able Battery? We can join the column when it goes by." Anderson and Record lit up at this suggestion. Captain Beard considered for a moment, then told us to go on. For some reason he chose to remain with the battalion and wait for the trucks.

The three OF parties mounted their jeeps and took off in a wave of mud. We had to keep the vehicles in four-wheel drive all the way to the main highway, which was no better. We found the battery sitting in the center of a huge hairpin curve as the road twisted up a mountain. The battery was skillfully hidden in between some Korean houses in the turn. The vehicles were dispersed at the open end of the horseshoe made by the road.

We turned off the road and into the group of mud-and-stick houses. The CP was located in one of them. Plummer was sitting on the stoop in front of it. We pulled under a shed nearby and Plummer came hopping over the puddles to meet us on the double. We talked there for a few minutes, then Record and Anderson went over to the CP.

Plummer asked me if I had any dry clothes and I shook my head. At this he produced a complete outfit, except for boots. He had a Korean boy, who was traveling with the battery, bring water to the shed for me. I took a bucket bath, shaved, brushed my teeth, and put on the new clothes Plummer had provided. All the time we talked incessantly.

Plummer had been in command of the battery for almost a month now, although on paper he was carried as the executive officer. (Captain Hull, the battery commander, had been sick with stomach trouble and spent most of his time with Service Battery.) I fervently wanted Plummer to make captain. He had been in grade for eight years (two years of this in reserve) and had had four tanks shot out from under him in the ETO. As a result he was carrying only half as much fanny around Korea as the rest of us. On top of this I felt that he was as professionally competent as any officer in the artillery.

The mess truck was parked nearby and chow was being served, although it was just 1630. I was starved after five days of C rations, and I almost fell in a puddle in my effort to get to the truck. The rain had stopped, making the chow serving much easier. Plummer and I got our mess gear loaded to the hilt, then went over to the CP's stoop where the other officers were eating with a new lieutenant in the battery who had just come over as a replacement.

We finished our meal, then sat around the stoop talking. Someone had an old *Stars and Stripes* that was being passed around for all to read. The article that most interested us concerned a bill being prepared in Congress to grant combat pay to the ground forces in Korea. To us, this seemed just the thing to do, especially because the air force was receiving flight pay and the navy sea pay while getting three meals a day and sleeping in clean beds. On the other hand, the army was suffering 99 percent of the casualties and living in the mud for the same pay the garrison soldiers were receiving safe in the States. It seemed that we should receive some type of hazardous-duty pay, and all of us who read the paper that day felt that it was surely forthcoming.

After exhausting this topic, we delved into others, running from the future of "Terry and the Pirates" (the popular comic strip) to why Louis Johnson was still secretary of defense (at this date, 5 September 1950, he had not been fired). We talked about the possibility of another front and the end of the war; of going back to Japan and the victory party that should be thrown; about our families, some were in Japan and others in the States. Someone mentioned General MacArthur and he was thoroughly discussed. There was not a man among us who had ever seen him, but he had become a legend to those of us in the Far East and we admired him greatly. Everyone agreed that we were fortunate in having such a competent and capable leader. He was the one American that every Red in Asia respected and feared. He was our ace in the hole.

It started to pour again and we pulled our legs up and huddled against the wall to stay dry. It was 1800, and in the rainy weather the light was fading fast. In the jeep under the shed, Minor and Roberts were getting things ready to roll. From the stoop of the house we could see the road, and expected to see the trucks with the 1st Battalion at any moment, signaling that we would have to leave our dry sanctuary and ride in the cold rain through the mud to another fight. No one wanted to see those trucks come around the curve.

The battery's radio operator stuck his head out of FDC saying that Captain Beard had just called and wanted the FOs on the road and ready to pull out. The column would pass the battery area in a few minutes. When I heard this I glanced up to find Plummer looking at me sternly. I met his gaze and we exchanged a look that was full of meaning. I smiled and got up. "Let's go shoot some North Koreans," I suggested with enthusiasm, and ran through the rain to the jeep. The others did likewise.

I put on my poncho and hopped into the jeep, which Minor had running. We backed out of the shed and pulled up to the road. The battalion was just coming around the curve with the colonel in the lead. Captain Beard and his wire crew were in the fourth and fifth jeeps from the head of the column. When he passed, he motioned us in behind him. All three of the OF parties buzzed into the column behind him with much splashing of mud and a few rebel war yells from Roberts, who at times just felt like yelling and couldn't help himself. Matter of fact, I think I gave out with a rebel yell at the time, and I remember that it made me feel much better.

The column moved up the mountain toward the main road to Masan. Then we turned sharply to the left at a schoolhouse. After going some ten or fifteen miles we took a right-hand fork. As to our location or destination I was not sure, but it was apparent that we were going north and then west, back toward the line. At a rest break, just at dark, the rumor reached me that we were going up to relieve a pocket behind the 2d Division.

The rain continued to pour down and everyone was cold, wet, and generally miserable. The effects of the last week's fighting were beginning to show on the troops, and the morale was dragging, as usually was the case when it rained. You just can't be happy when your fanny is wet and cold.

At a little town, after dark, the trucks stopped and the infantry dismounted. Then the trucks turned around and sped to the rear. The battalion proceeded on for about four or five miles. We entered another town and found it thick with ROK troops. It was pitch black and we could hardly see the mud houses that lined the road on both sides, but everywhere was the chatter of the Koreans. The noise of them, plus their odor, was all the clue we needed to know of their presence. I heard one of the men cuss as he slushed forward, "Goddamn, Sam, if we aren't fighting with that sorry 24th we are fighting with the South Koreans. Aren't we ever going to have a decent outfit on our flanks that will do their share of the fighting?"

Another man said, "Shit, maybe you'll get hit this time and you won't have to worry about it."

"Lord, I hope to hell I am," came the reply. "I'm so damn pooped now I'd just as soon be dead."

We crept through the town, and at its other side turned left into a large dry riverbed. There was an artillery battery and a tank platoon set up there that gave us a great feeling of security. We were a mile or so behind what might be called the front. We were told to bed down here for the night.

The three OF jeeps were together and we decided to pull them abreast of one another with a five- or six-foot gap in between jeeps. Now we could stretch shelter halves across the space between the jeeps and have a place protected from the rain to sleep in. This was done and we all crawled under the two shelters for some sack time. Our position was in the center of the area with the rest of the battalion around us. The artillery battery and the tanks were about three hundred yards farther down the riverbed.

I fell asleep almost immediately. The others did likewise for we were all dead tired. The effects of the last two months were beginning to show on all of us.

CHAPTER
ELEVEN

Surprise Peak

I came to consciousness gradually amid wild small-arms fire. "By God, I think we are being shot at," drawled Record. Three or four rounds ricocheted off the jeeps to verify his belief. I reached for my carbine, then started lacing up my boots, making certain that I kept well down all the time. The others followed suit.

The first light of dawn was appearing, bringing with it the enemy. They had come off of high ground to the west and south, probably after the artillery and tanks. The fact that we had come in during the night was undoubtedly a surprise to them. They were loaded with burp guns and machine guns, which were raking the area from a dike at the west of the perimeter. We stayed under the jeeps and watched the fight develop. The .50s, on the tanks and on the ring mounts of the trucks that were with the artillery battery, took their toll, and the 81s of Dog Company were set up and in action in a surprisingly quick time.

The Reds seemed to be circling us to the north, and it looked as though they made a breach of our perimeter at one place, but they failed to capitalize on it. The attitude of those of us under the jeeps was that our boys would discourage the North Koreans in due time and no one was the least bit concerned over his own welfare. In fact, the calmness with which this attack had been taken by our group seemed a little comical to me at the time. Now I think it was plain foolhardiness.

The fight went on and on, our side holding our own, but the Reds refusing to give up in spite of their losses. There did not seem to be many casualties among us in spite of the thickness of the flying lead, and I don't remember hearing anyone call for a medic.

By 0800, it was light and the NKPAs were withdrawing across a stream, over a dike, through some rice paddies, and up a large hill to the west. As they withdrew, the tankers started using their .75s on them and the battery fired its 105s. The firefight was over. We got out from under our jeeps and complained a little about having to get up so "damn early." There was a well at a nearby house. We took our toilet articles and made for it. Captain Beard was at the well. His wire sergeant had been hit.

We washed, then went over to Headquarters Company's mess. There was an abundance of rations and we stuffed ourselves. After chow we were issued field jackets. It was September, the nights were chilly. The troops settled down and, as far as I could tell, we were going to remain put until we received further orders. Maybe this mission would be a restful one after all.

It was about 0940 when the colonel called for Buckley and me to come up to his CP. There we learned that Able Company had been selected to take the huge hill to the west where the Reds had withdrawn. It was the colonel's contention, and rightly, that as long as we did not hold that prominent piece of landscape our position in the low bivouac area would be untenable. On the other hand, once we controlled this high ground our position would be secure. This was obvious, for after all the North Koreans made their attack over this hill and they also made their withdrawal up it.

From the riverbed, the hill's crest seemed to be about two miles away, as the crow flies. It had two peaks with a saddle connecting them. There were a few scrubby trees at its base, but for the most part, there was no vegetation other than grass. At the foot of the hill was a village, with paddies from there to a dike. A stream ran parallel with the dike across our front. Between us and the stream was nothing but several hundred yards of rocks.

Buckley said that he would have the company ready to move out in ten minutes and took off. I suggested that I would meet him at the dike.

I went to the jeep and had Roberts and Minor make a radio check. I knew that the radio would be the easiest method of communication if it worked, and because of the short range to the hill there was a good chance that it might. Minor checked with

Captain Beard's radio, then broke it down for Roberts and me to carry on packboards. I carried the transmitter and receiver. Roberts carried the battery box. We picked up our weapons and took off. I stopped by Captain Beard's jeep and learned that Baker Battery of the 8th Field Artillery was in position close at hand, and he had contact with them over his 608. He would relay fire missions, if any were to follow.

At this Roberts and I took off. The radio was heavy and I wanted to reach the dike before the company so that we would have an opportunity to take the packboards off and rest a while before going on through the paddies. We made the river in about five minutes and waded across. The water was only hip deep at the deepest point. At the dike we nearly stepped on a dead Red who was stretched out in the tall grass near the water's edge. We climbed halfway up the dike and sat down to rest and wait for the company. Roberts was just about to light a cigarette when we heard enemy jabbering just the other side of the dike. It sounded as though they were arguing about something. The jabbering got more excited. I listened, without much thought of what our next move should be. I looked over to check Robert's reaction just in time to see him pitch a grenade over the dike. Then he lit his cigarette, proving to me that he was the roughest, toughest kid in Texas. There was the burst of the grenade. Roberts and I listened. There was no more jabbering.

We sat comfortably on the dike and watched as the company approached the stream. The outfit's front was about 500 yards across with the three rifle platoons abreast and the weapons platoon in the center and to the rear. As they crossed the stream Roberts and I fell in with the 2d Platoon, which was in the center. We went over the dike to find two dead North Koreans and one badly wounded one where Roberts had tossed his grenade.

Pathways ran through the paddies, and, rather than slog through them, Roberts and I elected to walk along them where the going was easier, although it was not as safe. By now we were not too careful of our own safety. Those of us who had lived through the campaign to this point more or less considered ourselves untouchable.

As the doughfeet sifted through the paddies they flushed several North Korean soldiers, mostly wounded, from the early morning engagement. I saw two making for the other end of the paddy at about two hundred yards, and after pointing them out to Roberts, dropped one of them. Roberts got the other one. Roberts was a master with his M1 and my respect for his shooting grew each day. I had never been a good shot, but in the course of the war I had reached the point where I never doubted my ability with my carbine at anything less than one hundred yards.

We made the village after fifteen minutes in the paddies and ran into a little trouble. The Reds had left a machine gun behind in their withdrawal and it was set up in a house that stood on a rise overlooking the paddies. They had held their fire until we were within fifty yards. I hit the paddy head on as did everyone else. Because the weapons platoon was in the paddies, they could not set up the 60s and we were strictly hurting for a while. After several minutes of burrowing in the muck somebody got a BAR into action on the left, and as the enemy machine gunner shifted his fire, another BAR opened up on the right. The rounds went right through the mud-and-stick house, and after a minute or so of continuous firing, several large holes were torn in the wall and the gun was silent. Someone crawled up close and pitched a grenade to make certain. We advanced on the building to find its occupants quite dead. The village was completely deserted except for two flea-bitten puppies that cried pitifully at us as we passed through.

There were four or five fingers of land running down from the main slope of our objective, and each platoon advanced up the crest of one of these fingers, which led to the main mass of the hill. This caused the platoons to be thrown apart by as much as two hundred yards, being separated by deep gullies or ravines. We advanced up our finger, gingerly at first, then with less and less caution as the territory to our front produced no Reds. There were pieces of shrapnel and burst marks all over the side of the hill where the tanks and 105s had fired at the retreating NKs, but there were no dead on the side of the hill as far as I could tell. One wounded hostile was captured on the way up, however.

Due to the zigzagging route we had to take in order to follow the contours of the hill in our ascent, the distance to the top was much greater than I had originally guessed. We had to stop often for a break and the heat was terrific. The noon sun was giving us the full treatment and I felt a little dizzy several times during the climb. Other than the physical exertion there were no other difficulties. The NKPAs just weren't around.

At last we were in sight of the crest and everyone's pace quickened a little. Our platoon was going to come out right in the middle of the saddle between the two peaks on the north and south ends of the crest, which appeared to be narrow. The 1st Platoon, on our left, abreast of us, were to reach the crest at the southern peak. The 3d Platoon, on the right, had fallen about three hundred yards to the rear. They were to take the peak on the north.

We expected the Reds to be set up on the top, waiting for us, but this proved to be a bet the enemy had missed. We reached the crest of the saddle without mishap. Roberts, Burris, and I stuck our heads over the top simultaneously and withdrew them about a hundred times faster. The crest was swept clean with machine-gun fire. The rounds whined through the air over our heads and the crest danced with dust as other rounds drove into it. There was a third peak to this damn hill that we didn't know about and it was on the other side of

283

the saddle to the west. The NKPAs were well dug in there and evidently loaded for bear.

The 1st Platoon reached their objective on the left and went into position, keeping their heads well down. The weapons platoon (about 200 yards below us) was called by Sergeant Burris and told to get the 60s into action. The 3d Platoon was still below, huffing and puffing to reach their objective on our right.

I decided to get some artillery on those little bastards across the way with all haste. I took off my packboard with the radio aboard and gave it to Roberts with instructions to put it together with the battery box, which he carried, and to make radio contact with Captain Beard. I decided to move over to the right and try to get my head up long enough to get an azimuthal reading to the enemy position. Burris said that he would go with me.

We went about a hundred yards to the right and I edged my head over the top. I could see the enemy plainly at about three hundred yards, firing at the men in the 1st Platoon who popped up to fire and then dropped back behind the crest. I had my compass out before I ever stuck my head up and I proceeded to take a reading. I got the sight squarely on the center of the Red position and read the needle as it came to a stop at 2910 mils. I was about to lower the compass when there was a noise like a string of fire crackers bursting in my right ear, and the compass seemed to shatter in slow motion right in front of my face. There was a burning sensation in my right hand that hurt horribly. Reflex caused me to drop behind the crest and to roll. To my left, not more than thirty yards away, I got a glimpse of two North Koreans, scurrying around a knoll. The people of the 3d Platoon, who were coming up fast, were firing at them as they dropped from sight.

The pain in my hand was the most intense I had ever known. My hand was a grim mess of ripped and torn flesh; brilliant red blood; and white bone, broken and splintered, glistening in the sun. The ring finger was off completely. It dangled from the knuckle by a thread of skin. The middle finger was broken at the first joint, the jagged bone protruding. There was a hole through my hand between the index finger and the base of the thumb from which blood oozed, red and warm.

I looked up to find Burris sitting beside me. He was cool as a cucumber.

"Come on, Lieutenant, let's get out of here."

I accepted this suggestion and we scooted back to where I had left Roberts with the radio. I sat down and tried to help Roberts get the cable plugged into the battery box. Burris took my right hand and wrapped it with my first-aid pack, which he had taken from my cartridge belt. He turned my hand so that the palm was up and placed the two fingers in it. They felt warm and stiff. The bandage was not large enough to cover the entire wounded area, but Burris did the best he could. At least he stopped the fingers from swinging crazily around with every movement of my hand.

Roberts had the radio almost set up. After I connected the cable to the battery box we were ready to transmit. I took the mike in my left hand and began giving Captain Beard the call sign. We got a reply and I gave them the fire mission. I remember thinking that I was pretty cool, that the transmission was undoubtedly clear. This was not the case. Captain Beard's voice came back over the radio, "Wait a damn minute, will you? Repeat the whole thing again." This gave me my first clue that I was somewhat excited. I had been under the impression that I was the perfect picture of composure. I gave the fire mission again, this time very slowly and distinctly exactly following prescribed procedure. After the commands, I said rather nonchalantly, I thought, that I was hit. There was a silence. Then Captain Beard told me to come off the hill, he would send up a replacement. I gave him a "Roger and out."

I put the mike down on top of the set. The 3d Platoon had gone into position all along the crest and knoll to the right. The fire from the enemy had dropped off and our machine-gun sections were getting into action. A man came running up from the weapons platoon with a wire for Burris, close behind him came a medic. Burris got on the phone and gave the 60s their fire mission. The medic took off the dressing that Burris had put on my hand and applied a fresh one. He gave me a shot of morphine and asked me if I could walk. I told him that I could and got up.

Burris and Roberts agreed that they could handle our fire mission when it came over. The medic took my left arm and started leading me down the hill. I pulled my arm away from him and went back and picked up my carbine. I was feeling weak and I got dizzy as I stumbled after the medic. It seemed as if only a few seconds had passed and we had reached the mortar positions. They were at least fifty yards back, yet I didn't even remember walking to them. I was put in a column of four or five ammo bearers who were going back for 60mm ammunition. I was shepherded down the hill in the middle of their small column. I remember vaguely hearing the artillery go over. We walked on and on, yet the time seemed short and I continued to have that weak and tipsy feeling. We were bearing to the south in a different way than I had come up. At the foot of the hill there was a road that led through the paddies and across the dike and stream. This trail was scattered with dead Reds from the morning's attack. I watched each one carefully as we passed, expecting them to jump up and start firing. We passed a few who had been hit by the tank fire and they were torn to pieces. The hot sun burned down. The stink from the paddies plus the dead bodies was overwhelming. I felt sick. We walked on. There was a footbridge over the stream at this point and I remember stumbling as we reached it. Across the river was the artillery battery.

A man pulled out of the area in a jeep and we stopped him for a lift. Everyone crawled on and we took off for the battalion CP and the aid station. It seemed only a minute for us to get there. I got off the jeep and looked into a sea of faces that spun round and round, getting close then fading away to be replaced by new faces. I recognized one of the faces as Captain Beard's and another as the colonel's. I remember telling the colonel of the situation on the hill and giving my belt with its equipment, my shoulder holster and .45, and my carbine to Minor with instructions to give them to Plummer. I remember thinking that I would probably return in a few days, just as I had the last time I was hurt, and I wanted to keep my gear. Captain Beard said something about calling his wife in Osaka and I was whisked off by a medic.

At the aid station a new dressing was put on and a card was tied to my fatigue jacket. I was placed on a litter jeep and carried to a field collection station. There I was transferred to an ambulance with several other wounded and within a short time we pulled up to a large tent. I know now that this was a MASH outfit, but at the time, I had no idea where I was. I remember being carried inside and placed on the ground with what looked like hundreds of other wounded men. There was a good deal of groaning and some crying going on.

The next thing I recall was being aware of two huge bosoms in my face and a familiar voice saying something like "Baby doll, what in the world are you doing here? Don't worry, I'll have the colonel work on you." It was Nurse "X" from Jinmachi.

Shortly thereafter, two orderlies picked up my litter and I was passed from the rear of the line to the front of those patients going into surgery. I was given a shot and a few minutes later carried into an operating room and placed on the table.

Someone said, "Lieutenant, we are going to give you Pentothal, count to three." I remember getting to two. My next recall was waking up on a cot in a tent with about eight other men. It seemed to be morning. As I looked around, there was Nurse "X." "How're you doing, darling? You came through the surgery just fine. Let me get you something to drink." She had a No. 10 can of cold grapefruit juice. It was wonderful. I realized I was thirsty. A few minutes later she was back and took my vital signs. She asked if I felt that I could travel. I said yes.

She took a card out of her apron and wrote something on it, then attached the card to a string and placed it around my neck. Within half an hour, I was picked up, placed in an ambulance, and delivered to the Rail Transportation Office. There a train was waiting with litters fitted into two-by-four frames in the boxcars. Some twenty-five wounded could be carried in each car. A medic was in my car and I think in each of the other cars.

After what seemed like a several-hour wait, the train pulled out. Later that night we arrived in Masan and were carried to an old Catholic convent that had been converted into a hospital. The next day, someone checked the tag around my neck and

I was immediately picked up and loaded on an ambulance bound for K2, an airstrip north of Pusan.

The evacs in the litters were taken out of the ambulance and placed on the ground. There was no plane in sight. The strip was made of a steel landing mat placed on top of the ground. There was a wind sock and what I assumed was an operations tent. A few air force ground crew people scurried around. We were given some grapefruit juice and waited.

Two days after being shot I was on a litter at K2 waiting for a plane that would take me to Japan and connections to the States. For me the war was over. I had drawn the "million-dollar wound." There would be no more paddy water. For me, the sleeping in mud was over. From here on out I would sleep at night and this sleeping would be on clean sheets with no fear of having a rusty bayonet shoved between my ribs. There would be no more mortars crashing down in the black of night and the crackle of small arms would only be a memory.

But — what about the brave men who were still fighting? Would they be reinforced with the necessary troops and equipment to go on and win the war and . . . peace? Would they return home after victory, knowing that their efforts had purchased peace for the world and security for themselves, their families, and our nation? Or, would they come home to face the prospect of an even larger and more horrible war in the future? Would they come home to find that all their suffering had only earned them a breathing spell in which to prepare for the all important, definitive struggle for existence with the well-known enemy? What of the men who would not return? Would history record that they had been spent dearly? Would history record that they had died cheaply on the bargain table of international diplomacy?

A C-47 arrived. I was placed aboard with the other wounded. I was going home.

CHAPTER
TWELVE

Evacuation, Surgical Repair, Further Duty

The C-47 was rigged with litters, three-high on each side of the fuselage, and there were two army nurses aboard. All the patients were given shots of some kind, and we slept until there was a jolt from the wheels hitting the runway at Johnson Air Force Base outside of Tokyo. The air base hospital was like a resort. Clean sheets, clean latrines, nice people, and great food (I weighed 140 pounds upon arrival). There was an unlimited supply of ice cream and Armed Forces Radio with all the world news and the new popular songs from the Zone of the Interior (the States), and we could sleep as long as we wanted! I felt like I had fallen into the lap of luxury. This was the first time I had been in a bed for two-and-a-half months.

I really don't know how long I was at Johnson. I think three days. The medical team judged that my wounds required surgical repair so they "tagged" me for ZI (Zone of the Interior) evacuation. I was issued a clean pair of GI drawers, a summer flight suit, and a Red Cross ditty bag with a razor, toothbrush, and comb. With this uniform and equipment, I was carried out to the flight line and loaded on a United Airlines DC-6 with bona fide stewardesses and an air force nurse. I guess there must have been seventy to eighty wounded aboard.

First stop was Wake Island. We were allowed off the plane while it was being fueled and serviced. The walking wounded went to the base mess hall for chow. I picked up a piece of coral, which I have to this day, as my first touch of the United States. We then flew to Honolulu and an overnight at Letterman General Hospital. The following day we were carried aboard the same DC-6 and were off to Fairfield-Suisun (now Travis Air Force Base) outside of Sacramento. I was there for two days with a quick medical examination, and then was loaded aboard an air force double-decker aircraft, and flown to San Antonio, Texas. About half of the patients were offloaded there and sent to Brooke Army Hospital. My group remained on board. We were served a light lunch and departed for Millington Naval Air Station, north of Memphis.

After arriving at Millington, I was assigned to an officers' ward of noncritical patients and told that I would be there for some time. The Red Cross arranged for me to call my wife and ten-month-old son who were camped with her grandfather, Will Thompson, in Sullivan, Indiana. My wife was blown out of the tub to learn that I was in the States. She made immediate arrangements to depart the following day by automobile with Add Jr. I was allowed to call my mother, who was a housemother at Ward-Belmont Junior College in Nashville. She, too, was on her way the next day. What a homecoming! I thought I would never get enough hugging, kissing, and crying for joy.

Little Add, of course, had no idea who I was. I don't suppose I looked too appealing with a shaved head, a smelly cast over my right arm and hand, and generally a bone-and-gristle physique. I refused to be turned away, however, and by the second day he seemed about half glad to see me.

It developed that the best hand surgeon in the army was at Fort Benning, Georgia. This was just over a hundred miles from my family home in Macon. Orders were cut for me to be transferred to Fort Benning, and within four days I was off to Georgia aboard a Tennessee National Guard B-26.

The stay at Fort Benning is kind of a blur. I was operated on three times, with thirty- to forty-five-day healing periods in between while skin grafts "took." After each surgery, I was given a convalescent leave to go home. In this time frame this book was written and I learned to change diapers with my left hand only. Little Add and I became fast buddies.

In June of 1951, I was approved for limited duty and assigned to the 58th Field Artillery in Fort Bragg, North Carolina. This was a "long tom" outfit, that is, 155mm rifled artillery (not a howitzer). Within weeks I came down with malaria, contracted in Korea and suppressed by all the drugs I was given in the hospital. Malaria is a *big-time sick*. The folks at the hospital got me through the sweats, chills, and fever in about a week and told me to expect to be back every two weeks for a few months. Sure enough, in two weeks I was sick as a dog and back on sick call. I was put in the malaria ward and treated accordingly. After a week, I was running a fever of 104 degrees and could not move my legs. A consulting doctor came in and ordered a spinal tap. *I had Polio!* The next month was full of pain and conversation about life in a wheelchair. After all, FDR pulled it off and he never had the benefit of army training.

There is no need to recount the recovery period or the therapy administered to a polio patient. I recovered some movement and was able to walk with crutches by Thanksgiving. I was again assigned to limited duty, this time with army field forces, Board One, at Fort Bragg. The mission of the army field forces is to test new weapons and equipage in temperate, tropical, desert, and arctic climates to determine their suitability for standard procurement and issue. My assignment in operations dealt with the contractors and the test programs. This developed into a great learning experience and I encountered my first great mentor, Col. Bill Grove.

By this time, I was walking without crutches. However, the calf of my right leg had disappeared and I could not get up on my right toes or push off with the right foot. This produced a kind of twisting gait that worked, but my walk and stance was far from military-parade form.

From army field forces, I received a posting to Fort Lee, Virginia, to attend the Army's Procurement School (thanks to Colonel Grove).

It was here that my twin sons, Tim and Jeb, were born.

From Fort Lee, I was assigned to the Washington Military District and posted as a procurement officer to the Quartermaster General. I purchased the basic commodities, that is, flour, coffee, corn, beans, and peas, and so on, for the whole armed services, plus the federal prisons. I was dumb enough to think the entire military establishment was depending on my performance and I was frequently at my duty post from 0700 to 2200. It was at this post that I met my second great mentor, Col. Grant Healy. He taught me "that without the discipline of writing, ideas and plans become nebulous and vague and ensuing action equally sloppy."

I learned two things in Washington: first, the civilian bureaucrats really run things at the Pentagon. The officers are rotated every three years, but their civilian "assistant" is there for life. Second, never try to save the taxpayers a dime. I saved several million dollars in the purchase and transport of coffee and had the Brooklyn congressman, both New York senators, the chairman of the Armed Services Committee, and the secretary of the army on top of me within days.

This led to an enlightening conversation with Maj. Gen. George A. Horkan, Quartermaster General, who basically said, "Son, you're RA (regular army) and I'm trying to save your ass. Pick any post you want outside of the ZI and get out of town by tomorrow." I picked Puerto Rico, the subject of my graduate thesis, and asked to go to the Infantry School at Fort Benning before shipping out. My orders were cut in five minutes.

My family and I, with three little boys, all still in diapers, were on our way to Georgia the following morning. Everything we owned was in or on top of a two-door 1951 Ford.

The Infantry School was great. Just wish I had gone there before Korea. By this time I was pretty mobile and was able to pass a physical exam that granted me full field-duty status (with a limp). To this day, I credit the Infantry School as the finest educational institution I ever attended.

We arrived at Losey Field, Puerto Rico, the day after Thanksgiving 1953. The posting was to the 65th Infantry Regiment. This was the last ethnic regiment in the army. The officers were mixed, Puerto Rican and Anglos. Several of the Puerto Rican officers were West Point graduates. Most of the others were products of the University of Puerto Rico ROTC. Many had served in Korea. I was given command of K Company. I was a junior captain at the time. I must say, I have never enjoyed my work as much as the time I was a company commander. It's the greatest job in the army!

The 65th was an amphibious outfit and we regularly assaulted Vieques, St. Thomas, and St. Croix. In this time, 1953–54, the primary SAC bomber was the B-36, ("six turning and four burning"). The air force had determined that their base in Mayagüez on the west coast of Puerto Rico was the only piece of U.S. territory outside of the one-way range of the Russian Yak. Accordingly, all major maintenance on the B-36 was performed at Mayagüez. The mission of the 65th was to protect this installation. We were good at it. The soft, spoiled, overpaid airplane drivers and their base were not attacked once while the "Fighting 65th" was on duty.

As the Puerto Rican tour progressed, I looked forward to every day and totally enjoyed the complete immersion with the troops. K Company won damn near every competition in the regiment. In the annual platoon and company proficiency tests, which are held throughout the army each year, we were tops in the command. There were no AWOL or discipline problems in K Company.

On the other hand, my wife did not like Puerto Rico, did not like the army, but above all she did not like a captain's pay.

Marital and family pressures being what they are, in January of 1955 I resigned my regular commission. My wife and the boys were flown back to Maxwell Air Force Base, where they were given train tickets to Gainesville, Florida (the place where I entered active duty). I was made officer in charge of a shipload of Puerto Rican troops being sent to the ZI to be integrated into the army as the 65th was losing its Puerto Rican identity. The ship was the USS *Sanborn*. We arrived in New York Harbor on a Friday night in a freezing rain. My troops had only their tropical uniforms and most of them had never seen snow or ice.

It developed that the crew on an army ship is civil service. The stevedores had all gone home for the weekend. To dock and disembark on a weekend would involve time-and-a-half pay. Therefore, we anchored in the Narrows for two days and the captain decided that the troops should chip ice to "keep them busy." As OIC, I had to oversee the detail. The stupidity of this exercise made my discharge from the army at Fort Hamilton on 2 February 1995 easier.

My friend Bill Hawthorne (a fraternity brother from Purdue) had arranged for me to purchase a new Chevrolet station wagon in New Jersey. After a farewell supper, I was off to Florida to pick up my family and start a civilian career.

We settled in Atlanta, and I opened the Addison Terry Company. I remained in the army reserves where I achieved the rank of major. In 1965 I resigned due to the demands of business.

I have never gotten over the army. It is my home. I cannot say "27th Regiment" without tearing up. I cannot hear "The Star Spangled Banner" without a chill and lump in my throat.

Now, I am remarried, semiretired, and teach college courses in economics and business. In the course of my lectures, the government's defense budget always comes up. I go to the light switch and turn off the lights. I ask the students what should be done to get the lights back on. They all say "flip the switch." At this point I state that this is exactly what the military is all about. When the president or the Congress "flips the switch" the soldiers are immediately turned on and they will be called upon to die in defense of this country. The debt 270 million citizens owe those who serve and protect them is seldom acknowledged.

Appendix and Maps

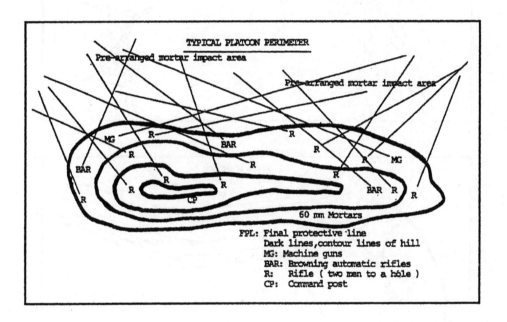

TYPICAL PLATOON PERIMETER

Pre-arranged mortar impact area

Pre-arranged mortar impact area

MG
R
BAR
R
R
BAR
R
MG
R
R
R
BAR
R
R
R
R
R
R
CP
BAR R
R

60 mm Mortars

FPL: Final protective line
Dark lines, contour lines of hill
MG: Machine guns
BAR: Browning automatic rifles
R: Rifle (two men to a hole)
CP: Command post

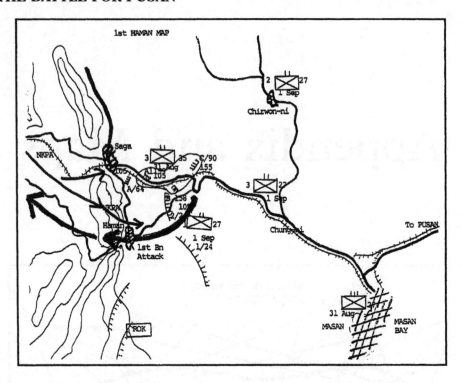

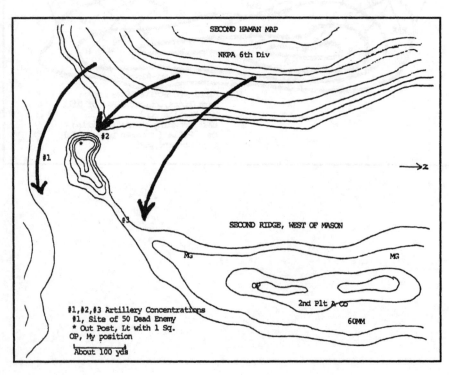

Commentary on Haman Maps

These two maps illustrate the movement and action of the 1st Battalion from the 31st of August to the 4th of September 1950. The 24th Regiment had occupied the ground in the second ridge for several weeks. This was the southern end of the area that became known as the Naktong Bulge. This was the last great attack of the NKPA before the Pusan breakout.

This action firmly solidified the esprit de corps of our outfit. The confidence we had in Colonel Check was unshakable. The manner in which he made his "estimate of the situation" and issued his battle orders were text book. For me, the engagement firmly cemented the doctrine that artillery lengthens the battlefield. Our ability to take Haman under fire for a couple of hours and then advance that fire over the first ridge and on to the second, completely disorganized the Inmun Gun (KNPA) and caused significant enemy casualties. With three batteries in support of the 1st Battalion and four on the following days, there was no doubt in anyone's

303

mind that we could advance at will and hold as ordered. The only negative afterthoughts concerning this action relate to the radios. If we had reliable radio commo there would have been a great reduction in time required for fire missions. Further we would have engaged many more targets of opportunity. And last, we would not have had to commit good soldiers to stringing wire and taking casualties, only to have to put the wire back the following morning.

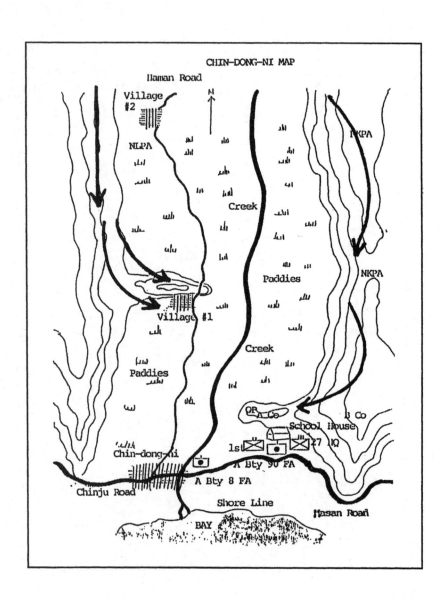

CHIN-DONG-NI MAP

Haman Road

Village #2

NLPA

Creek

NKPA

NKPA

Paddies

Village #1

Creek

Paddies

OP
A Co

B Co

School House

1st

27 HQ

Chin-dong-ni

A Bty 90 FA

Chinju Road

A Bty 8 FA

Shore Line

BAY

Hasan Road

306

Commentary on Chingdong-ni Battle Map

The 1st Battalion of the 27th jumped off on 2 August from the school house to plug the Chinju pass. The account of this engagement is recorded in chapter four. My return with the prisoner, G2 documents, and the wounded was a northwest passage over the mountains west and north of the area shown on this map. It was about midnight of the 2d when I arrived back at the regimental headquarters and delivered the prisoner and documents. I gave Colonel Michaelis a report of the situation to the west and north.

During the night the first battalion and A Battery of the 8th Field Artillery arrived back in the perimeter after fighting through the road block the enemy had set up on the Chinju road. The 90th Field Artillery had greatly assisted this break-through with its fire. (I believe this was the first 155mm artillery this bunch of enemy had encountered.) At first light on the 3d, the North Koreans were pouring off the ridge to our north and east. They were bound to be after the 90th and did not know that the 1st Battalion had returned during the night. The first part of the battle was the small arms and grenade encounter to gain the ridge just above the school house. The second part was the artillery engagement as the enemy counterattacked through village number one. I fired A Battery of the 8th most of the time and A Battery of the 90th as blocking fire, north, up the east ridge at 3,000 to 6,000 yard range.

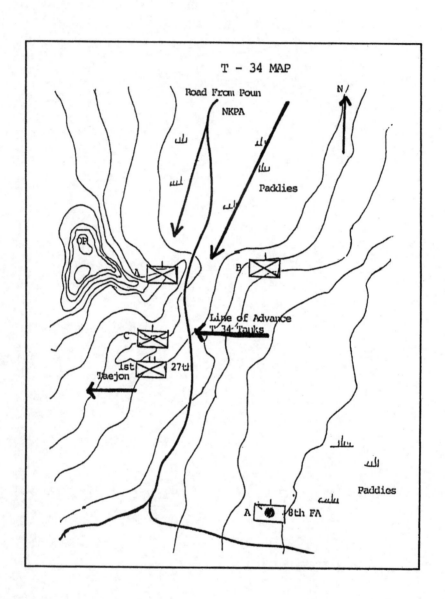

T – 34 MAP

Road From Poun

NKPA

Paddies

N

OP

A

B

Line of Advance
T–34 Tanks

C

1st
Taejon

27th

Paddies

A 8th FA

Commentary on T-34 Map

On the 22d and 23d of July, four fresh NKPA divisions, the 1st, 2d, 13th, and 15th bypassed the battle going on at Taejon, defended by the remnants of the 24th Division. They moved east to intersect the Poun Road, cutting off the 24th route of withdrawal. The two battalion 27th was moved from their positions just south of the Taejon-Taegu rail line. The 1st Battalion moved into a perimeter on each side of the Poun Road.

In my judgment, the NKPA had no idea we were there. They came down the road on the 24th about six abreast following eight T-34 tanks. The tanks actually penetrated to the battalion command post. My observation post on the hill described in chapter two provided a press box seat for this significant battle. This was the first time the enemy was defeated and stopped. Much credit goes to the Australian Air Corps in P-51s. It was here we developed our "how able" tactic that served so well as we withdrew down Heartbreak Highway.

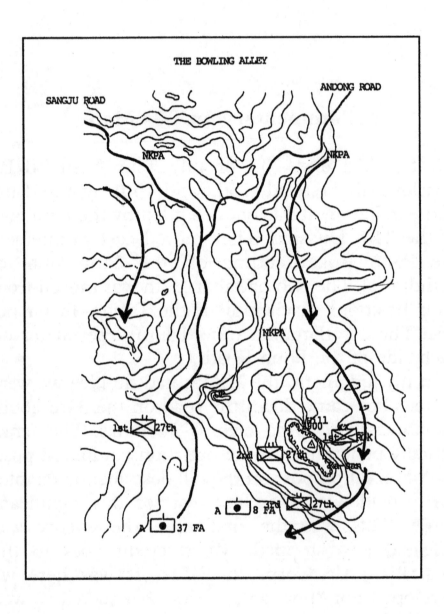

Commentary on "The Bowling Alley" Battle Map

On the 10th of August, the NKPA 13th and 8th Divisions mounted an attack down the Sangju-Taegu Road. They were supported with T-34s and several self-propelled guns. At the same time the NKPA 12th Division joined the NKPA 5th Division and broke through the Pohang on the east coast. The ROK 3d Division fell back and the rear of the ROK 8th and Capital Divisions was exposed. To the west, the 1st Cat was falling back on all fronts.

The 27th had just restored the "Naktong bulge" for the 24th Division and was southbound for R&R in the Pea Patch at Masan. We were turned around and rushed north to Taegu. We now had three battalions (although understrength by perhaps 30%). Colonel Michaelis anchored the perimeter on hill 902, in an old walled village of Ka-San on the east. The west end was on the high ground west of the town of Tabu. This terrain was about ten miles from Taegu, 8th Army headquarters. The NKPA could shell Taegu from hill 902. My position (OP on map) was a narrow ridge looking due north on the Sangju Road. (This was the only time I was attached to the 2d Battalion.) On the night of 18 August, the 13th NKPA division attacked straight down the road with flanking infantry on the ridge to the east and hills to the west. They got into Ka-San and lead units attacked our artillery positions in the defilade to the rear of the 3d Battalion. The prearranged fire on the road and the use of illuminating star flares saved the day. By the 20th, the NKPA had evaporated, except for the dead in the Bowling Alley. General Walker inspected the battlefield on that day and declared Taegu "saved."